Introduction to Health Behavior Theory

Joanna Hayden, PhD, CHES

Professor and Chairperson

Department of Public Health

William Paterson University

JONES AND BARTLETT PUBLISHERS

Sudbury, Massachusetts

BOSTON   TORONTO   LONDON   SINGAPORE

World Headquarters

Jones and Bartlett Publishers
40 Tall Pine Drive
Sudbury, MA 01776
978-443-5000
info@jbpub.com
www.jbpub.com

Jones and Bartlett Publishers Canada
6339 Ormindale Way
Mississauga, Ontario
L5V 1J2
CANADA

Jones and Bartlett Publishers
International
Barb House, Barb Mews
London W6 7PA
UK

Jones and Bartlett's books and products are available through most bookstores and online booksellers. To contact Jones and Bartlett Publishers directly, call 800-832-0034, fax 978-443-8000, or visit our website, www.jbpub.com.

Substantial discounts on bulk quantities of Jones and Bartlett's publications are available to corporations, professional associations, and other qualified organizations. For details and specific discount information, contact the special sales department at Jones and Bartlett via the above contact information or send an email to specialsales@jbpub.com.

Production Credits
Acquisitions Editor: Jacqueline Ann Geraci
Associate Editor: Amy L. Flagg
Editorial Assistant: Kyle Hoover
Production Manager: Julie Champagne Bolduc
Production Assistant: Jessica Steele Newfell
Marketing Manager: Jessica Faucher
Marketing Associate: Meagan Norlund
Manufacturing Buyer: Therese Connell
Composition: Publishers' Design and Production Services, Inc.
Cover Design: Brian Moore
Photo Research Manager and Photographer: Kimberly Potvin
Cover Image: © Alexander Sysoev/ShutterStock, Inc.
Printing and Binding: Courier Stoughton
Cover Printing: Courier Stoughton

Photo credits:
Figure 2-1 © Tomasz Trojanowski/ShutterStock, Inc.; Figure 2-2 © Répási Lajos Attila/ShutterStock, Inc.; Figure 4-1 © Wendy M. Simmons/ShutterStock, Inc.; Figure 5-1 © Supri Suharjoto/ShutterStock, Inc.; Figure 6-1 © Christy Thompson/ShutterStock, Inc.; Figure 6-2 © M Stock/Alamy Images; Figure 8-1 © Phil Date/ShutterStock, Inc.; Figure 9-2 © carolyn brule/ShutterStock, Inc.; Figure 10-1 © Ablestock.

Library of Congress Cataloging-in-Publication Data
Hayden, Joanna.
    Introduction to health behavior theory / Joanna Hayden.
       p. ; cm.
    Includes bibliographical references.
    ISBN 978-0-7637-4383-3 (pbk. : alk. paper)
    1. Health behavior--Textbooks.   I. Title.
    [DNLM: 1. Health Behavior. 2. Attitude to Health. 3. Behavioral Research. 4. Health Education.
5. Health Promotion. W 85 H414i 2009]
    RA776.9.H39 2009
    613--dc22
                        2008010757
6048
Printed in the United States of America
12 11 10 09 08   10 9 8 7 6 5 4 3 2 1

Contents

Preface

Theory is the foundation for professional practice and, as such, is an essential component of professional preparation at any level. However, this does not make the teaching and learning of theory any easier; it just makes it necessary. Of all the subject matter in health education and health promotion I have taught in my more than 20 years in professional preparation, theory is often the most difficult for undergraduate students to comprehend. It is difficult because they do not have a reservoir of knowledge from which to draw as they do for, say, math, history, English, or the sciences. This text is written for these students.

The purpose of this text is to provide an easy-to-understand, interesting, and engaging introduction to a topic that is usually perceived as difficult, dry, and boring. The language used and depth and breadth of the information are intentional. It is not meant to be a comprehensive tome on theory, but rather an *introduction* to theory. It is meant to be the headwaters of that reservoir of knowledge.

Although written with the undergraduate in mind, this book would also be of value to graduate students or practicing professionals whose own reservoir of theory knowledge and understanding could use a refill. It would be an excellent text to use along with others in preparing for certification examinations in which health behavior is included.

The text begins with an explanation of what theory is, how theories are developed, and factors that influence health behavior. Chapters 2 through 9 cover the more frequently used health behavior theories and present the concept and constructs for each theory. Multiple examples from the literature are used to demonstrate how the theory is used in practice. Although some examples relate easily to college students, many purposely do not. Since this book is intended for students in professional preparation programs, the examples are meant to demonstrate how theories are used in a variety of settings, with different populations, addressing an assortment of health issues. Because many examples were taken from the literature, students can refer to the extensive reference list at the end of each chapter, which contains numerous citations of both health education research studies and programs in which the theory was used.

Each theory chapter contains a Theory in Action section featuring a full-length, peer-reviewed journal article. This provides students with an in-depth example of how theory was used to guide the development of a health education or promotion program. The articles chosen present a complete picture of how theory is used while addressing a different health issue and population in each chapter. The articles are the basis for the class activities included in each chapter.

Each theory chapter begins with a theory essence sentence and ends with a constructs chart. The theory essence sentence reduces the complex theory to one sentence, that is, to its essence. Presented at the beginning of the chapter, it prepares the student for the more detailed discussion that follows. The constructs chart at the end of each chapter provides a summary of the theory's main ideas.

Because a picture is worth a thousand words, each chapter contains a unique illustration. Typically not found in a theory text, the illustrations were developed to provide a visual representation of the theory in common situations.

While illustrations are unusual, flowcharts are standard fare in theory texts and thus are included here. Some are classic; others I developed to provide a more user-friendly interpretation of the theoretical constructs.

The final chapter in the book, "Choosing a Theory," answers the often-asked question "How do I know which theory to use when?" This chapter provides a framework to help answer that question and a theory chart. The chart groups the theories by levels and is a compilation of the theory essence sentences and the constructs charts provided in each chapter.

In no way does this book purport to cover all of the theories that could be used to explain health behavior, nor does it claim to provide an in-depth, exhaustive discourse on the theories it does contain. It does, however, provide an introduction to the more commonly used theories in health education and health promotion practice. It is my hope that students will find this book interesting and engaging enough to read it and that it will entice them to read further and fill deeper their theory reservoirs.

Acknowledgments

This book certainly would not have been written if it were not for all of my former students who struggled to understand theory. They were the reason I stopped trying to find the right book for them and decided to write it myself.

I must thank my associate editor, Amy Flagg, and my acquisitions editor, Jacqueline Geraci, at Jones and Bartlett for their immeasurable patience and for believing in the value of this project over the past 3 years. Thank you also to Julie Bolduc, production manager, and Jess Newfell, production assistant.

A huge thank you also goes to the many reviewers who provided me with wonderful suggestions that guided the many revisions of this first edition:

Kathleen Allison, PhD, MPH, CHES, Lock Haven University of Pennsylvania

Jill M. Black, PhD, CHES, Cleveland State University

Mark Doherty, PhD, CHES, University of Louisiana at Monroe

Anne L. Drabczyk, PhD, MA, BS, CHES, Indiana State University

Retta Evans, PhD, University of Alabama at Birmingham

Judith K. Lerbke, PhD, CHES, Minnesota State University, Mankato

Melody S. Madlem, PhD, CHES, Central Washington University

Kim H. Miller, PhD, CHES, University of Kentucky

Lilliam Rosado, EdD, New Jersey City University

Phillip J. Waite, CHES, FAIT, Utah State University

Cecilia Watkins, PhD, CHES, Western Kentucky University

The illustrations throughout this book are the work of Nate Bliss. He expertly took my stick-figure sketches and turned them into the unique artwork you see in each chapter. I cannot thank him enough for his creative genius.

To my colleague at William Paterson University, dear friend, and textbook mentor Michele Grodner, I would like to express my sincerest gratitude. It was Michele who gently pushed me to "write what you know," and so I did.

Finally, I'd like to dedicate this book to my father, a prince among princes who left this world much too soon. He would have been so proud.

Introduction to Theory

After reading this chapter the student will be able to:

1. Describe how models and theories are different but related.

2. Explain why theories are used in health education.

3. Explain concepts, constructs, and variables.

4. Discuss factors that influence health and health behavior.

5. Explain how theories are developed.

The idea of studying theory can be a bit daunting. But understanding and being able to use theory is essential because theories provide the foundation for professional practice. They help us develop approaches to solving problems and formulating interventions to best provide the services we offer. In fact, having a theoretical foundation upon which practice is based is among several criteria that have been identified as differentiating a profession from an occupation (Upton, 1970).

WHAT IS THEORY?

So, what is theory? A theory is "a set of statements or principles devised to explain a group of facts or phenomena, especially one that has been repeatedly tested or is widely accepted and can be used to make predictions about natural phenomena" (*American Heritage Dictionary of the English Language*, 2000). Theory is "a set of interrelated concepts, definitions, and propositions that present a systematic view of events of situations by specifying relations among variables in order

to *explain* and *predict* events of situations" (Glanz, Rimer, & Lewis, 2002, p. 25).

From a health promotion and disease prevention perspective, "the term *theory* is used to represent an interrelated set of propositions that serve to explain health behavior or provide a systematic method of guiding health promotion practice" (DiClemente, Crosby, & Kegler, 2002, p. 8). "Theory, then, provides a framework for explaining phenomena and may serve as the basis for further research as well as practice application" (Baumgartner, Strong, & Hansley, 2002, p. 18). Simply put, theories *explain* behavior and thus can suggest ways to achieve behavior change (Glanz, Rimer, & Lewis, 2002). By understanding why people engage in unhealthy behaviors, we can better develop educational interventions that will enable them to change their behavior, if they choose, and adopt healthier lifestyles.

In addition to theories, there are also *models*. A model is a composite, a mixture of ideas or concepts taken from any number of theories and used together. Models help us understand a specific problem in a particular setting (Glanz, Rimer, & Lewis, 2002), which perhaps one theory alone can't do.

Theories and models help us explain, predict, and understand health behavior. They provide a foundation or framework from which to design educational interventions that will improve health status.

TYPES OF THEORIES

Theories and models can be separated into three levels of influence: intrapersonal, interpersonal, and community. Each type of theory explains behavior by looking at how different factors influence what we do.

Intrapersonal Theories

At the intrapersonal or individual level, theories focus on factors within the person that influence behavior, such as knowledge, attitudes, beliefs, motivation, self-concept, developmental history, past experience, and skills (National Cancer Institute [NCI], 2003). These theories and models include, among others, the Health Belief Model, Theory of Reasoned Action, Self-Efficacy Theory, Attribution Theory, and the Transtheoretical Model.

Interpersonal Theories

Theories addressing factors at the interpersonal level operate on the assumption that other people influence our behavior. Other people affect behavior by sharing their thoughts, advice, and feelings and by the emotional support and assistance they provide. These other people may be family, friends, peers, health care providers, or co-workers (NCI, 2003). Social Cognitive Theory is a very commonly used theory addressing behavior at this level.

Community-Level Theories

Community-level models and theories focus on factors within social systems (communities, organizations, institutions, and public policies), such as rules, regulations, legislation, norms, and policies. These theories and models suggest strategies and initiatives that can be used to change these factors (Cottrell, Girvam, & McKenzie, 2005; NCI, 2003). These are change theories more than explanatory theories. Changing a social system from one that maintains and supports *un*healthy behaviors to one that supports healthy behaviors ultimately supports individual behavior change (McLeroy et al., 1988). A commonly used community-level theory is Diffusion of Innovation. More recent additions to this category are ecological models and Social Capital Theory.

In health education and health promotion, theories and models are used to explain why people behave, or don't behave, in certain ways relative to their health. They help us plan educational interventions to enable people to adopt healthier behaviors. However, in order to understand how theories explain health behavior, it is important to understand where theories come from and what factors influence health behavior in the first place.

WHERE DO THEORIES COME FROM?

Theories are born from the need to solve a problem or to find an explanation that would account for some repeated occurrence. The development of a theory in this manner begins with inductive reasoning and qualitative methods (Mullen &

Iverson, 1982; Thomas, 1992). For example, let's look at visits to the student health service on campus. It is noted every year that the number of students needing treatment for alcohol overdose is greater during the month of September than any other time of the academic year. It is also noted that all of the students needing treatment are freshmen. As a result, it might be proposed that risky behavior (drinking) occurs when environmental controls (parents) are absent. This is reasonable based on the information at hand. However, this may or may not be true, which means the conclusion drawn from observation needs to be verified, that is, tested to find out how accurate it is in predicting or explaining the behavior. Can risk-taking behavior be explained by the lack of external controls? To further develop this theory, research would be done to determine what happens, why, and under what conditions (Mullen & Iverson, 1982).

Observation, inductive reasoning, and qualitative research methods are what led to the development of the Health Belief Model. (The Health Belief Model is discussed in detail in Chapter 4.) The Health Belief Model was developed by researchers at the U.S. Public Health Service in the late 1950s. During this time, the emphasis in public health was moving toward disease prevention and early detection through screening programs. Although public health practitioners were in favor of this, the public was not very receptive to being screened for early diagnosis of diseases for which they did not have symptoms. This was particularly true for tuberculosis (TB) screenings (Hochbaum, 1958; Rosenstock, 1960).

Public health screening programs for TB did not attract the considerable number of people who were known to be most at risk for TB. Knowing that this population did not respond to the screening services prompted researchers at the U.S. Public Health Service to try to understand why people were avoiding early detection of TB and why they were avoiding it even though the screening was either free or very low cost (Hochbaum, 1958; Rosenstock, 1960). But equally as important as understanding why some people did not go for screenings was to understand why some people did (Hochbaum, 1958). To begin to answer these questions, qualitative methods were used. A research study was conducted with the objective of identifying what specific combinations or interactions of psychological, social, and physical factors determined whether a person wanted to be screened for TB, when, and at what type of facility (Hochbaum, 1958).

Because the researchers responsible for explaining this behavior were all social psychologists, their approach was based on the idea that behavior is the result of how the individual perceives his or her environment. That is, the beliefs or perceptions of the person are what determine behavior. From this foundation it was reasoned that in order for a person to take action to prevent a disease he or she didn't have, or to be screened for a disease he or she did not have symptoms of, certain beliefs or perceptions about the disease needed to exist. Four perceptions or beliefs were identified as possibly providing an explanation for the avoidance of preventive health screenings: perceived susceptibility to the disease, perceived seriousness of the disease, the perceived benefits of taking action (having the screening), and the perceived barriers to taking action (Hochbaum, 1958; Rosenstock, 1960). The outcome of this research was the Health Belief Model, one of the most widely used theories in health education and health promotion (Glanz, Rimer, & Lewis, 2002).

HEALTH BEHAVIOR

Health behavior includes all of those things we do that influence our physical, mental, emotional, psychological, and spiritual selves. These behaviors range from the daily brushing of our teeth to having unprotected sex; from practicing yoga for stress management to smoking for weight management. A myriad of factors influences the type of behavior in which we engage, whether it is helpful or harmful to our health. Some of these factors are socioeconomic status, skills, culture, beliefs, attitude, values, religion, and gender.

Socioeconomic Status

Socioeconomic status (SES) makes a significant contribution to health since it encompasses education, income, and occupation. Of the SES factors, education level seems to be the best predictor of good health (Winkleby et al., 1992). The higher the education level, the greater the employment opportunities, income, and, ultimately, health status. With knowledge, people can make informed decisions about their health and, as a result, are more likely to engage in health-enhancing behaviors.

However, behavior is driven by more than just knowledge. For example, it is common knowledge that unprotected sex increases the risk of contracting the human immunodeficiency virus (HIV). It is also common knowledge that condoms decrease the risk of contracting HIV. If knowledge were the only factor contributing to behavior, then every sexually active person at risk of contracting HIV would be using condoms. We know this is not the case, but why?

Skills

In the grand scheme of things, it is relatively easy to teach people new information, thereby increasing their knowledge. But without the skill or ability to use that knowledge, it is almost useless. So, behavior is influenced by having both the knowledge and the skills necessary to put the knowledge to use. Going back to the condom example, unless people know how to use condoms, all the knowledge in the world about their HIV risk-reducing benefits is not going to make a difference.

We find a perfect example of this with child safety seats. Parents know the importance of using child safety seats. What they don't know is how to use them correctly. In fact, a study conducted by the National Highway Traffic Safety Administration found that 72.6% of them are *not* used correctly (Decina, Lococo, & Block, 2005).

Culture

Sometimes, even armed with the information and the skills, people still don't use what they know and what they know how to do. That's because behavior is significantly influenced by culture. In every culture there are norms, or expected, accepted practices, values, and beliefs that are the foundation for behavior.

Think about some of the American cultural norms that dictated what you did this morning in preparing for the day. In our culture, people typically shower on a daily basis and follow it with a daily application of deodorant. These behaviors are not necessarily based on knowledge because bathing every day is actually not the best thing for our skin, and using deodorant has no health benefit and in fact can cause problems for people who are allergic to the ingredients.

Looking at this scenario, why do we bathe every day? Other cultures bathe much less frequently and don't use deodorant. So, there must be something else that underlies these behaviors—that something else is our culture. Bathing every day and using deodorant is culturally expected if we are mainstream Americans.

Imagine, if you will, that there was a movement underway that sought to change these behaviors to the more health-enhancing ones of bathing less frequently and not using deodorant. Imagine that this campaign was based on the factual information that daily bathing is bad for the skin and that deodorants and antiperspirants inhibit a natural bodily process. Would you adopt these new behaviors? Would you simply stop taking that morning shower and stop rolling on that deodorant? Why not?

Beliefs

Beliefs are intimately woven with culture. Beliefs are one's own perception of what is true, although they might not be viewed as being true by others. A very common health belief is that going outside with a wet head causes pneumonia. Certainly, knowledge, based on our Western medicine, tells us pneumonia has many causes, but a wet head is not one of them. However, if one's belief is that a wet head causes pneumonia, then the behavior it supports is not going out of the house with a wet head. This seems like a very innocuous behavior on the surface. But take it one step further: an elderly woman with this belief would not get a pneumonia vaccine, believing instead that staying indoors until her hair is dry is all that is needed to avoid "catching pneumonia."

Attitude

When there are a series of beliefs, you have an attitude. Add to the previous belief about a wet head causing pneumonia the belief that wet socks also lead to pneumonia, as does "getting a chill." This results in an attitude that pneumonia can be easily avoided by drying your hair, quickly changing your wet socks, and keeping warm.

Values

Along with attitudes are values. Values are what people hold in high regard, things that are important to them, such as nature, truth, honesty, beauty, education, integrity, friendship, and family. What we value influences the types of behaviors we adopt. For example, if someone values nature, she might be more likely to recycle, use organic fertilizers, feed the birds, and plant trees. If someone values health, he might be more likely to exercise, maintain a normal weight, and drink in moderation.

Religion

Values and beliefs are often reflective not only of a culture, but of a religion. Religion is another enormously important factor in health behavior. Take, for example, the practice of male circumcision. There is no question in Judaism that a male infant will be circumcised, or, in the Muslim faith, that followers will fast from sunrise to sunset during Ramadan. Religion dictates diet, as in Hinduism, whose followers adhere to a strict vegan diet, or Orthodox Judaism, whose followers adhere to strict kosher laws. Religion influences the way we handle stress, such as by prayer or meditation, and whether or not we use contraception, as is the case in Christian religions.

Because the purpose of intercourse is procreation within marriage, contraception use is prohibited among married couples and unnecessary outside of marriage since intercourse is forbidden.

Gender

Gender is another important determinant of health behavior. Research consistently shows that men engage in fewer health-promoting behaviors and have less healthy lifestyles than women. A review of national data and hundreds of large studies has revealed that men of all ages are more likely than women to engage in more than 30 controllable behaviors conclusively linked with a greater risk of disease, injury, and death. Men eat more fat and less fiber, sleep less, and are more often overweight than women (Courtenay, 1998).

PUTTING IT ALL TOGETHER: CONCEPTS, CONSTRUCTS, AND VARIABLES

The factors we have been discussing not only influence health behavior, they are also the concepts of the theories we use to explain behavior. For example, we saw that beliefs influence health behavior. Beliefs form the concept (or idea) of the Self-Efficacy Theory (Chapter 2) and Health Belief Model (Chapter 4), while attitudes are the basis of the Theory of Reasoned Action and the Theory of Planned Behavior (Chapter 3). As the concept of a theory develops and evolves, as it becomes less nebulous and more concrete, constructs emerge. *Constructs* are the ways concepts are used in each specific theory (Glanz, Rimer, & Lewis, 1997).

Each theory, then, has at least one concept at its heart, and a series of constructs that indicate how the concept is used in that theory. To use an analogy here, if a theory is a house, the concepts are the bricks and the constructs are the way the bricks are used in the house. In one house, the bricks are used for the front steps; in another house, the bricks are used for the façade.

A *variable* is the operationalized concept, or how the concept is going to be measured (Glanz, Rimer, & Lewis, 1997). Going back to the house analogy, the bricks can be measured (operationalized) by square footage, number, size, or weight.

Theories, concepts, and constructs. How the concepts (bricks) are used in each theory (house) are the constructs (steps, walkway), and how they are measured (number, color, size) are the variables.

SUMMARY

Theories and models help us understand why people behave the way they do. They are based on concepts and take into account the many factors influencing health behavior. They enable us to focus on these factors from three different levels: intrapersonal, interpersonal, and community. In addition to providing an explanation for behavior, theories and models provide direction and justification for health education and health promotion program planning activities.

Although many theories and models are used to explain health behavior, unfortunately it is beyond the scope of this text to include them all. Rather, this text provides an introduction to the ones most commonly used for health education and health promotion interventions.

CHAPTER REFERENCES

American Heritage Dictionary of the English Language (4th ed.). (2000). Retrieved March 23, 2005, from http://dictionary.reference.com.

Baumgartner, T., Strong, C.H., & Hansley, L.D. (2002). *Conducting and Reading Research in Health and Human Performance.* New York: McGraw Hill.

Cottrell, R.R., Girvam, J.T., & McKenzie, J.F. (2005). *Principles & Foundations of Health Promotion and Education.* San Francisco: Pearson/Benjamin Cummings.

Courtenay, W.H. (1998). College men's health: An overview and call to action. *Journal of American College Health, 46*(6).

Decina, L.E., Lococo, K.H., & Block, A.W. (2005). *Misuse of Child Restraints: Results of a Workshop to Review Field Data Results* (DOT HS 809 851). Washington, DC: National Highway Traffic Safety Administration. Retrieved April 12, 2007, from http://www.nhtsa.dot.gov/people/injury/research/TSF_MisuseChildRetraints/images/809851.pdf.

DiClemente, R.J, Crosby, R.A., & Kegler, M.C. (2002). *Emerging Theories in Health Promotion Practice and Research.* San Francisco: Jossey-Bass.

Glanz, K., Rimer, B.K., & Lewis, F.M. (Eds.). (1997). *Health Behavior and Health Education* (2nd ed.). San Francisco: Jossey-Bass.

Glanz, K., Rimer, B.K., & Lewis, F.M. (Eds.) (2002). *Health Behavior and Health Education* (3rd ed.). San Francisco: Jossey-Bass.

Hochbaum, G.M. (1958). *Participation in Medical Screening Programs: A Socio-psychological Study* (Public Health Service Publication No. 572). Washington, DC: U.S. Government Printing Office.

McLeroy, K.R., Bibeau, D., Steckler, A., & Glanz, K. (1988). An ecological perspective on health promotion programs. *Health Education Quarterly, 15,* 351–377.

Mullen, P.D., & Iverson, D. (1982). Qualitative methods for evaluative research in health education programs. *Health Education, 13,* 11–18.

National Cancer Institute. (2003). *Theory at a Glance: A Guide for Health Promotion Practice.* Washington, DC: U.S. Department of Health and Human Services.

Thomas, B.L. (1992). Theory development. In J.L. Brooking, S.A. Ritter, & B.L. Thomas (Eds.), *Textbook of Psychiatric & Mental Health Nursing.* New York: Churchill-Livingstone.

Rosenstock, I.M. (1960). What research in motivation suggests for public health. *American Journal of Public Health, 50,* 295–301.

Upton, L.A. (1970). *A Study of Secondary School Counselors' Perception of School Counseling as a Profession and Their Desire for Professionalization of School Counseling.* Doctoral dissertation, State University of New York, Buffalo, New York.

Winkleby, M.A., Jatulis, D.E., Frank, E., & Fortmann, S.P. (1992). Socioeconomic status and health: How education, income, and occupation contribute to risk factors for cardiovascular disease. *American Journal of Public Health, 82*(6), 816–820.

CHAPTER 2

Self-Efficacy Theory

Theory Essence Sentence

People will only try to do what they think they can do, and won't try what they think they can't do.

STUDENT LEARNING OUTCOMES

After reading this chapter the student will be able to:

1. Explain the concept of Self-Efficacy Theory.
2. Identify the constructs of Self-Efficacy Theory.
3. Explain how vicarious experience influences self-efficacy.
4. Describe the influence of mastery experience on self-efficacy.
5. Demonstrate how verbal persuasion impacts self-efficacy.
6. Explain how the somatic and emotional states affect self-efficacy.
7. Use Self-Efficacy Theory to explain one health behavior.

THEORETICAL CONCEPT

If you were given the opportunity to fund your college education by swimming 10 laps in a pool, you surely would give it a try, assuming you can swim. Now imagine you were given the same opportunity to raise tuition money, but had to swim the English Channel instead. Would you still go for it? If your swimming ability is like the average person's, there's no way you'd even attempt it. Why the difference? In the first case, you believe you can swim the 10 laps. In the second, you don't believe you can swim the English Channel, and so you won't even try. Think back to your childhood and the book *The Little Engine That Could*: "I think I can. I think I can." This is the concept of self-efficacy.

Self-efficacy is the belief in one's own ability to successfully accomplish something. It is a theory by itself, as well as being a construct of Social Cognitive Theory, which is discussed in detail in Chapter 7. Self-Efficacy Theory tells us that people generally will only attempt things they believe they can accomplish and won't attempt things they believe they will fail. Makes sense—why would you try something you don't think you can do? However, people with a strong sense of efficacy believe they can accomplish even difficult tasks. They see these as challenges to be mastered, rather than threats to be avoided (Bandura, 1994).

Efficacious people set challenging goals and maintain strong commitment to them. In the face of impending failure, they increase and sustain their efforts to be successful. They approach difficult or threatening situations with confidence that they have control over them. Having this type of outlook reduces stress and lowers the risk of depression (Bandura, 1994).

Conversely, people who doubt their ability to accomplish difficult tasks see these tasks as threats. They avoid them based on their own personal weaknesses or on the obstacles preventing them from being successful. They give up quickly in the face of difficulties or failure, and it doesn't take much for them to lose faith in their capabilities. An outlook like this increases stress and the risk of depression (Bandura, 1994).

THEORETICAL CONSTRUCTS

The theory introduces the idea that the perception of efficacy is influenced by four factors: mastery experience, vicarious experience, verbal persuasion, and somatic and emotional state (Bandura, 1994, 1997; Pajares, 2002).

Mastery Experience

We all have mastery experiences. These occur when we attempt to do something and are successful; that is, we have mastered something. Mastery experiences are the most effective way to boost self-efficacy because people are more likely to believe they can do something new if it is similar to something they have already done well (Bandura, 1994).

Perhaps you never thought about this, but babysitting is a significant mastery experience (Figure 2.1). Babysitting is among the strongest predictors of a new mom's belief in her ability to take care of her own children. Women who have experience taking care of infants prior to becoming mothers themselves are more confident in their maternal abilities, and even more so in completing infant care tasks they did frequently (Froman & Owen, 1989, 1990; Gross, Roccissano, & Roncoli, 1989). So, babysitting as a teenager pays off in many ways.

Mastery is the basis for preoperative teaching of men undergoing surgery for prostate cancer. Since this type of surgery can result in urinary incontinence, it is important for men to do pelvic exercises postoperatively to restore urine control. If they are taught these exercises before surgery and practice them, their self-efficacy increases and they are more likely to regain urine control more quickly after surgery (Maliski, Clerkin, & Litwin, 2004).

Providing opportunities for people to gain mastery is the reason why workshops, training programs, internships, and clinical experiences are offered. These are ways people can become proficient at new skills and increase their self-efficacy. For example, training programs are one way of providing mastery experiences for people with disabilities who are entering the labor market (Strauser, 1995). Hours in the clinical practice areas provide opportunities for student nurses to master nursing skills, and internships afford health education students the chance to master the competencies needed for professional practice.

Using this logic, it would seem that mastering something new is relatively simple: all you have to do is practice. How-

FIGURE 2.1 Babysitting provides mastery experiences.

ever, this isn't always the case. If the new tasks are always easy and similar to ones already mastered, and difficult, unfamiliar ones are avoided, then a strong sense of efficacy does not develop. To develop a strong sense of efficacy, difficult tasks also need to be attempted, and obstacles worked through (Bandura, 1994). In reality, it's great if you tried to make brownies, were successful, and now make them all the time. But you can't live on brownies alone. At some point, you need to try making a meal.

Vicarious Experience

Another factor influencing perception of self-efficacy is vicarious experience, or the observation of the successes and failures of others (models) who are similar to one's self. Watching someone like yourself successfully accomplish something you would like to attempt increases self-efficacy. Conversely, observing someone like you fail detracts or threatens self-efficacy. The extent to which vicarious experiences affect self-efficacy is related to how much like yourself you think the model is (Bandura, 1994). The more one associates with the person being watched, the greater the influence on the belief that one's self can also accomplish the behavior being observed.

This construct can be used to explain how group weight loss programs work. If an obese person sees someone just like himself or herself lose weight and keep it off by following a sensible diet and exercise, then the belief in his or her own ability to also do this is strengthened. Watching friends who have taken a nutrition course choose healthy foods at a fast food establishment may increase your belief in your ability to also choose healthy foods: "If they can do it, so can I."

Not only do workshops and training sessions increase mastery, they can also provide vicarious experiences, as well. Watching others in a training session, a class, or during role playing can provide observational experiences that enhance self-efficacy, especially if the person performing or learning the behavior is similar to the observer.

Verbal Persuasion

The third factor affecting self-efficacy is verbal or social persuasion. When people are persuaded verbally that they can achieve or master a task, they are more likely to do the task. Having others verbally support attainment or mastery of a task goes a long way in supporting a person's belief in himself or herself. Coaches frequently use this tactic with their teams. They psyche them up, verbally, before a game or a meet. The coach tells the players that they are going to win, that the other team is no match for them, that they are stronger, faster, better prepared, and so on.

If a team performs poorly, the team members' perception of ability can be negatively affected depending on the coach's reaction. For example, saying we lost the game because you are all lousy players doesn't do much for improving self-efficacy, whereas saying we lost because we need more practice does (Brown, Malouff, & Schutte, 2005).

Conversely, when people are told they do not have the skill or ability to do something, they tend to give up quickly (Bandura, 1994). Imagine the same coach telling his team that they can't possibly win against the opposition. What would the likely outcome be?

Somatic and Emotional States

The physical and emotional states that occur when someone contemplates doing something provide clues as to the likeli-

FIGURE 2.2 Fear of the dentist can lead to avoidance behavior.

hood of success or failure. Stress, anxiety, worry, and fear all negatively affect self-efficacy and can lead to a self-fulfilling prophecy of failure or inability to perform the feared tasks (Pajares, 2002). Stressful situations create emotional arousal, which in turn affects a person's perceived self-efficacy in coping with the situation (Bandura, 1977).

A prime example of how the emotional state affects self-efficacy and, ultimately, health behavior is the classic fear of the dentist (Figure 2.2). For millions of people in this country, the mere thought of going to the dentist is associated with intense pain and anxiety. It is certainly a stressful situation. As a result, they cannot bring themselves to make appointments or keep appointments for even routine, preventive dental care. This avoidance behavior results in a situation in which dental health deteriorates, causing them to have the very pain they wanted to avoid, and the need for more extensive treatment or possible tooth loss (Rowe & Moore, 1998).

As is evident from this example, emotional arousal affects self-efficacy, and self-efficacy affects the decisions people make. If the emotional state improves—that is, emotional arousal or stress is reduced—a change in self-efficacy can be expected (Bandura, 1977).

In summary, according to Self-Efficacy Theory, verbal persuasion, mastery experiences, vicarious experiences, and somatic and emotional states affect our self-efficacy and, therefore, our behavior (Figure 2.3).

FIGURE 2.3 Self-Efficacy Theory.

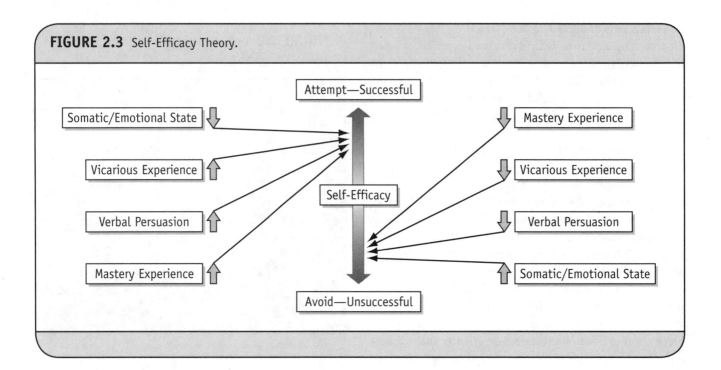

Self-Efficacy Constructs Chart

Mastery experience	Prior success at having accomplished something that is similar to the new behavior
Vicarious experience	Learning by watching someone similar to self be successful
Verbal persuasion	Encouragement by others
Somatic and emotional states	The physical and emotional states caused by thinking about undertaking the new behavior

Self-efficacy is increased by verbal persuasion.

Effect of Maternal Confidence on Breastfeeding Duration: An Application of Breastfeeding Self-Efficacy Theory

ROSEMARY BLYTH, BN, MMID(HONS), DEBRA K. CREEDY, RN, PHD, CINDY-LEE DENNIS, RN, PHD, WENDY MOYLE, RN, PHD, JAN PRATT RN, MHLTHSC, AND SUSAN M. DE VRIES, RN, MPH

Rosemary Blyth is Nurse Researcher at Royal Women's Hospital, Brisbane; Debra Creedy is Professor of Nursing & Health and Wendy Moyle is Senior Lecturer at the Centre for Practice Innovation in Nursing & Midwifery, Griffith University, Brisbane; Jan Pratt is Nursing Director of Primary Care Program and Susan De Vries is Nurse Researcher in the Community Child Health Service at Royal Children's Hospital Health District, Brisbane, Australia; and Cindy-Lee Dennis is Assistant Professor in the Faculty of Nursing at University of Toronto, Toronto, Canada.

ABSTRACT

Background: Although much research has focused on identifying factors that influence breastfeeding initiation and duration, many high-risk factors are nonmodifiable demographic variables. Predisposing factors for low breastfeeding duration rates that are amenable to supportive interventions should be identified. The purpose of this study was to assess the effect of maternal confidence (breastfeeding self-efficacy) on breastfeeding duration. Method: A prospective survey was conducted with 300 women in the last trimester of pregnancy recruited from the antenatal clinic of a large metropolitan hospital in Brisbane, Australia. Telephone interviews were conducted at 1week and 4 months postpartum to assess infant feeding methods and breastfeeding confidence using the Breastfeeding Self-Efficacy Scale. Results: Although 92 percent of participants initiated breastfeeding, by 4 months postpartum almost 40 percent of mothers discontinued and only 28.6 percent were breastfeeding exclusively; the most common reason for discontinuation was insufficient milk supply. Antenatal and 1-week Breastfeeding Self-Efficacy Scale scores were significantly related to breastfeeding outcomes at 1 week and 4 months. Mothers with high breastfeeding self-efficacy were significantly more likely to be breastfeeding, and doing so exclusively, at 1 week and 4 months postpartum than mothers with low breastfeeding self-efficacy. Conclusions: Maternal breastfeeding self-efficacy is a significant predictor of breastfeeding duration and level. Integrating self-efficacy enhancing strategies may improve the quality of care that health care professionals deliver and may increase a new mother's confidence in her ability to breastfeed, and to persevere if she does encounter difficulties. (BIRTH 29:4 December 2002)

Although approximately 90 percent of Australian women initiate breastfeeding, only 48 percent continue to 1 month postpartum and fewer than 23 percent maintain any type of breastfeeding until 6 months (1). Similar breastfeeding duration rates have been reported in the United States (2), Canada (3), and the United Kingdom (4). In developing countries comparable trends are described by UNICEF (5), with only 50 percent of mothers exclusively breastfeeding for the first 6 months postpartum. Thus, most new mothers discontinue breastfeeding before the duration recommended by the American Academy of Pediatrics (6) and World Health Organization (7) of exclusive breastfeeding for the first 6 months postpartum.

Much research has focused on identifying factors that influence breastfeeding initiation and duration, and consistently, mothers who are young, low income, single, or recently immigrated are particularly vulnerable to poor breastfeeding outcomes (8). However, many of these high-risk factors are *nonmodifiable* demographic variables. To address low breastfeeding duration rates effectively, health care professionals need to assess high-risk women reliably and to identify predisposing factors that are amenable to supportive interventions (9). One possible *modifiable* variable is maternal breastfeeding confidence.

Maternal Breastfeeding Confidence

The importance of maternal confidence on breastfeeding outcomes has been highlighted by several researchers. Buxton et al reported that 27 percent of women with low maternal confidence in the prenatal period discontinued breastfeeding within the first postpartum week compared with only 5 percent of the highly confident women ($p < 0.001$) (10). Similarly, in a longitudinal study of 64 low-income mothers, breastfeeding confidence rather than perceived problems was found to be associated with the early termination of breastfeeding (11). Specifically, pregnant mothers who lacked confidence in their ability to breastfeed were twice as likely to discontinue before 2 months postpartum. Furthermore, in a prospective study of 198 women involving multivariate analysis of 11 psychosocial and demographic factors, antenatal confidence was one of the most significant predictors of breastfeeding duration (12).

Postnatal breastfeeding confidence is also of consequence. Mothers who could not establish lactation reported significantly lower levels of breastfeeding confidence compared with mothers who breastfed for more than 6 months (13). In a phenomenological study involving in-depth interviews, deterioration in breastfeeding confidence during the early postnatal period was a major factor in the decision to stop breastfeeding (14). Using the H & H Lactation Scale to measure perceptions of insufficient milk supply, Hill and Humenick reported that mothers who had lower scores on the maternal confidence/commitment subscale also had lower breastfeeding levels at 6 weeks postpartum ($r = 0.66$, $p < 0.05$) (15). Although the preceding results provide initial evidence that breastfeeding confidence is a noteworthy variable in the continuation of breastfeeding, this concept has suffered from a theoretical perspective in the extant literature. To promote the conceptual development of breastfeeding confidence and guide effective supportive interventions, Dennis (16) incorporated Bandura's social cognitive theory (17) and developed the breastfeeding self-efficacy theory.

Breastfeeding Self-Efficacy Theory

Breastfeeding self-efficacy refers to a mother's perceived ability to breastfeed her newborn, and is a salient variable in breastfeeding duration as it predicts (a) whether a mother chooses to breastfeed or not, (b) how much effort she will expend, (c) whether she will have self-enhancing or self-defeating thought patterns, and (d) how she will respond emotionally to breastfeeding difficulties (16). In particular, efficacious (confident) mothers are more likely to choose breastfeeding, persist when confronted with difficulties, employ self-encouraging thoughts, and react positively to perceive difficulties (16). It is important to note that mothers may believe a behavior will assist them in continuing to breastfeed, but have little confidence in their own ability to execute that behavior (16). Thus, to employ a behavior successfully, a mother must both believe that it will help produce a certain outcome (e.g., continue to breastfeed) and have confidence in performing the specific behavior.

Breastfeeding self-efficacy is influenced by four main sources of information: (a) performance accomplishments (e.g., past breastfeeding experiences); (b) vicarious experiences (e.g., watching other women breastfeed); (c) verbal persuasion (e.g., encouragement from influential others, such as friends, family, and lactation consultants); and (d) physiological responses (e.g., fatigue, stress, anxiety) (16, 18). As such, health care professionals may modify a mother's breastfeeding confidence through adjusting these sources of self-efficacy information (16).

Bandura advocated a behavior-specific approach to the study of self-efficacy, arguing that a measure of general self-efficacy in overall ability would be inadequate for tapping an individual's efficacy in managing tasks associated with a specific behavior (17). Thus, to measure breastfeeding self-efficacy, an instrument specific to tasks associated with breastfeeding must be used. A comprehensive literature review found no direct application of self-efficacy theory to the measurement of breastfeeding confidence. The Breastfeeding Self-Efficacy Scale was developed by Dennis (9) and psychometrically tested. The purpose of this study was to assess the effect of maternal confidence on breastfeeding duration using the Breastfeeding Self-Efficacy Scale.

METHODS

Sample

Participants were recruited in Brisbane, Australia, from a large teaching hospital antenatal clinic between January and July 2001. Eligible participants were all pregnant women who intended to breastfeed, were at least 36 weeks' gestation, were age 18 years or older, understood English, planned to give birth at the participating hospital, and resided in the surrounding region for the duration of the study. Mothers were excluded if they had a factor that could significantly interfere with breastfeeding, such as multiple or high-risk pregnancy (serious medical condition, known birth defect). After screening, 348 potentially eligible women were approached; 17 mothers were ineligible due to bottle-feeding intentions, and 300 agreed to participate, with a study participation rate of 90.6 percent.

Procedure

Potential participants were identified by midwives during an antenatal clinic visit and approached by the research assistant to further assess eligibility and explain the study. After informed consent procedures, approved by Griffith University and the ethical review board at Royal Women's Hospital, questionnaires were completed while women waited for clinic appointments. All participants were telephoned by a research assistant at 1 week postpartum to determine infant feeding method and readminister the Breastfeeding Self-Efficacy Scale. Data collection procedures were repeated at 4 months with mothers who were still breastfeeding at 1 week. Of the

300 participants enrolled into the study, telephone interviews were completed at 1 week postpartum with 276 mothers (8% attrition rate). At this time, 92 percent ($n = 253$) of mothers were still breastfeeding their infants; 4-month telephone interviews were completed with 233 mothers for a 7.9 percent attrition rate.

Measures

The Breastfeeding Status Questionnaire was developed by the researchers to determine breastfeeding duration and level. For this study, breastfeeding was defined as the receipt by the infant of any breastmilk within the past 24 hours. During the telephone interview, breastfeeding was further classified into one of six categories advocated by researchers to promote consistency in the definition of breastfeeding and to facilitate comparison of research results (19): exclusive breastfeeding (breastmilk only); almost exclusive breastfeeding (breastmilk and other fluids but not formula, e.g., vitamins); high breastfeeding (less than 1 bottle of formula per day); partial breastfeeding (at least 1 bottle of formula per day); token breastfeeding (breast given to comfort baby not for nutrition); and bottle-feeding (no breastmilk at all). Breastfeeding duration was calculated using the number of breastfeeding days from birth to the time of weaning, or the time of questionnaire completion for mothers who had not weaned. If mothers were not exclusively breastfeeding, rationales were requested to explain the change in infant feeding method.

The Breastfeeding Self-Efficacy Scale (9) is a 33 item, self-report instrument developed to measure breastfeeding confidence. As Bandura (17) recommended, all items are presented positively and scores are summed to produce a range from 33 to 165, with higher scores indicating higher levels of breastfeeding self-efficacy. An initial psychometric assessment was conducted with a convenience sample of 130 Canadian breastfeeding women who completed questionnaires in-hospital and at 6 weeks postpartum (9). Cronbach's alpha coefficient for the scale was 0.96, and principal components factor analysis yielded two subscales: breastfeeding technique and intrapersonal thoughts. Support for predictive validity was demonstrated through positive correlations between Breastfeeding Self-Efficacy Scale scores and infant feeding method at 6 weeks postpartum. In this study, the scale was administered antenatally and postnatally at 1 week and 4 months; Cronbach's alpha coefficients were 0.97, 0.96, and 0.96 respectively.

Statistical Analysis

The data are presented using descriptive statistics (means, standard deviations, proportions). To determine breastfeeding self-efficacy, a total score on the Breastfeeding Self-Efficacy Scale was calculated. A one-way analysis of variance was used to examine differences between two groups for categorical data; t tests were conducted for data at the interval level of measurement. Pearson's correlations were applied to examine the relationship between breastfeeding self-efficacy and breastfeeding level. Hierarchical regression was used to determine the predictive power of breastfeeding self-efficacy on breastfeeding duration at 4 months postpartum.

RESULTS

Sample Characteristics

Characteristics of the sample were representative of the Queensland birthing population (20). The mean age of participants was 28.5 years (± 5.03), with a range from 18 to 41 years. Of the 300 women, 257 (86%) were Caucasian, 12 (4%) were Australian Aboriginal, 12 (4%) were Asian, and 18 (6%) were other ethnic minorities; 264 (88%) women were married or common-law, and 29 (10%) were single. With respect to education level, 189 (63%) were high school graduates, 24 (8%) had a diploma/certificate, 66 (22%) had a university degree, and 20 (7%) had postgraduate education. With respect to occupational status, 70 (23%) were professionals, 67 (22%) worked in the clerical/sales and service sector, and 99 (33%) were stay-at-home mothers. In Australia, most new mothers have 1-year maternity leave provisions; therefore, being employed outside the home was not a confounding issue for breastfeeding duration. Whereas most participants (62%) intended to breastfeed for more than 6 months, 70 (23%) planned to breastfeed for less than 6 months and a further 45 (15%) did not specify, but responded with comments, such as "until the baby is old enough to wean" or "as long as I can."

Outcomes and Self-Efficacy at 1 Week Postpartum

Most women (91.7%) were breastfeeding their infants at 1 week postpartum; only 3 mothers chose not to initiate, and 10 women breastfed for less than 3 days. Significant differences in antenatal breastfeeding self-efficacy were found among mothers who at 1 week postpartum were breastfeeding (mean = 128.10 ± 22.74) or bottle-feeding (mean = 109.57 ± 27.18) (t [274] = 3.68, $p < 0.001$). Table 1 shows breastfeeding status at 1 week postpartum. Rationales for the change in infant feeding method (Table 2) included insufficient milk supply; maternal factors such as sore or cracked nipples, fatigue, and mastitis; infant factors such as poor latch, slow weight gain, and feeding frequency; and other factors, such as inconvenience and hospital practices. Women who were exclusively breastfeeding reported higher antenatal breastfeeding self-efficacy (mean = 129.50 ± 21.71) than women who were partially breastfeeding (mean = 120.62 ± 27.47) or bottle-feeding (mean = 109.08 ± 26.11) (Table 3). The difference in mean scores for women who were exclusively breastfeeding and women who were bottle-feeding was statistically significant ($F[2] = 10.218$, $p < 0.001$).

TABLE 1. Breastfeeding Status at 1 Week and 4 Months Postpartum

Infant Feeding Method	1 Week Postpartum No. (%)	4 Months Postpartum No. (%)
Exclusive breastfeeding	199 (72.1)	73 (28.6)
Almost exclusive breastfeeding	18 (6.5)	65 (25.5)
High partial breastfeeding	2 (0.7)	9 (3.5)
Partial breastfeeding	32 (11.6)	6 (2.4)
Token breastfeeding	2 (0.7)	7 (3)
Bottle-feeding	23 (8.3)	95 (37.3)

TABLE 2. Rationale for Change in Infant Feeding Method at 1 Week and 4 Months Postpartum

Rationale	1 Week Postpartum No. (%)	4 Months Postpartum No. (%)
Insufficient milk supply	22 (8.0)	58 (24.9)
Infant factors	18 (6.5)	9 (3.8)
Maternal factors	23 (8.3)	23 (9.8)
Return to work/study	0	10 (4.3)
Started solids	0	50 (21.5)
Other	14 (5.1)	9 (3.9)

Outcomes and Self-Efficacy at 4 Months Postpartum

Including all participants not lost to follow-up, 153 (60%) mothers were still breastfeeding at 4 months, whereas 102 (40%) were token or bottle-feeding. Over one-half ($n = 138$, 54.1%) of women were exclusively or almost exclusively breastfeeding their infants at 4 months postpartum (Table 1). Frequent reasons cited for alterations in infant feeding method were primarily insufficient milk supply and the introduction of solids (Table 2).

A consistent increase in breastfeeding self-efficacy occurred over time (Table 3). Antenatally, the mean self-efficacy score was 126.16 (±23.85), whereas postnatally the mean score was 139.86 (±23.87) at 1 week and 140.88 (24.63) at 4 months. Differences in antenatal mean scores were found between breastfeeding and bottle-feeding mothers at 4 months postpartum ($t[253] = 4.91$, $p < 0.001$). Similarly, employ-ing the 1-week self-efficacy scores, significant variations were found among mothers who at 4 months postpartum were breastfeeding (mean = 146.97 ± 15.56) or bottle-feeding (mean = 126.48 ± 25.82) ($t[252] = 7.17$, $p < 0.001$).

A standard multiple regression was performed to predict breastfeeding duration at 4 months postpartum and included both antenatal and 1-week Breastfeeding Self-Efficacy Scale scores to determine the influence of maternal confidence on breastfeeding outcomes. Antenatal breastfeeding self-efficacy accounted for 9 percent of variance ($\beta = 0.30$, $t = 4.91$, $p < 0.001$) in breastfeeding status at 4 months, whereas 1-week self-efficacy scores accounted for 17 percent variance ($\beta = 0.41$, $t = 7.17$, $p < 0.001$). Hierarchical regression determined if the addition of breastfeeding self-efficacy improved the prediction of breastfeeding duration beyond that afforded by high-risk maternal demographic variables including age, marital status, educational level, ethnicity, and intended breastfeeding duration (Table 4). Specifically, did the antenatal or 1-week self-efficacy score improve the prediction of breastfeeding duration over and above that provided by the traditional demographic factors? Entered first, the maternal factors accounted for 24 percent ($p < 0.001$) of the variance in breastfeeding duration. Next, antenatal self-efficacy scores were entered and accounted for a 3 percent ($p < 0.001$) increase in variance. However, the 1-week scores were entered to the maternal factor, and the variance increased 9 percent ($p < 0.001$). This enhanced prediction of breastfeeding duration at 4 months postpartum provided additional support for the prognostic ability of the Breastfeeding Self-Efficacy Scale, and suggested that assessments early in the postnatal period have increased predictive power than antenatal appraisals.

Breastfeeding Self-Efficacy and Demographic Factors

Differences in breastfeeding self-efficacy were assessed in relation to maternal demographic variables. No relationship was found between maternal age and breastfeeding self-efficacy antenatally ($r = 0.06$; $p = 0.34$) or postnatally at 1 week ($r = 0.07$; $p = 0.27$) and 4 months ($r = 0.07$; $p = 0.27$). Similarly, no significant differences in antenatal self-efficacy scores were found between mothers who were married/common-law (mean = 126.00 ± 23.44) or single/separated (mean = 127.33 ± 26.98) ($t[298] = 0.32$; $p = 0.75$) or postnatally at 1 week ($t[273] = 0.67$; $p = 0.50$) and 4 months ($t[227] = 0.60$; $p = 0.55$). In relation to educational level, mothers who had high school education or less did not differ in their antenatal breastfeeding self-efficacy (mean = 127.48 ± 23.77) than mothers with some postsecondary education (mean = 124.02 ± 24.01) ($t[297] = 1.21$; $p = 0.23$); similar results were found at 1 week ($t[273] = 0.66$; $p = 0.50$) and 4 months ($t[227] = 0.42$; $p = 0.68$). No

TABLE 3. Mean Breastfeeding Self-Efficacy Scale Scores and Infant Feeding Method

Time	BSES Mean (SD)	Bottle-feeding	Partial Breastfeeding	Exclusive Breastfeeding
Antenatal interview	126.16 (23.85)			
1 Week postpartum	139.86(23.87)	87.42	125.50	147.91
4 Months postpartum	140.88 (24.63)	116.32	134.47	155.11

BSES = Breastfeeding Self-Efficacy Scale.

TABLE 4. Predictive Power of the Breastfeeding Self-Efficacy Scale

Model	Demographic Variables	R	R^2	Increase R^2	Beta	t	p
1		0.50	0.25	0.25			
	Age				0.13	2.17	0.03
	Marital status				0.14	2.38	0.02
	Educational level				0.00	0.04	0.97
	Ethnicity				0.04	0.70	0.48
	Intended duration				0.32	5.21	0.000
2*	BSES Antenatal	0.53	0.28	0.03	0.19	2.92	0.004
	1-week	0.58	0.33	0.08	0.32	5.01	0.000

* Hierarchical regression models were run separately for the antenatal and 1-week BSES. BSES = Breastfeeding Self-Efficacy Scale.

significant differences in antenatal self-efficacy scores were found between Caucasian mothers (mean = 125.42 ± 23.96) and ethnic minority mothers (mean = 130.98 ± 23.04) (t [297] = 1.34; p = 0.16) or postnatally at 1 week (t [273] = 1.48; p = 0.12) and 4 months (t [227] = 0.29; p = 0.78). However, significant differences in antenatal breastfeeding self-efficacy scores were found between primiparas (mean = 122.25 ± = 19.69) and multiparas with previous breastfeeding experience (mean = 129.11 ± = 23.23) (t [298] = 2.59, p = 0.01). This difference was maintained at 1 week (t [273] = 2.66, p = 0.01) and 4 months (t [227] = 2.51, p = 0.01) postpartum.

DISCUSSION

Most participants initiated breastfeeding, by 4 months postpartum, but almost 40 percent of mothers discontinued and only 28.6 percent were breastfeeding exclusively. These findings are consistent with those from other Australian reports (13,21,22). Even though the combined exclusive and almost exclusive breastfeeding rate at 4 months approached the Australian year 2000 target of 60 percent of mothers fully breastfeeding at three months (23), these results suggest that most Australian mothers do not breastfeed for the recommended 6 to 12 months postpartum (6,7).

Of the various rationales mothers cited for the decrease in their breastfeeding level, approximately one-fourth reported perceived insufficient milk supply at 4 months. This significant finding is corroborated by other researchers (8,24–27).

Unfortunately, the cause of perceived insufficient milk supply remains equivocal. Whereas Wight (28) indicated it is related to breastfeeding mismanagement due to inappropriate timing and duration of feeds, formula supplementation, and improper positioning and latching, several other researchers suggested that perceived insufficient milk supply may reflect a lack of breastfeeding confidence (14,29,30). Clearly a salient factor for breastfeeding duration and level, maternal perceptions of insufficient milk supply requires further research to determine the extent to which the etiology is physiological or psychological in nature.

The results from our study unmistakably indicate that maternal breastfeeding self-efficacy is significantly related to breastfeeding duration and level. Antenatal breastfeeding self-efficacy scores were associated with breastfeeding outcomes at 1 week and 4 months postpartum. In particular, high breastfeeding self-efficacy was related to breastfeeding initiation and exclusivity, whereas low self-efficacy was related to bottle-feeding at 1 week postpartum. Even more predictive of breastfeeding outcomes were the scores at 1-week. New mothers with higher breastfeeding self-efficacy were significantly more likely to continue to breastfeed to 4 months postpartum and do so exclusively than mothers with lower scores. This finding is consistent with breastfeeding self-efficacy theory (16) and suggests that immediate performance accomplishments and physiological responses are powerful sources of efficacy information and influence mothers' perceived ability to breastfeed. The results from our study support the findings of Dennis and Faux (9), who also identified a significant relationship between breastfeeding self-efficacy in the immediate postpartum period and breastfeeding outcomes at 6 weeks postpartum.

One limitation of this study is that whereas breastfeeding self-efficacy can be measured and has been shown to be predictive of breastfeeding behaviors, interventions need to be evaluated to determine if maternal confidence can be enhanced to alter breastfeeding outcomes. However, if a high level of self-efficacy suggests choosing, performing, and maintaining breastfeeding (17), it is logical that the self-efficacy framework by Dennis (16) could be used by health care professionals in developing assessment, intervention, and evaluation guidelines.

Implications for Care

The following strategies are potential self-efficacy building interventions that could be evaluated by health care professionals. Prenatally, health care professionals could initially review any previous breastfeeding experience. Consistent with breastfeeding self-efficacy theory, mothers in this study with previous breastfeeding experience had significantly higher breastfeeding self-efficacy than primiparous women. However, negative past experiences and existing misinterpretations can have detrimental effects on breastfeeding self-efficacy. Assessing such experiences may enhance self-efficacy by defusing negative emotional responses, such as fear and anxiety, and correcting misinformation (16).

Performance mastery, and consequently breastfeeding self-efficacy, may be enhanced through successful accomplishments (16,17). Thus, new mothers could be encouraged to initiate breastfeeding immediately after birth and given multiple opportunities to breastfeed before hospital discharge. A knowledgeable health care professional could support all initial breastfeeding attempts to ensure that negatively perceived aspects of performance do not undermine breastfeeding self-efficacy. To aid health care professionals in planning individualized interventions, the Breastfeeding Self-Efficacy Scale could be administered. This tool not only identifies high-risk mothers with low breastfeeding confidence but also provides important assessment information to help individual health care professionals plan to meet the special needs of their new breastfeeding clients (16). Women who have been identified as having low breastfeeding self-efficacy should receive additional support, since this study showed that they are at an increased risk to discontinue breastfeeding prematurely.

After implementing breastfeeding self-efficacy assessment and individualized plan of care, health care profession-als could introduce confidence-building strategies to maintain breastfeeding. A potential intervention that may be evaluated includes positively reinforcing successful breastfeeding performances with decisions made about how to improve future activities. During such a review, health care professionals could note whether the mother experiences discomfort, anxiety, frustration, or a sense of failure. Through the provision of anticipatory guidance, the tendency to experience anxiety, pain, and fatigue could be explicitly acknowledged and normalized while strategies for controlling these states could be taught and practised (16).

Breastfeeding self-efficacy may also be increased through vicarious experience (16,17). Health care professionals could be instrumental in bringing new mothers together to share experiences—a need identified by many breastfeeding women (31,32). Peer support is recognized as an effective strategy to increase breastfeeding duration (8). In a recent trial, when participants were requested to evaluate their peer support experience, most thought that their peer volunteer increased their confidence to breastfeed and were highly satisfied with their experience (33).

CONCLUSIONS

To improve breastfeeding duration rates, health care professionals need to identify high-risk mothers based on modifiable variables. Breastfeeding self-efficacy (maternal confidence) is a potentially modifiable variable that can predict breastfeeding outcomes, provides a clear theoretical framework to guide the development of interventions to improve breastfeeding outcomes, and has a valid and reliable instrument to assess and identify high-risk new mothers. Integrating self-efficacy enhancing strategies not only has the potential to improve the quality of care but may also increase a new mother's confidence in her ability to breastfeed, so that if she does encounter difficulties, she will be able to persevere and continue. Future research is needed to evaluate these proposed confidence-building strategies to determine if breastfeeding self-efficacy can be enhanced to alter breastfeeding outcomes and whether these study findings can be generalized to other populations.

REFERENCES

1. Lund-Adams M, Heywood P. Australian breastfeeding rates: The challenge of monitoring. *Breastfeeding Rev* 1996;4:69–71.
2. Ryan A. The resurgence of breastfeeding in the United States. *Pediatrics* 1997;99:E12.
3. Barber C, Abernathy T, Steinmetz B, Charlebois J. Using a breastfeeding prevalence survey to identify a population for targeted programs. *Can J Public Health* 1997;88:243–245.
4. Savage S, Reilly J, Edwards C, Durnin J. Weaning practices in the Glasgow longitudinal infant growth study. *Arch Dis Child* 1998;79:153–156.

5. UNICEF. The State of the World's Children, 1998. Access at www.unicef.org/sowc98/silent5.htm.

6. American Academy of Pediatrics, Work Group on Breastfeeding. Breastfeeding and the use of human milk. *Pediatrics* 1997;100:1035–1039.

7. World Health Organization. The optimal duration of exclusive breastfeeding. Note for the Press No. 7, 2 April 2001; access at www.who.int/inf-pr-2001/en/note2001-07.html.

8. Dennis C-L. Breastfeeding initiation and duration: A 1990–2000 literature review. *J Obstet Gynecol Neonatal Nurs* 2002; 31:12–32.

9. Dennis C-L, Faux S. Development and psychometric testing of the breastfeeding self-efficacy scale. *Res Nurs Health* 1999; 22:399–409.

10. Buxton K, Gielen A, Faden R, et al. Women intending to breastfeed: Predictors of early infant feeding experiences. *Am J Prev Med* 1991;7:101–106.

11. Ertem IO, Votto N, Leventhal, JM. The timing and prediction of the early termination of breastfeeding. *Pediatrics* 2002;107:543–548.

12. O'Campo P, Faden R, Gielen A, Wang M. Prenatal factors associated with breastfeeding duration: Recommendations for prenatal interventions. *Birth* 1992;19:195–201.

13. Papinczak TA, Turner CT. An analysis of personal and social factors influencing initiation and duration of breastfeeding in a large Queensland maternity hospital. *Breastfeeding Rev* 2000;8:25–33.

14. Dykes F, Williams C. Falling by the wayside: A phenomenological exploration of perceived breast-milk inadequacy in lactating women. *Midwifery* 999;15:232–246.

15. Hill P, Humenick S. Development of the H & H Lactation Scale. *Nurs Res* 1996;45:136–140.

16. Dennis C-L. Theoretical underpinnings of breastfeeding confidence: A self-efficacy framework. *J Hum Lact* 1999; 15:195–201.

17. Bandura A. Self-efficacy: Toward a unifying theory of behavioral change. *Psychol Rev* 1977;84:191–215.

18. Bandura A. Englewood Cliffs, NJ: Prentice-Hall, 1986.

19. Labbok M, Krasovec K. Toward consistency in breastfeeding definition. *Stud Fam Plann* 1990;21:226–230.

20. Queensland Health. *Perinatal Statistics, Queensland 1997.* Brisbane: Author, 1998.

21. Donath SM, Amir LH. Does maternal obesity adversely affect breastfeeding initiation and duration? *Breastfeeding Rev* 2000;8:29–33.

22. Scott J, Landers M, Hughes R, Binns C. Factors associated with breastfeeding at discharge and duration of breastfeeding. *J Paediatr Child Health* 2001;37:254–261.

23. Nutbeam D, Wise M. Australia: planning for better health: Opportunities for health promotion through the development of national health goals and targets. *Promot Educ* 1993; Spec No: 19–24.

24. Arlotti J, Cottrell B, Lee S, Curtin J. Breastfeeding among low-income women with and without peer support. *J Community Health Nurs* 1998;15:163–178.

25. Chan SM, Nelson EA, Leung SS, Li CY. Breastfeeding failure in a longitudinal post-partum maternal nutrition study in Hong Kong. *J Paediatr Child Health* 2000; 36:466–471.

26. Matthews K, Webber K, McKim E, et al. Maternal infant-feeding decision: Reasons and influences. *Can J Nurs Res* 1998;30:177–198.

27. Quinn A, Koepsell D, Haller S. Breastfeeding incidence after early discharge and factors influencing breastfeeding cessation. *J Obstet Gynecol Neonatal Nurs* 1997;26:289–294.

28. Wight NE. Management of common breastfeeding issues. *Pediatr Clin North Am* 2001;48:321–344.

29. Stamp G, Crowther C. Breastfeeding–Why start? Why stop? A prospective survey of South Australian women. *Breastfeeding Rev* 1995;3:15–19.

30. Dykes F, Griffiths H. Societal influences upon initiation and continuation of breastfeeding. *Br J Midwifery* 1998;6:76–80.

31. Britton C. The influence of antenatal information on breastfeeding experiences. *Br J Midwifery* 1998;6:312–315.

32. Hoddinott P, Pill R. Qualitative study of decision about infant feeding among women in east end of London. *BMJ* 2000;318:30–34.

33. Dennis C-L. Breastfeeding peer support: Maternal and volunteer perceptions from a randomized controlled trial. *Birth* 2002;3:169–176.

Article Source: Blyth, R., Creedy, D.K., Dennis, C.L., Moyle, W., Pratt, J., & De Vries, S.M. (2002). Effect of maternal confidence on breastfeeding duration: An application of breastfeeding self-efficacy theory. *Birth, 29*(4), 278–284. Reprinted with permission of Blackwell Publishing.

QUESTIONS

1. According to the article, how does breastfeeding self-efficacy relate to breastfeeding behavior?

2. What are the suggested ways to increase breastfeeding self-efficacy using the constructs? How are these suggestions similar to or different from the ones your group identified?

CHAPTER REFERENCES

Bandura, A. (1977). Analysis of Self-Efficacy Theory of behavior change. *Cognitive Therapy and Research, 1*(4), 287–310.

Bandura, A. (1994). Self Efficacy. In V.S. Ramachaudran (Ed.), *Encyclopedia of Human Behavior* (Vol. 4, pp. 71–81). New York: Academic Press. (Reprinted in H. Friedman [Ed.], *Encyclopedia of Mental Health.* San Diego: Academic Press, 1998)

Bandura, A. (1997). *Self-Efficacy: The Exercise of Control.* New York: Freeman.

Brown, L.J., Malouff, J.M., & Schutte, N.S. (2005). The effectiveness of a self-efficacy intervention for helping adolescents cope with sport-competition loss. *Journal of Sport Behavior, 28*(2), 136–150.

Froman, R.D., & Owen, S.V. (1989). Infant care self-efficacy. *Scholarly Inquiry for Nursing Practice: An International Journal, 3*(3), 199–210.

Froman, R.D., & Owen, S.V. (1990). Mothers' and nurses' perceptions of infant care skills. *Research in Nursing and Health, 13*, 247–253.

Gross, D., Rocissano, L., & Roncoli, M. (1989). Maternal confidence during toddlerhood: Comparing preterm and fullterm groups. *Research in Nursing and Health, 18*(6), 489–499.

Maliski, S.L., Clerkin, B., & Litwin, M.S. (2004). Describing a nurse case manager intervention to empower low-income men with prostate cancer. *Oncology Nursing Forum, 31*(1), 57–63.

Pajares, F. (2002). Overview of Social Cognitive Theory and of self-efficacy. Retrieved January 23, 2006, from http://www.emory.edu/EDUCATION/mfp/eff.html.

Rowe, M.M., & Moore, T.A. (1998). Self-report measures of dental fear: Gender difference. *American Journal of Health Behavior, 22*(4), 243–247.

Strauser, D. (1995). Applications of Self-Efficacy Theory in rehabilitation counseling. *Journal of Rehabilitation, 61*(1), 7–11.

The Theory of Reasoned Action and the Theory of Planned Behavior

Theory Essence Sentence

Health behavior results from intention influenced by attitude, norms, and control.

STUDENT LEARNING OUTCOMES

After reading this chapter the student will be able to:

1. Explain the concept of the Theory of Reasoned Action (TRA) and the Theory of Planned Behavior (TPB).

2. Explain how the constructs of attitude, subjective norm, volitional control, and behavioral control influence intention.

3. Differentiate between the TRA and the TPB.

4. Use the theory to explain at least one behavior.

THEORETICAL CONCEPT

The Theory of Reasoned Action (TRA) and the Theory of Planned Behavior (TBP) propose that behavior is based on the concept of intention. *Intention* is the extent to which someone is ready to engage in a certain behavior, or the likelihood that someone will engage in a particular behavior (Fishbein, 1967; Ajzen & Fishbein, 1980). People are more likely to do something if they plan or aim to do it than if they do not.

THEORETICAL CONSTRUCTS

Intention in the TRA/TBP is influenced by the following factors: attitudes, subjective norms, volitional control, and behavioral control.

Attitudes

As we saw in Chapter 1, attitudes are formed by a series of beliefs and result in a value being placed on the outcome of the behavior (Ajzen, 2002a). If the outcome or result of a behavior is seen as being positive, valuable, beneficial, desirable, advantageous, or a good thing, then a person's attitude will be favorable and his or her likelihood of engaging in that behavior would be greater. For example, if someone believes eating soy is healthier than eating animal protein, is better for the environment, and carries less of a chance of foodborne illness, the individual's attitude toward eating soy products would be favorable. Conversely, an unfavorable attitude toward soy consumption may result from the beliefs that soy products have an unpleasant taste and texture and are too expensive (Rah et al., 2004). These attitudes would either positively or negatively influence the intention to eat soy products.

Another example of how intention to engage in a behavior is impacted by attitude and beliefs is seen in infant feeding choice. If a woman believes breastfeeding will protect her baby against infection (Swanson & Power, 2004), is healthier for her, and is more convenient, these beliefs are consistent with a positive attitude and she is more likely to breastfeed. If she believes breastfeeding is embarrassing (Swanson & Power,

2004), hurts, and restricts her activity (negative attitude), she is more likely to bottle feed.

Subjective Norms

In addition to attitude, intention is influenced by subjective norms. A *subjective norm* is the perceived social pressure to engage or not to engage in a certain behavior. It is determined by normative beliefs. These are the behaviors that *we perceive* important people in our lives expect from us (Ajzen, 2002a). These important people are often family members, friends or peers, religious figures, health care providers, or others we hold in high esteem—people we like to please. Subjective norms, then, result from the behaviors we perceive these important people expect from us, and our desire to comply with their perceived expectations. Note that these expectations may or may not be based in reality, as they are our *perceptions*.

Continuing with the soy consumption example used previously, if a health care provider and family member suggest that an individual eat soy products, and if the person wants to make these others happy, there is a greater willingness to comply and a greater likelihood of soy consumption (Rah et al., 2004). On the other hand, if the health care provider does not make the suggestion to consume soy and there is limited family support to try this food source, then the likelihood of soy being eaten is greatly diminished.

Just as we have seen earlier how attitude and beliefs influence infant feeding choice, so too do subjective norms. The decision women make about feeding method for their first baby is influenced by their own mothers, friends, partners, and medical professionals (Swanson & Power, 2004). These new moms will choose the method they perceive to be the preference of these important people.

The same is true when we look at condom use among adolescent mothers. The extent of importance given to the parents', peers', and sexual partner's approval or disapproval of condom use influences intention to use (Koniak-Griffin & Stein, 2006).

Volitional Control

Although the Theory of Reasoned Action tells us behavior is the result of a person's intention to do something, in order for this to happen, the behavior has to be under volitional control. A behavior under volitional control is one in which the person is able to decide, at will, to engage in or not (Ajzen, 1991). Whether you eat breakfast in the morning is under volitional control. The type of exercise you do (if any) is under volitional control. Having your blood pressure checked is under volitional control.

In some situations a person may not have complete control over a behavior even though the intention to engage in the behavior is great. For example, a woman may intend to practice safer sex. However, the actual use of the (male) condom is not in her control. Thus, she has limited volitional control over this behavior even though her intention is great. Condom use is significantly more likely if, in addition to her intention to use a condom, her male partner also intends to use a condom (DeVisser & Smith, 2004). On the other hand she can say no to sex without a condom. She does have volitional control over engaging in intercourse (except in the case of rape).

If we look at participating in a team sport, making the team is a good example of a behavior that is not under volitional control. A person may have great intention to join the university lacrosse team, have a really positive attitude toward team sports and exercise, and want to make his parents happy by engaging in a sport in college, but alas, does not make the team. Making the team is not completely under his control because there is no way to affect the skill level of the other people he is competing against.

Behavioral Control

In situations where there is less volitional control, even when intention is great, the TRA is not very useful in predicting or explaining behavior. To address this, the construct of behavioral control was added to the theory, and with this, the *Theory of Planned Behavior* was born (Ajzen, 1991; Ajzen, 2002b). Therefore, the Theory of Planned Behavior is nothing more than the Theory of Reasoned Action with another construct added.

The construct of behavioral control is similar to the construct of self-efficacy in Social Cognitive Theory (Ajzen, 2002b) and the concept of Self-Efficacy Theory. However, behavioral control differs from self-efficacy in that self-efficacy is concerned with one's perception of *ability* to perform a behavior, whereas behavioral control is concerned with "perceived *control* over performance of a behavior" (Ajzen, 2002b, p. 4), or how easy or difficult it is to perform the behavior (Ajzen, 1991).

Behavioral control is impacted by a set of control beliefs. These are beliefs the person has that help or hinder performance of the behavior (Ajzen, 2002b); that is, they affect the perception of how easy or difficult it is to carry out the behavior (Ajzen, 1991). For the lacrosse player who didn't make the team, behavioral control influenced his intention to try out. He believed it would be easy for him to make the team. In the condom example, although the woman has limited volitional

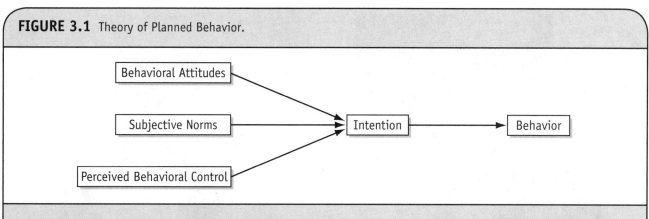

FIGURE 3.1 Theory of Planned Behavior.

Source: Reprinted from *Journal of Nutrition Education, 36*(5), Rah, J.H., Hasler, C.M., Painter, J.E., Chapman-Novakofski, K.M. Applying the Theory of Planned Behavior to Women's Behavioral Attitudes on and Consumption of Soy Products, 238–244. Copyright (2004) with permission from Society for Nutrition Education.

control, she may believe it is easy to get her partner to use a condom.

In summary, according to the Theory of Reasoned Action and the Theory of Planned Behavior, attitudes, subjective norms, volitional control, and behavioral control affect intention and, therefore, our behavior (Figure 3.1).

Constructs Chart

Attitude	A series of beliefs about something that affects the way we think and behave
Subjective norms	The behaviors we perceive important people expect of us and our desire to comply with these expectations
Volitional control	The extent to which we can decide to do something, at will
Behavioral control	The extent of ease or difficulty we believe the performance of a behavior to be

Theory of reasoned action. Intention to engage in a behavior is affected by beliefs and attitudes. A positive attitude increases intention to engage in the behavior, and a negative attitude decreases intention to engage in the behavior.

Application of the Theory of Planned Behavior to Adolescent Use and Misuse of Alcohol

B. C. MARCOUX AND J. T. SHOPE[1]

Department of Physical Therapy, School of Health Sciences, Oakland University, Rochester, MI 48309-4401 and [1]University of Michigan Transportation Research Institute and Department of Health Behavior and Health Education, School of Public Health, University of Michigan, Ann Arbor, MI 48109-2150, USA

ABSTRACT

This research assessed the plausibility and robustness of Ajzen's Theory of Planned Behavior (TPB) in predicting and explaining use, frequency of use and misuse of alcohol among 3946 fifth through eighth grade students in southeastern Michigan. The study also compared the effectiveness of the TPB and the Theory of Reasoned Action (TRA) in predicting intention to use alcohol. Data for this secondary analysis were part of a longitudinal study, and were collected in March and May of 1987. Results provided strong support for the use of the TPB in this context and suggest that the model is fairly robust. All model components reached significance at the 0.05 level. Intention to use alcohol explained up to 26% of the variance in use, 38% of the variance in frequency of use and 30% of the variance in misuse of alcohol. In addition, up to 76% of the variance in intention to use alcohol was explained by attitudes, subjective norms and perceived behavioral control. Although both models were effective in predicting intention to use alcohol, as expected, the TPB was more effective in predicting intention to use alcohol than was the TRA.

INTRODUCTION

The negative consequences of adolescent alcohol use and misuse are well documented, and include decreased academic achievement, depression, other substance use, unintentional injuries and serious traffic accidents (Richmond, 1979; Barnes and Welte, 1986; Vega *et al.*, 1993; DeSimone *et al.*, 1994). While a declining trend in adolescent alcohol use has been noted over the past decade, the 1992 survey by Johnson *et al.* (1993) found non-significant *increases* in prevalence and 'binge drinking' among eighth graders. In their most recent survey, Johnston *et al.* (1995) reported that 69% of eighth grade students had used alcohol in the previous 30 days and 13% reported consuming five or more drinks in a row at least once in the previous 2 weeks.

Through research on the correlates and predictors of adolescent alcohol use, a number of psychosocial factors which are included in general models of health-related behaviors have emerged as significant predictors of alcohol use. A model of substance use behavior would be beneficial in pinpointing those variables that are of greatest importance in predicting, explaining and understanding alcohol use and misuse. This information could also be used in developing curricula to prevent alcohol and other drug use, evaluating educational programs, and in long-range forecasting of these behaviors. Ajzen's Theory of Reasoned Action (TRA) and the Theory of Planned Behavior (TPB) both have potential value in predicting and explaining adolescent alcohol use.

In the late 1970s, Fishbein and Ajzen developed a model of behavioral intentions based on their TRA. The theory was developed to both predict and explain behaviors of social relevance that are under a person's volitional control. In 1985, the TPB expanded the TRA. This expanded model is appropriate for both volitional and non-volitional behaviors. In both theories, the central variable is *intention* to perform a behavior and it is the immediate determinant of the behavior (Ajzen and Fishbein, 1980; Fishbein, 1980).

In the TRA, *intention* is viewed as a function of two other determinants; *attitude* toward the behavior and *subjective norms*. *Subjective norms* are a function of the individual's beliefs that specific social referents (parents, friends, peers, etc.) think he/she should or should not perform the behavior as well as his/her motivation to comply with those referents (Fishbein, 1980). The TPB adds *perceived control* over the behavior as a third determinant of *intention* (see Figure 1) (Ajzen, 1985; Schifter and Ajzen, 1985; Ajzen and Madden, 1986).

The literature on substance use suggests that attitudes toward alcohol use (Lacey, 1981; Stacey and Elvy, 1982; Downs, 1987), normative influences (Bank *et al.*, 1985; Kandel 1985; Brook *et al.*, 1986; Needle *et al.*, 1986) and intention to use alcohol (Huba *et al.*, 1981; Lacey, 1981; Wolford and Swisher, 1986) are important predictors of adolescent alcohol use. These variables are contained in the TRA which was used by Laflin *et al.* (1994) to successfully predict drug and alcohol use in high school and college students.

The primary difference between the TRA and TPB is that the TPB contains the concept of perceived control. Jemmott *et al.* (1992) used the TPB to predict intention to use condoms among 179 African-American adolescents and found that perceived behavioral control added significantly to the explained variance. The influence of perceived control has also been examined in intention to exercise and was again found to be important (Godin *et al,* 1993).

The current study assesses the plausibility and robustness of the TPB in predicting and explaining use, frequency of use and misuse of alcohol among young adolescents, and provides a partial test of the model. It is a partial test because motivation to comply with significant others was not measured. In addition, the determinants of behavioral intentions (attitudes, subjective norms and perceived control) are approximations of Ajzen's components. While the items used to measure attitudes, subjective norms and perceived control in this study are not worded precisely as suggested by Ajzen, it is believed they have captured the essence of these concepts. This alternative wording serves as an additional test of the robustness of the model.

This research is unique in that it provides information about alcohol use and misuse among very young adolescents, those in fifth through eighth grades. The major hypotheses of this study were as follows: (1) *intention* to use alcohol will predict *alcohol use, frequency of use* and *alcohol misuse* among adolescents; (2) *attitudes, subjective norms* and *perceived behavioral control* will account for *intention* to use alcohol; and (3) the TPB will be more effective in accounting for and predicting *intention* to use alcohol among young adolescents than the theory of reasoned action.

METHODS

Respondents and Procedures

This study was part of a longitudinal project evaluating the effectiveness of a school-based substance abuse prevention program. Participants in this longitudinal study were 3946 fifth through eighth grade students from 179 classes in 16 buildings in six school districts in southeastern Michigan. The

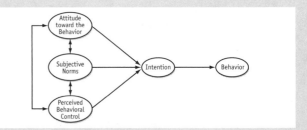

FIG. 1. Theory of Planned Behavior.

data used in this study were collected in March and May of 1987, and were the first two waves of data collected in a study that continued through March 1994. Identical questionnaires and procedures were used at each data collection point. Of the 5370 potential subjects for this study, only three (0.06%) refused to participate. In addition, 295 students were absent on the day of pretesting. Therefore, pretest data were collected from 4371 subjects yielding an 81% response rate. Post-test data were collected from 4226 subjects. A total of 3946 subjects (90%) completed both surveys.

The subjects were primarily white (51% male) and ranged in age from 9 to 16 years (mean age 11.9, standard deviation 1.31). A power analysis revealed that there was more than adequate power (>0.95) to detect a significant relationship between the dependent variables (alcohol use, frequency of use, misuse of alcohol and intention to use alcohol) and the independent variables.

The questionnaire was pilot-tested on a separate sample of same-age children and revised based on student's questions and comments until it was age-appropriate. Each student was assigned a unique identification number to allow for longitudinal matching of individual data. Project staff administered the confidential questionnaires in the students' regular classroom with teachers present, but appropriately situated in the room to assure that students' confidentiality of responses was not threatened. One full class period (approximately 50 min) was allowed for completion of the 25 page questionnaire.

Variables

All variables in this study were based on self-report. The use of self-reported data has been examined in both adults and children by a number of authors (Midanik, 1982; Polich, 1982; Baranowski, 1985; Campanelli *et al.*, 1987; Embree and Whitehead, 1993; Carifio, 1994). Most relevant is the study by Campanelli *et al.* (1987) as it assessed the validity of self-reports of alcohol use and misuse in adolescents. Using the 'bogus pipeline' technique, they found that alcohol use and misuse among those who were told that biochemical tests would be performed on their saliva samples to verify alcohol use or misuse were *not* different from the control group. The possibility, however, exists for both over and underestimation by adolescents in reporting alcohol use, frequency of alcohol use and alcohol misuse, and should be considered in interpreting the results of this and any study using self-reported data.

Dependent Variables

The dependent variables were *alcohol use* (N = 3914, mean = 1.41, SD = 1.08), *frequency of alcohol use* (N = 3726, mean = 1.53, SD = 0.90) and *misuse of alcohol* (N = 3893, mean = 0.14, SD = 0.34) in Hypothesis 1, and *intention to use alcohol* (N = 3900, mean = 1.95, SD = 0.99) in Hypotheses 2 and 3. *Alcohol use* was a single item which asked 'In the past 2 months, have you had *a full drink* (NOT JUST A TASTE) of alcohol?' The four possible responses and scoring of this item were: yes = 3, I've only had a taste = 2, no = 1 and I've never tasted alcohol = 0. *Frequency of alcohol use* was an index created from three items which measured the frequency of consuming one full drink of beer, wine or liquor. Each of the three questions asked 'How often did you have at least one bottle or can of beer (one glass of wine, or one full mixed drink or shot of liquor) in the past 2 months?'. The response categories and scoring for each item in the index were: 1 = none, 2 = less than one, 3 = about once a year and 4 = once a week or more. Individual responses to the three questions were averaged to provide the index (Cronbach α = 0.79).

Alcohol misuse was an index which averaged the responses to three items measuring alcohol overindulgence ('How many times did you drink more than you planned to?', 'How many times did you feel sick to your stomach after drinking?' and 'How many times did you get very drunk?'). The response categories and scoring for these three items were: 0 = never and 1 = at least once (Cronbach α = 0.77).

Intention to use alcohol was a mean of two items: 'If a friend offered you a drink of alcohol (beer, wine or liquor) would you drink it?' and 'If you had a chance to drink some alcohol (beer, wine or liquor) in the next 2 years would you do it?'. Both items had four response categories: 1 = no, 2 = probably not, 3 = probably and 4 = definitely would use alcohol (Cronbach α = 0.88).

Independent Variables

The independent variables were *attitude, subjective norms* and *perceived behavioral control. Attitude* was an average of two items (Cronbach α = 0.54) measuring beliefs regarding the health consequences of using alcohol. The items were: 'How much do you think a person your age risks hurting themselves (health or other ways) by having five or more alcoholic drinks

every weekend?' and 'At your age, if you had five or more alcoholic drinks every weekend, do you think it would hurt you (health or other ways)?'. The response categories for the first item were: a lot = 4, some = 3, a little = 2 and not at all = 1. The response categories for the second item were: yes = 4, probably = 3, probably not = 2 and no = 1. *Subjective norms* were measured by a series of four single-item variables. Each variable measured the respondents' beliefs about people their age using alcohol by a different normative influence: parents, older brothers, older sisters and friends. The stem for each of the items was: 'How do your (parents/friends/older brothers/older sisters) feel about kids your age drinking alcohol?'. The response categories were as follows: 1 = very bad idea, 2 = bad idea, 3 = neither good nor bad idea, 4 = good idea and 5 = very good idea. The items were not combined in an index so that the individual influence of each normative influence could be examined.

Perceived control included an index of peer pressure to use alcohol (mean of three items, Cronbach α = 0.84), an index of items related to opportunity to use alcohol as well as friends' experience with alcohol (mean of four items, Cronbach α = 0.91), a single item that measured ease or difficulty of getting alcohol (availability), and a single item that measured belief in one's ability to say 'no' to friends and make it stick (Table II). These measures were selected based on the theoretical definition of perceived control given by Ajzen (1985) and Shifter and Ajzen (1985), and on the results of statistical analyses of these variables including a smallest space analysis, factor analysis with varimax rotation, and α coefficients. The relative importance of each of these components of perceived behavioral control will be examined.

DATA ANALYSIS

Data were analyzed using the OSIRIS.IV statistical package. Multiple regression analysis with pairwise deletion of missing data was used to test all hypotheses. The research project from which these data were obtained included a classroom-based prevention program which, in the long run, was expected to reduce alcohol misuse among the intervention group (Shope *et al.*, 1994, 1997a,b). It was anticipated that the intervention would have minimal or no effect on behavioral outcomes at the first post-test because the interval between the baseline data collection and the first follow-up (the data in this study) was only 2 months. In order to determine the influence, if any, of the intervention, dummy variables for the two experimental groups were created and included in the regression equations. The first experimental group received the substance abuse prevention program as part of a comprehensive health education curricula and are labeled 'health education' group. The second experimental group received only the substance abuse prevention program and are labeled 'substance education' group.

RESULTS

Predicting Alcohol Use, Frequency of Alcohol Use and Alcohol Misuse

To test the hypothesis that intention to use alcohol will predict *alcohol use* 2 months later, *intention* (measured at time 1) plus the dummy variables for the experimental groups were regressed on *alcohol use* (measured at time 2). As seen in Table I, the resulting R^2 of the analysis for all subjects was 0.2618 and *intention* was the only predictor which reached significance. This regression was repeated with *frequency of alcohol use* (measured at time 2) as the dependent variable. Again, *intention* (measured at time 1) was the only predictor to reach significance with 38.40% of the variance explained (Table I).

The hypothesis that intention to use alcohol will predict *alcohol misuse* (measured at time 2) was first tested using multiple regression. As above, *intention* (measured at time 1) plus the dummy variables for the interventions were regressed on *alcohol misuse*. In this analysis, 30.67% of the variance was explained by intention (Table I). This hypothesis was also tested using logistic regression because the dependent variable (*misuse*) was a dichotomous variable. Results of the logistic regression analysis were similar to those of the multiple regression and showed that intention was the only significant predictor. Interestingly, the health education group nearly

reached significance at 0.054, indicating a trend in the expected direction. In the OSIRIS.IV program, the covariance ratio for a predictor is the R^2 for that predictor when it is regressed on all the other predictors. For all regression analyses run to test this hypothesis, the covariance ratios were less than 0.53, indicating that multicollinearity was not a problem.

Predicting Intention to Use Alcohol

The second hypothesis in this study examined the ability of the TPB to explain *intention* to use alcohol and was tested (using cross-sectional data) by regressing *attitudes, subjective norms* and *perceived control* on *intention* to use alcohol. Betas were used to evaluate the relative importance of each variable in explaining *intention* to use alcohol. The results of this analysis showed that all variables reached significance at $P < 0.05$ and the resulting R^2 value for this regression equation was 0.7639 (Table II). It is important to note that while all of these variables reached significance at the 0.05 level, the unique contribution of each of the independent variables to the overall explained variance was minimal for all but two indices: friends' experience with alcohol and peer pressure.

The TPB Versus the TRA

The final hypothesis in this study compared the ability of the TPB with the ability of the TRA to predict intention to use alcohol. In this multiple regression analysis (using cross-sectional data), the indices of attitudes, normative beliefs of parents, older brothers, older sisters and friends were regressed

TABLE I. Results of regression analysis for alcohol use, frequency of use and alcohol misuse (N = 3946)

Variable	B	β	Marginal R^2	T ratio	Probability
Alcohol use[a]					
intention	0.599	0.515	0.257	37.06	0.000
health education	−0.032	−0.014	0.000	0.74	0.461
substance education	−0.076	−0.031	0.000	1.56	0.118
Frequency of use[b]					
intention	0.599	0.618	0.371	48.70	0.000
health education	0.002	0.001	0.000	0.07	0.945
substance education	0.023	0.110	0.000	0.62	0.537
Alcohol misuse[c]					
intention	0.172	0.552	0.296	41.04	0.000
health education	−0.022	−0.036	0.001	1.93	0.054
substance education	−0.014	−0.022	0.000	1.13	0.258

[a]$R^2 = 0.2618$; $F = 465.98$; significance = 0.00.
[b]$R^2 = 0.3840$; $F = 818.95$; significance = 0.00.
[c]$R^2 = 0.3067$; $F = 581.254$; significance = 0.00.

TABLE II. Results of regression analysis for TPB predicting intention to use alcohol (N = 3946)

Variable	B	β	Marginal R^2	T ratio	Probability
Attitude index	−0.0378	−0.0272	0.0006	3.274	0.001
Subjective norms					
parents	0.1163	0.0766	0.0046	8.739	0.000
brothers	0.0449	0.0429	0.0010	4.083	0.000
sisters	0.0704	0.0648	0.0023	6.191	0.000
friends	0.0378	0.0438	0.0008	3.602	0.001
Peer pressure index	0.5091	0.4375	0.0958	39.961	0.000
Friends' experience index	0.3504	0.3448	0.0415	26.307	0.000
Confidence saying no	0.0192	0.0158	0.0002	1.962	0.049
Availability	0.0519	0.0644	0.0032	7.253	0.000

$R^2 = 0.7639$; $F = 1,414.903$; significance = 0.000.

on *intention* to use alcohol. This equation represents those variables in the TRA. Results of this analysis showed that all variables emerged significant $(P < 0.01)$ and approximately 52% of the variance in intention to use alcohol was explained (Table III). Comparing the results of Tables II and III, it can be seen that the TPB was more effective in explaining the variance in intention to use alcohol than was the TRA.

DISCUSSION

The major purpose of this study was to explore the use of the TPB to predict and explain alcohol use and misuse among young adolescents, and to evaluate the robustness of the model. It was hypothesized that (1) intention to use alcohol will predict alcohol use, frequency of alcohol use and alcohol misuse among young adolescents, (2) attitudes, subjective norms and perceived behavioral control will account for intention to use alcohol, and that (3) the TPB will be more effective in accounting for and predicting intention to use alcohol among young adolescents than the TRA.

Generally, the results of the study lend strong support to Ajzen's TPB and suggest that the theory is useful in predicting and explaining alcohol use, frequency of use and misuse among adolescents. The central component in this model is intention to perform a behavior. In this study, the relationship between intention and behavior explained as much as 26% of the variance in alcohol use, 37% of the variance in frequency of alcohol use and approximately 30% of the variance in alcohol misuse. While intention accounted for as much as 26–37% of the variance in these behaviors, approximately 63–74% of the variance was unexplained. In this prospective study, intention to use alcohol was measured in March of 1987 and was used to predict behaviors that were reported 2 months later. During this 2 month interval, respondents may have

changed their intention to use alcohol, changed their beliefs regarding the positive or negative aspects of alcohol use, been exposed to new information about alcohol use, experienced changes in the availability of alcohol or had changes in social situations such as friends' alcohol use and perceived pressure to use alcohol.

The next major point in Ajzen's TPB states that attitudes, subjective norms and perceived control will explain intention to perform or not perform a behavior. The results were very good, with approximately 76% of the variance in intention to use alcohol being explained by the three model components.

Examination of the relative importance of the independent variables revealed that the indices of peer pressure and friends' experience with alcohol (both part of the model component 'perceived behavioral control') were the two most important variables in this model. Normative beliefs of parents emerged as the third most important predictor. These findings are consistent with recent literature showing that peer influence and friends' alcohol use have a significant influence on the decision to use alcohol (Biddle *et al.*, 1980; Rooney, 1982; Dielman *et al.*, 1991; Hansen and Graham, 1991; Aas and Klepp, 1992). This finding is also consistent with literature showing that peer behavior is more important in predicting adolescent alcohol use than are the normative beliefs of parents (Needle *et at.*, 1986; Moncher *et al.*, 1992; Keefe, 1994).

According to Ajzen and Fishbein (1980), variables that are external to the model will influence the behavior indirectly through the model components. In the context of this study, situational factors such as physical location, presence of others, and thoughts and feelings about using alcohol are likely to be important in the adolescent's decision to use alcohol. While the model component attitudes reached significance, it

TABLE III. Results of regression analysis for TRA predicting intention to use alcohol (N = 3946)

Variable	B	β	Marginal R^2	T ratio	Probability
Attitudes	−0.1677	−0.1204	0.0134	10.455	0.000
Subjective norms					
parents	0.1639	0.1079	0.0092	0.0108	0.0103
brothers	0.1454	0.1389	0.1314	8.6451	9.3995
sisters	0.1482	0.1365	9.1846	32.7623	0.000
friends	0.3876	0.4492	0.000	0.000	0.000

$R^2 = 0.5175$; $F = 845.278$; significance = 0.000.

was among the least important of the independent variables and its unique contribution to the overall explained variance in intention to use alcohol was less than 1%. The most likely explanation for this finding is that the way in which the attitude component was measured in this study did not capture the influence of these situational factors. A second reason for the low level of importance of attitudes in explaining intention may be that attitudes are not firmly established until later adolescence (ages 15–20). The subjects in this sample were very young (mean age 11.9 years), and it is likely that attitudes regarding the consequences of using alcohol were not yet fully developed and established.

Overall, the study showed that external factors (peer pressure, friends' experiences with alcohol, normative beliefs of parents and availability of alcohol) are more important in predicting intention to use alcohol than internal factors such as attitudes. These findings suggest that prevention programs that provide students with knowledge and skills to resist peer pressure and skill in decision making would be beneficial in reducing alcohol use and misuse in this age group. In addition, these findings suggest that a reduction in the availability of alcohol, avoidance of peer groups in which alcohol use is frequent and those in which alcohol is frequently talked about were important in the decision not to use alcohol. Further, those subjects who believed that their parents disapproved of adolescents' using alcohol were less likely to use it. Encouraging parents to discuss their concerns related to alcohol use in this age group and, where possible to become involved in prevention programs, would also be helpful. Unlike generations before them, adolescents in the 1990s are exposed to far more media portrayals of and advertisement for alcohol than past generations were. Parental discussion of the messages given to adolescents through television could be important in reducing alcohol use and misuse.

A unique aspect of this study is the young age of the subjects (fifth to eighth grade students). The results of this study are cause for concern about alcohol use at this early age. As in studies of alcohol use among high school and college age students, use increases with increasing age. The findings in this study suggest that those factors that are important in older adolescents are important in the decision to try alcohol in younger adolescents as well. Because alcohol is known to be one of the gateway substances which leads to use of illicit drugs, this information is vital in the design and development of interventions to prevent abuse of all substances.

Fishbein and Ajzen's TRA has been used to successfully predict and explain use of alcohol in high school and college students (Laflin *et al.*, 1994). The results of this partial test of the TRA provide evidence that the model is also valuable in predicting and explaining intention to use alcohol among young adolescents. Further, these results support the contention that the TPB is more effective in predicting and explaining intention to use alcohol among young adolescents than is the TRA.

Based on the literature of the past two decades, it can be concluded that normative beliefs continue to play an important role in the decision to use alcohol for all adolescents. While there had been a declining trend in the use of illegal substances among high school students in the past decade, the most recent data (1993–1994) indicate increases in the use of illicit drugs for these students (Johnston *et al.*, 1995). It has been suggested that this rebound may be due to a decline in media attention given to adolescent substance use (UMISR, 1992). This information, combined with the results of this study reinforce the need to implement substance abuse prevention programs in the elementary schools.

ACKNOWLEDGEMENTS

This study was supported originally by grants from the Michigan Department of Public Health, the Michigan Department of Education, the Michigan Office of Substance Abuse Services and several local funding sources.

REFERENCES

Aas, H. and Klepp, K.-I. (1992) Adolescents' alcohol use related to perceived norms. *Scandinavian Journal of Psychology, 33*, 315–325.

Ajzen, I. (1985) From intention to actions: a theory of planned behavior. In Kuhl, J. and Beckmann, J. (eds), *Action Control: From Cognition to Behavior.* Springer-Verlag, New York, pp. 11–39.

Ajzen, I. and Fishbein, M. (1980) *Understanding Attitudes and Predicting Social Behavior.* Prentice-Hall, Engelwood Cliffs, NJ.

Ajzen, I. and Madden, T. J. (1986) Prediction of goal-directed behavior attitudes, intentions, and perceived behavioral control. *Journal of Experimental Social Psychology, 22*, 453–474.

Bank, B. J., Biddle, B. J., Anderson, D. S., Hauge, R., Keats, D. M., Marlin, N. N. and Valantira, S. (1985) Comparative research on the social determinants of adolescent drinking. *Social Psychology Quarterly, 48*, 164–177.

Baranowski, T. (1985) Methodologic issues in self-report of health behavior. *Journal of School Health, 55*, 179–182.

Barnes, G. M. and Welte, J. W. (1986) Patterns and predictors of alcohol use among 7th–12th grade students in New York State. *Journal of Studies on Alcohol, 47*, 53–62.

Biddle, B. J., Bank, B. J. and Marlin, M. M. (1980) Social determinants of adolescent drinking: what they think, what they do, and what I think and do. *Journal of Studies on Alcohol, 41*, 215–241.

Brook, J. S., Whiteman, M., Gordon, A. S., Nomura, C. and Brook, D. W. (1986) Onset of adolescent drinking: a longitudinal study of intrapersonal and interpersonal antecedents. *Advances in Alcohol and Substance Abuse, 5*, 91–110.

Campanelli, P. C., Dielman, T. E. and Shope, J. T. (1987) Validity of adolescents' self-reports of alcohol use and misuse using a bogus pipeline procedure. *Adolescence, 22*, 7–22.

Carifio, J. (1994) Sensitive data and students' tendencies to give socially desirable responses. *Journal of Alcohol and Drug Education, 39*, 74.

Dielman, T. E., Butchart, A. T, Shope, J. T. and Miller, M. (1990–91) Environmental correlates of adolescent substance use and misuse: implications for prevention programs. *International Journal of the Addictions, 25*, 855–880.

DeSimone, A., Murray, P. and Lester, D. (1994) Alcohol use, self-esteem, depression, and suicidality in high school students. *Adolescence, 29*, 939–942.

Downs, W. R. (1987) A panel study of normative structure, adolescent alcohol use, and peer alcohol use. *Journal of Studies on Alcohol, 48*, 167–175.

Embree, B. G. and Whitehead, P. C. (1993) Validity and reliability of self-reported drinking behavior dealing with the problem of response bias. *Journal of Studies on Alcohol, 54*, 334–344.

Fishbein M. (1980) A theory of reasoned action: some applications and implications. In Howe, H. E., Jr (ed.), *1979 Nebraska Symposium on Motivation.* University of Nebraska Press, Lincoln, pp. 65–116.

Godin, G., Valois, P. and Lepage, L. (1993) The pattern of influence of perceived behavioral control upon exercising behavior: an application of Ajzen's theory of planned behavior. *Journal of Behavioral Medicine, 16*, 81–102.

Hansen, W. B. and Graham, J. W. (1991) Preventing alcohol, marijuana, and cigarette use among adolescents: peer pressure resistance training versus establishing conservative norms. *Preventive Medicine, 20*, 414–430.

Huba, G. J., Wingard, J. A. and Bentler, P. M. (1981) Intentions to use drugs among adolescents: a longitudinal analysis. *International Journal of the Addictions, 16*, 331–339.

Jemmott, J. B., Jemmott, L. S. and Hacker, C. I. (1992) Predicting intentions to use condoms among African-American adolescents: the theory of planned behavior as a model of HTV risk-associated behavior. *Ethnicity and Disease, 2*, 371–380.

Johnston, L. D., O'Malley, P. M. and Bachman, J. G. (1993) *National Survey Results on Drug Use from Monitoring the Future Study 1975–1992.* NIH publ. no. 93-3597, US Government Printing Office, Washington, DC, Vol. 1.

Johnston, L. D., O'Malley, P. M. and Bachman, J. G. (1995) *National Survey Results on Drug Use from Monitoring the Future Study 1975–1994.* NIH publ. no. 95-4026, US Government Printing Office, Washington, DC, Vol. 1.

Kandel, D. B. (1985) On processes of peer influences in adolescent drug use: a developmental perspective. *Advances in Alcohol and Substance Abuse, 4*, 139–163.

Keefe, K. (1994) Perceptions of normative social pressure and attitudes toward alcohol use: changes during adolescence. *Journal of Studies on Alcohol, 55*, 46–54.

Lacey, W. B. (1991) The influence of attitudes and current friends on drug use intentions. *Journal of Social Psychology, 113*, 65–76.

Laflin, M. T, Moore-Hirschl, S., Weis, D. L. and Hayes, B. E. (1994) Use of the theory of reasoned action to predict drug and alcohol use. *International Journal of Addiction, 29*, 927–940.

Midanik, L. (1982) Over-reports of recent alcohol consumption in a clinical population: a validity study. *Drug and Alcohol Dependence, 9*, 101–110.

Moncher, M. S., Holden, G. W. and Schinke, S. P. (1992) Psychosocial correlates of adolescent substance use: a review of current etiological constructs. *International Journal of Addiction, 4*, 377–14.

Needle, R., McCubbin, H., Wilson, M., Reineck, R., Lazar, A. and Mederer, H. (1986) Interpersonal influences in adolescent drug use. The role of older siblings, parents, and peers. *International Journal of Addiction, 2*, 739–766.

University of Michigan's Institute of Social Research (1993) New national survey on teen alcohol and other drug use. *The Bottom Line, 14*(2), 87–93.

Polich, J. M. 91982) The validity of self-reports in alcoholism research. *Addictive Behaviors, 7*, 123–132.

Richmond, J. F. and Healthy People (1979) *The Surgeon-General's Report on Health Promotion and Disease Prevention.* Public Health Service, US Government Printing Office, Washington, DC.

Rooney, J. F. (1982) Perceived differences of standards for alcohol use among American youth. *Journal of Studies on Alcohol, 43*, 1069–1083.

Schifter, D. E. and Ajzen, I. (1985) Intention, perceived control, and weight loss: an application of the theory of planned behavior. *Journal of Personality and Social Psychology, 49*, 843–851.

Shope, J. T., Copeland, L. A. and Dielman, T. E. (1994) Measurement of alcohol use and misuse in a cohort of students followed from grade 6 through grade 12. *Alcohol: Clinical and Experimental Research, 18*, 726–733.

Shope, J. T, Copeland, L. A., Kamp, M. E. and Lang, S. W. (1997a) Twelfth grade follow-up of the effectiveness of a middle school-based substance abuse prevention program. *Journal of Drug Education*, in press.

Shope, J T., Copeland, L. A., Marcoux, B. C. and Kamp, M. E. (1997b) Effectiveness of a school-based substance abuse prevention program. *Journal of Drug Education, 26*, 323–337.

Stacey, B. G. and Elvy, G. A. (1982) Attitudes, age, and sex as correlates and predictors of alcohol consumption among 14–17 year olds in New Zealand. *Addictive Behaviors, 7*, 333–345.

Vega, W. A., Gil, A. G. and Zimmerman, R. S. (1993) Patterns of drug use among Cuban-American, African-American, and White Non-Hispanic boys. *American Journal of Public Health, 83*, 257–259.

Wolford, C. and Swisher, J. D. (1986) Behavioral intention as an indicator of drug and alcohol use. *Journal of Drug Education, 16*, 305–326.

Article Source: Marcoux, B.C., & Shope, J.T. (1997). Application of the Theory of Planned Behavior to adolescent use and misuse of alcohol. *Health Education Research, 12*(3), 323–311. Reprinted by permission of Oxford University Press.

QUESTIONS

1. Which constructs of the TRA/TPB were used in the article?

2. Which of the constructs were most predictive of alcohol use?

3. How did each of the constructs explain alcohol use?

4. Did you think of these during your brainstorming session?

CHAPTER REFERENCES

Ajzen, I. (1991). The Theory of Planned Behavior. *Organizational Behavior and Human Decision Process, 50*, 179–21a. Retrieved October 24, 2004, from http://home.comcast.net/~icek.aizen/tpb.obhdp.pdf.

Ajzen, I. (2002a). Theory of Planned Behavior. Retrieved October 24, 2004, from http://www-unix.oit.umass.edu/~aizen/index.html.

Ajzen, I. (2002b). Perceived behavioral control, self-efficacy, locus of control and the Theory of Planned Behavior. *Journal of Applied Social Psychology, 32*, 1–20.

Ajzen, I., & Fishbein, M. (1980). *Understanding Attitudes and Predicting Social Behavior.* Englewood Cliffs, NJ: Prentice-Hall.

DeVisser, R.O., & Smith, A.M.A. (2004). Which intention? Whose intention? Condom use and theories of individual decision making. *Psychology, Health & Medicine, 9*(2), 193–204.

Fishbein, M. (1967). *Readings in Attitude Theory and Measurement.* New York: Wiley.

Koniak-Griffin, D., & Stein, J.A. (2006). Predictors of sexual risk behaviors among adolescent mothers in a human immunodeficiency virus prevention program. *Journal of Adolescent Health, 38*, 297e1–297e11.

Rah, J.H., Hasler, C.M., Painter, J.E., & Chapman-Novakofski, K.M. (2004). Applying the Theory of Planned Behavior to women's behavioral attitudes on and consumption of soy products. *Journal of Nutrition Education and Behavior, 36*(5), 238–244.

Swanson, V., & Power, K.G. (2004). Initiation and continuation of breastfeeding: Theory of Planned Behavior. *Journal of Advanced Nursing, 50*(3), 272–282.

CHAPTER 4

Health Belief Model

Theory Essence Sentence

Personal beliefs influence health behavior.

STUDENT LEARNING OUTCOMES

After reading this chapter the student will be able to:

1. Explain the original concept of the Health Belief Model.

2. Discuss how the constructs of perceived seriousness, susceptibility, benefits, and barriers might predict health behavior.

3. Analyze the impact of the modifying variables on health behavior.

4. Identify cues to action and how they motivate behavior.

5. Use the theory to explain at least one behavior.

THEORETICAL CONCEPT

The Health Belief Model (HBM) is by far the most commonly used theory in health education and health promotion (Glanz, Rimer, & Lewis, 2002; National Cancer Institute [NCI], 2003). It was developed in the 1950s as a way to explain why medical screening programs offered by the U.S. Public Health Service, particularly for tuberculosis, were not very successful (Hochbaum, 1958).

The underlying concept of the original HBM is that health behavior is determined by personal beliefs or perceptions about a disease and the strategies available to decrease its occurrence (Hochbaum, 1958). Personal perception is influenced by the whole range of intrapersonal factors affecting health behavior, as discussed in Chapter 1.

THEORETICAL CONSTRUCTS

The following four perceptions serve as the main constructs of the model: perceived seriousness, perceived susceptibility, perceived benefits, and perceived barriers. Each of these perceptions, individually or in combination, can be used to explain health behavior. More recently, other constructs have been added to the HBM; thus, the model has been expanded to include cues to action, motivating factors, and self-efficacy.

Perceived Seriousness

The construct of perceived seriousness speaks to an individual's belief about the seriousness or severity of a disease. While the perception of seriousness is often based on medical information or knowledge, it may also come from beliefs a person has about the difficulties a disease would create or the effects it would have on his or her life in general (McCormick-Brown, 1999). For example, most of us view the flu as a relatively minor ailment. We get it, stay home a few days, and get better. However, if you have asthma, contracting the flu could land you in the hospital. In this case, your perception of the flu might be that it is a serious disease. Or, if you are self-employed, having the flu might mean a week or more of lost wages. Again, this would influence your perception of the seriousness of this illness.

Perceived Susceptibility

Personal risk or susceptibility is one of the more powerful perceptions in prompting people to adopt healthier behaviors. The greater the perceived risk, the greater the likelihood of engaging in behaviors to decrease the risk. This is what prompts men who have sex with men to be vaccinated against hepatitis B (de Wit et al., 2005) and to use condoms in an effort to decrease susceptibility to HIV infection (Belcher et al., 2005). Perceived susceptibility motivates people to be vaccinated for influenza (Chen et al., 2007), to use sunscreen to prevent skin cancer, and to floss their teeth to prevent gum disease and tooth loss.

It is only logical that when people believe they are at risk for a disease, they will be more likely to do something to prevent it from happening. Unfortunately, the opposite also occurs. When people believe they are not at risk or have a low risk of susceptibility, unhealthy behaviors tend to result. This is exactly what has been found with older adults and HIV prevention behavior. Because older adults generally do not perceive themselves to be at risk for HIV infection, many do not practice safer sex (Rose, 1995; Maes & Louis, 2003). This same scenario was found with Asian American college students. They tended to view the HIV/AIDS epidemic as a non-Asian problem; thus, their perception of susceptibility to HIV infection was low and not associated with practicing safer sex behaviors (Yep, 1993).

What we have seen so far is that a perception of increased susceptibility or risk is linked to healthier behaviors, and decreased susceptibility to unhealthy behaviors. However, this is not always the case. In college students, perception of susceptibility is rarely linked to the adoption of healthier behaviors (Courtenay, 1998), even when the perception of risk is high. For example, although college students consider themselves at risk for HIV because of their unsafe sex behaviors, they still do not practice safer sex (Lewis & Malow, 1997), nor do they stop tanning even though they perceive themselves to be at increased risk for skin cancer (Lamanna, 2004). Perception of susceptibility explains behavior in some situations, but not all.

When the perception of susceptibility is combined with seriousness, it results in perceived threat (Stretcher & Rosenstock, 1997). If the perception of threat is to a serious disease for which there is a real risk, behavior often changes. This is what happened in Germany in 2001 after an outbreak of bovine spongiform encephalitis (BSE), better known as mad cow disease. Although mad cow disease does not occur in people, research suggests that eating cattle with the disease can result in variant Creutzfeldt-Jakob disease (CJD). Variant CJD, like BSE, affects the brain, causing tiny holes that make it appear spongelike. Both diseases are untreatable and fatal (National Institute of Neurological Disorders and Stroke, 2007). The perception of threat of contracting this disease through eating beef was one factor related to declining meat consumption in Germany (Weitkunat et al., 2003). People changed their behavior based on the perception of threat of a fatal disease.

Another example in which perception of threat is linked to behavior change is found in colon cancer survivors. Colorectal cancer is a very serious disease with a high risk of recurrence. It is the perception of the threat of recurrence that increases the likelihood of behavior change in people previously treated for this disease. In particular, changes occur in their diets, exercise, and weight (Mullens et al., 2003).

We see the same thing when people perceive a threat of developing non-insulin-dependent diabetes mellitus (NIDDM). Among people whose parents had or have the disease, the perception of threat of developing it themselves is predictive of more health-enhancing, risk-reducing behaviors. Most important, they are more likely than others to engage in behaviors to control their weight (Forsyth, 1997), given that obesity is a known risk factor for NIDDM.

Just as perception of increased susceptibility does not always lead to behavior change, as we saw earlier in the chapter with college students, neither does a perception of increased threat. This is the scenario with older adults and safe food-handling behaviors. Older adults are among the groups most vulnerable to foodborne illness (Gerba, Row, & Haas, 1996) and are among those for whom it can be particularly serious. Even though they perceive a threat of illness from foodborne sources, they still do not use safe food-handling practices (Hanson & Benedict, 2002) all of the time.

Perceived Benefits

The construct of perceived benefits is a person's opinion of the value or usefulness of a new behavior in decreasing the risk of developing a disease. People tend to adopt healthier behaviors when they believe the new behavior will decrease their chances of developing a disease. Would people strive to eat five servings of fruits and vegetables a day if they didn't believe it was beneficial? Would people quit smoking if they didn't believe it was better for their health? Would people use sunscreen if they didn't believe it worked? Probably not.

Perceived benefits play an important role in the adoption of secondary prevention behaviors, such as screenings. A good example of this is screening for colon cancer. One of the screening tests for colon cancer is a colonoscopy. It requires a few days of preparation prior to the procedure to completely cleanse the colon: a diet restricted to clear liquids followed by cathartics. The procedure involves the insertion of a very long, flexible tube instrument with a camera on the end into the rectum to view the length of the colon. The procedure itself is done under anesthesia, so it is not uncomfortable, but it does take time afterward to recover, and the preparation is time consuming. Regardless of the inconvenience, this is presently the best method for early detection of colon cancer, the third leading cause of cancer deaths in the United States. When colon cancer is found early, it has a 90% cure rate. However, only 36% of people over age 50 (who are most at risk) have this screening done (New York-Presbyterian Hospital, 2006). What makes some people undergo screening and others not? Among women, those who perceive a benefit from colonoscopy (early detection) are more likely to undergo screening than those who do not see the screening as having a benefit (Frank & Swedmark, 2004).

The same holds true for breast cancer. We know that the earlier breast cancer is found, the greater the chance of survival. We also know that a breast self exam (BSE), when done regularly, can be an effective means of early detection. But not all women do BSE regularly. They have to believe there is a benefit in adopting this behavior, which is exactly what was found to be true among black women: those who believed breast self exams were beneficial did them more frequently (Graham, 2002).

Perceived Barriers

Since change is not something that comes easily to most people, the last construct of the HBM addresses the issue of perceived barriers to change. This is an individual's own evaluation of the obstacles in the way of him or her adopting a new behavior. Of all the constructs, perceived barriers are the most significant in determining behavior change (Janz & Becker, 1984).

In order for a new behavior to be adopted, a person needs to believe the benefits of the new behavior outweigh the consequences of continuing the old behavior (Centers for Disease Control and Prevention, 2004). This enables barriers to be overcome and the new behavior to be adopted.

In trying to increase breast self examination practices in women, it would seem obvious that the threat of breast cancer would motivate adoption of this early detection practice. Certainly breast cancer is a very serious disease, one for which women are at risk and for which the perception of threat is high. Even with all of this, the barriers to performing BSE exert a greater influence over the behavior than does the threat of cancer itself (Champion, 1993; Champion & Menon, 1997; Ellingson & Yarber, 1997; Umeh & Rogan-Gibson, 2001).

Some of these barriers include difficulty with starting a new behavior or developing a new habit, fear of not being able to perform BSE correctly, having to give up things in order to do BSE, and embarrassment (Umeh & Rogan-Gibson, 2001).

Barriers also stand in the way of Hispanic women seeking Pap tests, even though they perceive cervical cancer as being serious and believe there are benefits to having a Pap test. The barriers—fear that the test is painful and not knowing where to go for testing—are not outweighed by the benefits of the test or minimized by the seriousness of the disease (Byrd et al., 2004). Among college women, fear of pain and embarrassment are the barriers to Pap tests. It is interesting that these barrier beliefs are greatest among women who have never had a Pap test (Burak & Meyer, 1997).

Modifying Variables

The four major constructs of perception are modified by other variables, such as culture, education level, past experiences, skill, and motivation, to name a few. These are individual characteristics that influence personal perceptions. For example, if someone is diagnosed with basal cell skin cancer and successfully treated, he or she may have a heightened perception of susceptibility because of this past experience and be more conscious of sun exposure because of past experience. Conversely, this past experience could diminish the person's perception of seriousness because the cancer was easily treated and cured.

In personal health classes on many campuses, students are required to complete a behavior change project. They choose an unhealthy behavior and develop a plan to change it and adopt a more healthy behavior. The modifying variable behind this is motivation. The motivation is a grade.

Cues to Action

In addition to the four beliefs or perceptions and modifying variables, the HBM suggests that behavior is also influenced by cues to action. Cues to action are events, people, or things that move people to change their behavior. Examples include illness of a family member, media reports (Graham, 2002), mass media campaigns (Figure 4.1), advice from others, reminder postcards from a health care provider (Ali, 2002), or health warning labels on a product.

Knowing a fellow church member with prostate cancer is a significant cue to action for African American men to attend prostate cancer education programs (Weinrich et al., 1998). Hearing TV or radio news stories about foodborne illness and reading the safe handling instructions on packages of raw meat and poultry are cues to action associated with safer food-handling behaviors (Hanson & Benedict, 2002). Having

FIGURE 4.1 Cue to action—don't drink and drive.

displays on college campuses of cars involved in fatal crashes from drunk driving is an example of a cue to action—don't drink and drive.

Self-Efficacy

In 1988, self-efficacy was added to the original four beliefs of the HBM (Rosenstock, Strecher, & Becker, 1988). As was discussed in Chapter 2, self-efficacy is the belief in one's own ability to do something (Bandura, 1977). People generally do not try to do something new unless they think they can do it. If someone believes a new behavior is useful (perceived benefit), but does not think he or she is capable of doing it (perceived barrier), chances are that it will not be tried.

As mentioned previously, a significant factor in not performing BSE is fear of being unable to perform BSE correctly (Umeh & Rogan-Gibson, 2001). Unless a woman believes she is capable of performing BSE (that is, has BSE self-efficacy), this barrier will not be overcome and BSE will not be practiced.

When we look at osteoporosis, exercise self-efficacy and exercise barriers are the strongest predictors of whether one practices behaviors known to prevent this disease. Women who do not engage in the recommended levels of weight-bearing exercise tend to have low exercise self-efficacy, mean-

FIGURE 4.2 Health Belief Model.

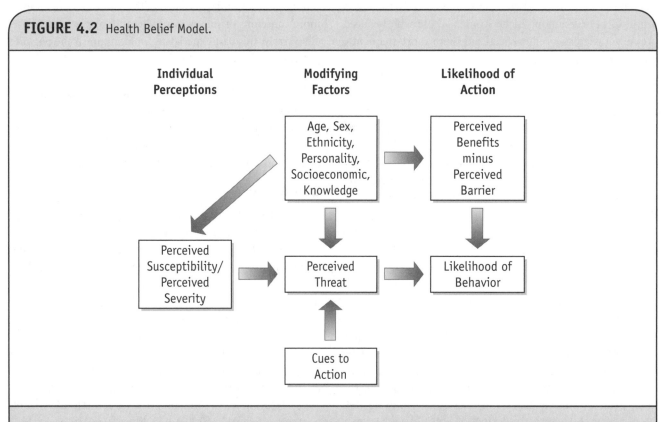

Source: Stretcher, V., & Rosenstock I.M. (1997). The Health Belief Model. In Glanz K., Lewis F.M., & Rimer B.K., (Eds.). *Health Behavior and Health Education: Theory, Research and Practice.* San Francisco: Jossey-Bass. Reprinted with permission.

ing they do not believe they can exercise, and perceive there to be significant barriers to exercise (Wallace, 2002). As a result, these women do not exercise.

In summary, according to the Health Belief Model, modifying variables, cues to action, and self-efficacy affect our perception of susceptibility, seriousness, benefits, and barriers and, therefore, our behavior (Figure 4.2).

Health Belief Model Constructs Chart

Perceived susceptibility	An individual's assessment of his or her chances of getting the disease
Perceived benefits	An individual's conclusion as to whether the new behavior is better than what he or she is already doing
Perceived barriers	An individual's opinion as to what will stop him or her from adopting the new behavior
Perceived seriousness	An individual's judgment as to the severity of the disease
Modifying variables	An individual's personal factors that affect whether the new behavior is adopted
Cues to action	Those factors that will start a person on the way to changing behavior
Self-efficacy	Personal belief in one's own ability to do something

Perception of benefits and barriers is a powerful determinate of health behavior.

THEORY IN ACTION: CLASS ACTIVITY

Using the HBM, brainstorm to identify possible perceptions of seriousness, susceptibility, benefits, and barriers that might explain why some women do not engage in behaviors to prevent osteoporosis, and possible cues to action and modifying variables that might change this behavior.

Now read the following article, and then answer the discussion questions that follow it.

Design and Implementation of an Osteoporosis Prevention Program Using the Health Belief Model

Lori W. Turner, PhD, RD

Sharon B. Hunt, EdD

Ro DiBrezzo, PhD

Ches Jones, PhD

Lori W. Turner, Ph.D., RD. is an Associate Professor of Health Science in the Department of Health Science, Kinesiology, Recreation and Dance at the University of Arkansas. Sharon B. Hunt, Ed.D. is Professor and Department Head in the Department of Health Science, Kinesiology, Recreation and Dance at the University of Arkansas. Ro DiBrezzo, Ph.D. is a Professor of Exercise Science and Director of Human Performance Laboratory in the Department of Health Science, Kinesiology, Recreation and Dance at the University of Arkansas. Ches Jones, Ph.D. is an Associate Professor of Health Science in the Department of Health Science, Kinesiology, Recreation and Dance at the University of Arkansas.

ABSTRACT

Osteoporosis is a crippling condition that often results in premature mortality and significant morbidity that is manifested in the form of fractures, bone deformity, and pain. Osteoporosis is a serious public health problem that affects 25 million people in the United States, 80% of whom are women. National health objectives indicate an urgent need to reduce deaths due to falls, reduce the incidence of hip fractures, and increase the number of women educated about osteoporosis. Strategies for preventing osteoporosis include maximizing peak bone mass and minimizing bone losses through health education and health promotion programs. This study describes the design and implementation of an Osteoporosis Prevention Program for middle-aged women using the Health Belief Model.

Osteoporosis is a crippling condition that often results in premature mortality and significant morbidity that is manifested in the form of fractures, bone deformity, and pain (Krall & Dawson-Hughes, 1999). It is a serious public health problem that affects 25 million people in the United States, 80% of whom are women (McBean, Forgac & Finn, 1994). Osteoporosis is responsible for more than 1.5 million fractures annually including hip fracture, a life-threatening outcome (Krall & Dawson-Hughes, 1999). Hip fracture results in severe disability and even death: 20% of persons who experience a hip fracture die within a year (McBean, Forgac & Finn, 1994).

National expenditures related to this disease are estimated at $17 billion annually; this cost is estimated to triple by the year 2040 (Melton, Thamer & Ray, 1997). National health objectives indicate an urgent need to reduce deaths due to falls, reduce the incidence of hip fractures, and increase the number of women educated about osteoporosis (U.S.D.H.H.S., 2000).

People who enter adulthood with low peak bone mass are at greatest risk of developing osteoporosis and associated fractures (Hansen, Overgaard, Riis, Christiansen, 1991). Lifestyle factors, including calcium intake and physical activity, account for approximately 20% of the variance in peak bone mass (Rubin, Hawker, Peltekova, Fielding, Ridout, Cole, 1999). Therefore facilitating healthy behaviors may maximize peak bone mass and slow bone loss. Medical treatment interventions are unable to completely reverse the effects of osteoporosis; therefore strategies designed to maximize peak bone mass and reduce bone loss later in life include prevention through health education and health promotion (Mark & Link, 1999).

Studies examining the design and implementation of osteoporosis prevention education are limited. Sedlak, Doheny and Jones (2000) implemented three osteoporosis prevention education programs and reported significant improvements in osteoporosis knowledge after completing the programs. Blalock and colleagues (2000) examined the effects of brief written education materials and reported changes in osteoporosis knowledge and beliefs. Jamal and colleagues (1999) provided an intervention that included osteoporosis education and bone mineral density testing. They examined changes in lifestyle behaviors one year following the intervention and reported significant improvements in self-reported lifestyle behaviors. The purpose of this article is to describe the design and implementation of an Osteoporosis Prevention Program for middle-aged women using the Health Belief Model.

HEALTH BELIEF MODEL FRAMEWORK

The Health Belief Model (HBM) is a conceptual framework used to understand health behavior and possible reasons for non-compliance with recommended health action (Becker & Rosenstock, 1984). It can provide guidelines for program development allowing planners to understand and address reasons for non-compliance. The HBM addresses four major components for compliance with recommended health action: perceived barriers of recommended health action, perceived benefits of recommended health action, perceived susceptibility of the disease, and perceived severity of the disease. In addition, there are modifying factors that can affect behavior compliance. Modifying factors would include media, health professionals, personal relationships, incentives, and self-efficacy of recommended health action. The Osteoporosis Prevention Program (OPP) addressed several of the components in order to address major reasons for non-compliance concerning recommendations for osteoporosis prevention.

Articulation of OPP to HBM Framework

Several perceived barriers deter participant participation in health promotion programs for women. These include inconvenient program days and time, inaccessible location, lack of childcare, lack of time and cost. This program was designed to address these common barriers. To make the class times convenient, eight sessions of each class were offered each month at a variety of times (morning, afternoon and evening) to accommodate the various scheduling needs of participants. Classes were held at a centrally located state-of-the-art community center that provided free childcare services. To address the barrier of lack of time, each of the four classes lasted one hour and the screening and individual consultation required approximately an hour and a half, therefore the total contact time commitment for the entire program was five and a half

hours. To overcome another common barrier, cost, the program was offered free to participants.

A common reason for non-compliance to osteoporosis prevention is the erroneous belief that osteoporosis is not serious. According to the Health Belief Model, people are most likely to make health behavior changes when they perceive that the disease is serious and are less likely to practice healthy behaviors if they believe that the disease is not severe (Maddux & Rogers, 1998; Rosenstock, 1974). To demonstrate the severity of this disease, negative outcomes associated with the disease were presented including death, crippling and fractures. Osteoporosis results in reduced quality of life, avoidance of social interaction due to low self-esteem and physical pain of daily activities. Emotional suffering and anxiety regarding fear of fracture and depression about being dependent on others are other negative outcomes associated with osteoporosis.

Program Administration

Recruitment efforts utilized a variety of avenues to reach women and encourage participation. A flyer was developed that included a list of dangers of osteoporosis, a graphic image of a spine, a photo of a disfigured woman with the disease, and contact information about the Osteoporosis Prevention Program. Targeted settings included the local university, the school systems, libraries, community centers, hair and beauty salons, shopping centers, the mall, and grocery stores. Flyers were also distributed to health department offices, hospitals, clinics and doctors' offices. Recruitment efforts were conducted by way of the local university daily e-mail announcements, newspapers, television and radio networks. These efforts generated interest from approximately 100 potential participants.

Recruitment announcements instructed interested potential participants to call to reserve a place in an Orientation Class. Eight sections of the Orientation Class were held at a centrally located, state-of-the-art community center. Class size was limited to 50 participants per class. The Orientation Class defined osteoporosis and described the disease outcomes, risk factors, general strategies for prevention, and information regarding the Osteoporosis Prevention Program. Attendees were instructed to tell their friends about the program and, as a result, 292 additional potential participants registered for a subsequent section of the Orientation Class. A total of 392 women attended the Orientation Classes and a total of 342 women completed the entire program.

The Osteoporosis Prevention Program was comprised of three components: educational classes, bone mineral density testing, and individual consultation. The educational classes component included four classes designed to educate and provide skill acquisition information to assist women in making lifestyle modifications to improve bone health. The four class topics were: general information about osteoporosis and orientation to the program, improving calcium intake through low fat food selections, selecting and utilizing calcium supplements, and initiating and adhering to a weight bearing exercise program. Several barriers deter participant participation in health promotion programs for women. These include inconvenient program days and time, inaccessible location, lack of childcare, lack of time and cost. This program was designed to address these common barriers. To make the class times convenient, eight sessions of each class were offered each month at a variety of times (morning, afternoon and evening) to accommodate the various scheduling needs of participants. Classes were held at a centrally located state-of-the-art community center that provided free childcare services. To address the barrier of lack of time, each of the four classes lasted one hour and the screening and individual consultation required approximately an hour and a half, therefore the total contact time commitment for the entire program was five and a half hours. To overcome another common barrier, cost, the program was offered free to participants. Funding was obtained from a local private organization.

To efficiently manage time, at the end of the orientation class, participants signed up for the nutrition class; upon completion of the nutrition class, participants signed up for the supplements class; and at the end of the supplements class, participants signed up for the exercise class. These cues to action encouraged participants to continue in the program. Classes started and ended on time; forty-five minutes were scheduled for lecture and fifteen minutes were provided for paperwork and to respond to questions.

The orientation class was prepared by the Principal Investigator and utilized information obtained from the National Osteoporosis Foundation. When participants arrived, they were greeted by the instructor and an assistant and asked to find a seat at a table. A handout packet was provided for each participant that included a flyer about the program and a power point handout that followed the presentation.

To demonstrate the severity of the health threat of osteoporosis, a picture of a woman with a severe stooped posture and a protruding abdomen was included in the educational materials. According to Klohn and Rogers (1991), motivation to prevent osteoporosis remained high among women in their study if they believed it was highly visible or disfiguring. Osteoporosis results in avoidance of social interaction due to low self-esteem and physical pain of daily activities. Emotional suffering and anxiety regarding fear of fracture and depression about being dependent on others are other negative outcomes associated with osteoporosis.

Another common barrier to osteoporosis education is low perceived susceptibility reflected in the false belief that osteoporosis only happens to old women. According to the Health Belief Model (Becker & Rosenstock, 1984) people who perceive that they are not susceptible to a disease are not likely to take positive prevention actions. In a study by Anderson, Auld & Schiltz (1996), women were aware about osteoporosis but they were unconcerned about the harm to them specifically as individuals. Kasper, Peterson, Allegrante, Galsworthy, & Gutin (1994) reported that most women in their study believed they would not develop osteoporosis and practiced behaviors that were detrimental to bone health.

To increase perceived susceptibility, a slide of normal healthy bone (from a 75 year old woman) and a slide of weak osteoporotic bone (from a 47 year old woman) were included as part of the class materials along with visuals of the three common sites for osteoporotic fracture (spine, hip and wrist). To further increase perceived susceptibility, incidences of osteopenia, osteoporosis, and osteoporotic fractures among U.S. women of all ages were included. The concept of osteoporosis as the silent thief was discussed to illustrate that this disease progresses without outward symptoms until the disease progress is severe, often resulting in fracture.

To maximize the probability that a participant will make a positive health behavior change, effective coping responses must be presented and participants must perceive they have the ability to perform these coping responses (Maddux & Rogers, 1998). Therefore, controllable risk factors for osteoporosis were presented. To enhance skill building, self-efficacy, and perceived ability to perform effective coping responses, strategies for osteoporosis prevention were also presented.

Slides were displayed of women receiving bone mineral density testing and this procedure was well described. Finally, the Osteoporosis Prevention Program was described and women were instructed to sign up for a nutrition class.

Adequate calcium is required for maintaining optimal bone density throughout life (National Osteoporosis Foundation, 2000). The National Institutes of Health (2000) report that fifty to sixty percent of women consume less than half of the recommended amount of calcium. Increasing calcium intake is an important part of osteoporosis prevention (NOF, 2000).

A Registered Dietitian prepared the nutrition class, titled "Increasing Calcium Consumption Through Foods." Information was obtained from nutrition textbooks, the National Osteoporosis Foundation, the American Dietetic Association, and National Institutes of Health. Each participant received a power point handout that included the slides presented in the class, a glossy handout of the Food Guide Pyramid, a list of calcium and fat contents of common foods, and a glossy recipe pamphlet of low-fat high calcium recipes with photos.

Dietary Reference Intakes state that 1000 milligrams of calcium are required for women ages 19 to 50 years and 1200 milligrams are required for women over age 50 (Institute of Medicine, 1997). This class addressed improving overall diet quality and emphasized ways to meet calcium requirements through food choices. The nutrition class provided information regarding specific ways to select low-fat dairy products. Detailed information was disseminated regarding calorie and fat contents of specific dairy products. A comparison of nutrients in milk and soda were displayed. Portions of a variety of dairy products to provide one serving or 300 milligrams of calcium were displayed and food models were circulated to demonstrate portion sizes. Ways to incorporate dairy products in recipes were presented such as substituting non-fat milk for water in soups, cereals, oatmeal, mashed potatoes and pancakes.

Information was distributed regarding how to obtain calcium from non-dairy food sources including red beans, pinto beans, cooked collards or turnips, broccoli, almonds, canned salmon and sardines with edible bones, calcium-enriched tofu, and calcium-enriched soy milk. Calcium fortified food products such as orange juice were also presented. Calcium-rich low-fat recipes were disseminated as well as sample grocery lists. Several women reported that the grocery lists were excellent reminders (or cues to action) to help make positive behavior changes. Women who expressed concerns about weight control and heart disease were given strategies for improving their calcium intake while reducing their risk of other chronic diseases.

The importance of avoiding fad diets was discussed and calcium contents of some popular fad diets were displayed. The ineffectiveness of fad diets for weight control was discussed along with the inadequate levels of calcium delivered by fad diets. Overcoming lactose intolerance was covered and handouts were available for women who had this condition.

At the end of the nutrition class, participants were instructed to sign up for the calcium supplements class. Women were instructed to bring calcium and other supplements they were using to the supplements class.

The class devoted to the selection of calcium supplements was designed to assist women who were lactose intolerant or who were otherwise unable to obtain sufficient calcium from their diets. This class was prepared by a Registered Dietitian and utilized a thorough literature review of 44 current articles in peer-reviewed journals regarding calcium supplementation.

Recommended daily calcium amounts were presented and participants were instructed to first calculate the amount of calcium they receive from foods, then to calculate the remaining amount needed from supplements. Guidelines for selecting a supplement were provided including the importance of selecting a dissolvable supplement. A dissolvability experiment was conducted and a variety of calcium supplements were put into clear cups with white vinegar and the amount of time required for supplements to dissolve was noted. (Supplements should fully dissolve in 45 minutes.) The benefit of liquid and chewable supplements was discussed because these dissolve in the mouth. The issue of absorbability was discussed and supplements with high absorbability ratings (calcium citrate and calcium carbonate) were recommended. Selecting products with selected other nutrients such as vitamin D and vitamin K was discussed.

The instructor discussed the issue of contaminants and presented products to avoid that may contain harmful substances. Dangers of toxicity, levels of intake that can lead to toxicity and conditions where supplementation is not recommended (such as kidney stones) were discussed. The issue of when to take a calcium supplement was covered and other dietary considerations that may impair calcium absorption were discussed. This class concluded with a list of strategies for maintaining bone health including not smoking and not consuming alcohol in excess. At the end of the supplements class, women were instructed to sign up for the exercise class.

Regular physical activity contributes to the prevention of osteoporosis by the bone's response to demands placed upon it (Greendale, Barrett-Connor, & Eldelstein, 1995). Physical activity promotes an increase in bone mineral density (Bassey & Ramsdale, 1994) and reduction in bone loss among women (Katz, Sherman, & DiNubile, 1998). Weight bearing exercises are especially beneficial for building and maintaining bone strength and density (Drinkwater & McCloy 1994).

The exercise class was prepared utilizing fitness textbooks and information from the National Osteoporosis Foundation and American College of Sports Medicine. Participants were provided with a power point handout and illustrations of safe stretches and exercises. Information presented in this class included benefits of exercise, exercise myths and facts, recommended types of exercises, developing components of fitness, guidelines for starting an exercise program, training principles, weight bearing exercises, resistive exercise with equipment, and utilization of common objects at home to provide resistance.

The instructor demonstrated exercises, and safety tips were provided. Several suggestions for improving adherence were discussed. The importance of selecting physical activities that are enjoyed was emphasized. A national survey indicated that yard work was associated with higher bone density levels and was more popular than walking and other activities among women (Turner, Ting, Bass & Brown, 2000). Women were encouraged to find a friend to exercise with. Information regarding local facilities and programs were also distributed.

Prior to the physical activity classes, sign up sheets were developed for the bone mineral density testing schedule. Participants were instructed to sign up for the bone density testing component of the program before departing.

Each participant received bone mineral density testing of the left hip, spine and total body using dual energy X-ray absorptiometry (DEXA) technology. A full table Lunar Prodigy was used for testing. Bone mineral density testing is safe, fast, easy and comfortable. The participants expressed appreciation for being able to have their bone density tested without having to pay a fee. The computer software generated detailed printouts regarding bone density and body composition. These included color printouts of bone density levels, graphic images of the hip, spine and total body, t-score and z-scores, and graphs displaying their readings along with future projections based on normal rates of loss. The total body printout included bone density and body fat and provided a graph of chronic disease risk based on percent of body fat. For many participants, receiving a bone mineral density test increased perceived susceptibility as 28% of participants had readings below the normal range.

Immediately after the bone density exam, participants received a 45 to 60 minute individual consultation from the Principle Investigator who is a Registered Dietitian. The individual consultation was provided to explain the test results and to provide individualized advice, empowerment and encouragement. During the individual consultation, participants were provided with the color printouts of their bone density results with graphic images and graphs. Participants were also provided with pre-prepared packets that included literature from the National Osteoporosis Foundation regarding osteoporosis prevention and bone density testing.

Additional literature was provided for specific situations as appropriate. For example, women who had osteoporotic readings received handouts regarding coping with osteoporosis. Other handouts were disseminated as needed including information about diets for hypertension, how to cope with lactose intolerance, and corresponding handouts in Spanish.

A form was developed to guide the consultation process. First, results of the bone density exam were described and projections of future bone density levels were explained utilizing graphs generated from the computer software. Next, individualized dietary recommendations were developed based on bone density readings and other medical issues and concerns as well as food preferences. Individualized guidelines for calcium supplementation were also provided, and these sometimes varied from recommendations provided in the Supplements Class. For example, women who are menopausal or postmenopausal and are not able to take hormone replacement therapy require 1500 mg/ calcium per day instead of 1200 mg/day.

A physical activity program was developed for each participant based on bone density levels and activity preferences. Women with severe osteopenia or osteoporosis must be cautious when engaging in physical activity. Several of these women responded favorably to acquiring an exercise video produced by the National Osteoporosis Foundation for people with osteoporosis. The final part of the individual consultation included advice about other lifestyle behaviors such as tobacco and alcohol use. Some women were advised to talk with their medical doctors about medications, and referrals to physicians were provided for women who did not have a medical doctor. Handouts regarding available medications produced by the National Osteoporosis Foundation were disseminated when appropriate.

DISCUSSION AND CONCLUSIONS

Osteoporosis is a serious public health problem that affects 20 million U.S. women (McBean, Forgac & Finn, 1994). National health objectives indicate an urgent need to increase the number of women educated about osteoporosis (U.S.D.H.H.S., 2010). The most effective osteoporosis reduction strategies include prevention through health education and health promotion (Mark & Link, 1999).

Studies examining the design and implementation of osteoporosis prevention education are limited. Researchers have established that improvements in knowledge, attitudes or behaviors have resulted from participation in osteoporosis education (Sedlak, Doheny & Jones, 2000; Blalock et al., 2000; Jamal et al., 1999). The use of health behavior theory in the planning and implementation of health promotion programs is recommended (Glanz, Lewis & Rimer, 1997). To enhance the effectiveness of an osteoporosis education program, applying constructs of the Health Belief Model can be valuable. The purpose of this paper was to describe the design and implementation of an Osteoporosis Prevention Program using the Health Belief Model.

The target goal was to obtain 300 middle aged women to participate in the study. The response was positive as 392 people attended the initial Orientation Class. Attendance and participation in classes were positive; 381 people attended the Nutrition Class; 375 women participated in the Supplements

Class; and 350 women attended the Exercise Class. Participants were attentive and interactive. They showed interest and asked questions. Many positive comments of appreciation were received.

Increasing perceived severity, perceived susceptibility, perceived benefits, self-efficacy and cues to action while decreasing perceived barriers were actions that encouraged participation. The program provided informational and instrumental support. Informational support was provided by way of class materials and individual consultation. Instrumental support was provided by classes being taught at a centrally-located facility with child-care services. More studies are needed to examine the use of the Health Belief Model as well as other behavior theories in the design and implementation of osteoporosis prevention education programs.

REFERENCES

Anderson, J. E., Auld, G. W., & Schiltz, C. M. (1996). Young women and osteoporosis: aware but unconcerned. *Journal of Wellness Perspectives*, *12*, 63–69.

Bassey, E. J., Ramsdale, S. J. (1994). Increase in femoral bone mineral density in young women following high impact exercise. *Osteoporosis International*, *4*, 72–75.

Becker, M. H., & Rosenstock, I. M. (1984). Compliance with medical advice. In A. Steptoe & A. Matthews (ed.). *Health care and human behavior*. London: Academic Press. Pp. 135–152.

Blalock, S. J., Currey, S. S., DeVellis, R. E, DeVellis, B. M., Giorgino, K. B., Anderson, J. J. B., Dooley, M. A., & Gold, D. T. (2000). Effects of educational materials concerning osteoporosis on women's knowledge, beliefs, and behavior. *American Journal of Health Promotion*, *14*, 161–169.

Blalock, S. J., DeVellis, R. E, Giorgino, K. B., DeVellis, B. M., Gold, D. T, Dooley, M. A., Anderson, J. J., & Smith, S. L. (1996). Osteoporosis prevention in premenopausal women: Using a stage model approach to examine the predictors of behavior. *Health Psychology*, *15*, 84–93.

Dijkstra, A. J., Roijackers, J., DeVries, H. (1998). Smokers in four stages of readiness to change. *Addictive Behaviors*, *23*, 339–350.

Doheny, M., & Sedlak, C. (1994). Osteoporosis preventing behavior survey. Unpublished instrument.

Drinkwater, B. L., McCloy, C. H. (1994). Does physical activity play a role in preventing osteoporosis? *Research Quarterly for Exercise and Sport*, *65*, 197.

Etter, J. E., Perneger, T. V. (1999). A comparison of two measures of stages of change for smoking cessation. *Addiction*, *94*, 1881–1889.

Gerrior, S., Putnam, J., & Bente, L. (1998). Milk and milk products: Their importance in the American diet. *Food Review*, *68*, 29–37.

Glanz, K., Lewis, E. M., & Rimer, B. K. (1997). (Eds.) *Health Behavior and Health Education: Theory, Research, and Practice*. San Francisco: Jossey-Bass Publishers.

Greendale, B. A., Barrett-Connor, E., & Eldelstein, S. (1995). Lifetime leisure exercise and osteoporosis: The Rancho Bernado study. *American Journal of Epidemiology*, *141*, 951–959.

Greene, G., Rossi, S. R., Rossi, J. S., Velicer, W. E., Fava, J. L., & Prochaska, J.O. (1999). Dietary applications of the Stages of Change Model. *Journal of the American Dietetic Association*, *99*, 673–679.

Greene, G. W., Rossi, S. R., Reed, G. R., Willey, C., Prochaska, J. O. (1994). Stages of change for reducing dietary fat to 30% of energy or less. *Journal of the American Dietetic Association*, *94*, 1105–1110.

Hansen, M. A., Overgaard, K., Riis, B. J., & Christiansen, C. (1991). Role of peak bone mass and bone loss in postmenopausal osteoporosis: 12 year study. *British Medical Journal*, *303*, 961–964.

Institute of Medicine (1997). Dietary Reference Intakes for calcium, phosphorus, magnesium, vitamin D, and fluoride, Washington, D.C., National Academy Press.

Jamal, S. A., Ridout, R., Chase, C., Fielding, L., Rubin, L. A., & Hawker, G. A. (1999). Bone mineral density testing and osteoporosis education improve lifestyle behaviors in premenopausal women: A prospective study. *Journal of Bone and Mineral Research*, *14*, 2143–2149.

Kasper, M. J., Peterson, M. G., Allegrante, J. R, Galsworthy, T. D., & Gutin, B. (1994). Knowledge, beliefs, and behaviors among college women concerning the prevention of osteoporosis. *Archives of Family Medicine*, *3*, 696–702.

Katz, W. A., Sherman, C., & DiNubile, N. A. (1998). Osteoporosis. *The Physician and Sportsmedicine*, *26*, 33–36.

Kim, K., Horan, M., & Gendler, P. (1991). *Osteoporosis knowledge tests, osteoporosis health belief scale, and osteoporosis self-efficacy scale*. Allendale, MI: Grand Valley State University.

Kim, K., Horan, M., Gendler, P., & Patel, M. (1991). Development and evaluation of the osteoporosis belief scale. *Research in Nursing*, *14*, 155–163.

Klohn, L. S., & Rogers, R. W. (1991). Dimensions of the severity of a health threat: the persuasive effects of visibility, time of onset, and rate of onset on young women's intentions to prevent osteoporosis. *Health Psychology*, *10*, 323–329.

Krall, E. A., & Dawson-Hughes, B. (1999). Osteoporosis. In M.E. Shils, J.A Olson, M. Shike, & A.G. Ross (Eds.), *Modern nutrition in health and disease* (pp. 1353–1364). Baltimore, MD: William & Wilkins.

Kristal, A., Glanz, K., Curry, S., & Patterson, R. (1999). How can stages of change be best used in dietary interventions? *Journal of the American Dietetic Association*, *99*, 679.

Lindsay, R. (1993). Prevention and treatment of osteoporosis. *The Lancet*, *341*, 801–806.

Maddux, J. E, & Rogers, R. W. (1998). Protection motivation and self efficacy: a revised theory of fear appeals and attitude change. *Journal of Experimental Social Psychology*, *19*, 469–479.

Mark, S., & Link, H. (1999). Reducing osteoporosis: Prevention during childhood and adolescence. *Bulletin of the World Health Organization*, *77*, 423–425.

McBean, L. D., Forgac, T., & Finn, S. G. (1994). Osteoporosis: visions for care and prevention—a conference report. *Journal of the American Dietetic Association*, *94*, 668–671.

Melton, L. J. III; Thamer, M., & Ray, N. F. (1997). Fractures attributable to osteoporosis: Report from the National Osteoporosis Foundation. *Journal of Bone and Mineral Research*, *12*, 16–23.

National Institutes of Health Consensus Statement. (2000). *Osteoporosis prevention, diagnosis, and therapy*. Retrieved March 5, 2001, from http:/odp.od.nih.gov/consensus/cons/l 11/11 l_statement.htm.

National Osteoporosis Foundation. (1998). Strategies for osteoporosis. *The Osteoporosis Report, Summer*.

Norman, G. J., Velicer, W. F., Fava, J. L., & Prochaska, J. O. (1998). Dynamic typology clustering within the stages of change for smoking cessation. *Addictive Behaviors*, *23*, 139–153.

Ray, N. E., Chan, J. K., Thamer, M., & Melton, L. J. (1997). Medical expenditures for the treatment of osteoporotic fractures in the United States in 1995; report from the National Osteoporosis Foundation. *Journal of Bone Mineral Research*, *12*, 24–35.

Rosenstock, I. M. (1974). Historical origins of the health belief model. *Health Education Monographs*, *2*, 328–335.

Rubin, L. A, Hawker, G. A., Peltekova, V., Fielding, L., Ridout, R., & Cole, D. E. (1999). Determinants of peak bone mass: Clinical and genetic analyses in a young female Canadian cohort. *Journal of Bone Mineral Research, 14,* 633–643.

Sedlak, G. A., Doheny, M. O., & Jones, S. L. (2000). Osteoporosis education programs: changing knowledge and behaviors. *Public Health Nursing, 17,* 398–402.

Turner, L. W., Ting, L., Bass, M. A., & Brown, B. (2000). Physical activity and bone mineral density among older women: Results from a national survey. *Research Quarterly for Exercise and Sport, 71,* A-46.

United States. Department of Health and Human Services. (2000). *Healthy People 2010. With Understanding and Improving Health and Objectives for Improving Health.* 2nd ed. Washington, D.C: U.S. Government Printing Office.

Wardlaw, G. M. (1993). Putting osteoporosis in perspective. *Journal of the American Dietetic Association, 93,* 1000–1007.*

---

* Acknowledgments: We express our appreciation to Community Care Foundation of Springdale, Arkansas for funding the Osteoporosis Prevention Program.

Article Source: Turner, L.W., Hunt, S.B., DiBrezzo, R., & Jones, C. (2004). Design and implementation of an osteoporosis prevention program using the health belief model. *American Journal of Health Studies, 19*(2), 115–121. Reprinted with permission.

QUESTIONS

1. What were the beliefs studied in the article?
2. Which beliefs of the HBM were used to develop the prevention program and why?
3. In your brainstorming session, did you think of these?

CHAPTER REFERENCES

Ali, N.S. (2002). Prediction of coronary heart disease preventive behaviors in women: A test of the Health Belief Model. *Women & Health, 35*(1), 83–96.

Bandura, A. (1977). Self-efficacy: Toward a unifying theory of behavioral change. *Psychological Review, 84,* 191–215.

Belcher, L., Sternberg, M.R., Wolotski, R.J., Halkitis, P., & Hoff, C. (2005). Condom use and perceived risk of HIV transmission among sexually active HIV positive men who have sex with men. *AIDS Education and Prevention, 17*(1), 79–89.

Burak, L.J., & Meyer, M. (1997). Using the Health Belief Model to examine and predict college women's cancer screening beliefs and behavior. *Health Care for Women International, 18*(3), 251–263.

Byrd, T.L., Peterson, S.K., Chavez, R., & Heckert, A. (2004). Cervical cancer screening beliefs among young Hispanic women. *Preventive Medicine, 38*(2), 192–198.

Centers for Disease Control and Prevention. (2004). *Program Operations Guidelines for STD Prevention: Community and Individual Behavior Change Interventions.* Retrieved September 29, 2004, from http://www.cdc.gov/std/program/community/9-PGcommunity.htm.

Champion, V. (1993). Instrument for breast cancer screening behaviors. *Nursing Research, 42,* 139–143.

Champion, V., & Menon, U. (1997). Predicting mammography and breast self-examination in African-American women. *Cancer Nursing, 20,* 315–322.

Chen, J.K., Fox, S.A., Cantrell, C.H., Stockdale, S.E., & Kagawa-Singer, M. (2007). Health disparities and prevention: Racial/ethnic barriers to flu vaccinations. *Journal of Community Health, 32*(1), 5–20.

Courtenay, W.H. (1998). College men's health: An overview and call to action. *Journal of American College Health, 46*(6), 279–287.

de Wit, J.B.F., Vet, R., Schutten, M., & van Steenbergen, J. (2005). Social-cognitive determinants of vaccination behavior against hepatitis B: An assessment among men who have sex with men. *Preventive Medicine, 40*(6), 795–802.

Ellingson, L.A., & Yarber, W.L. (1997). Breast self-examination, the Health Belief Model, and sexual orientation in women. *Journal of Sex Education & Therapy, 22,* 19–24.

Forsyth, L.H. & Goetsch, V.L. (1997). Perceived threat of illness and health protective behaviors in offspring of adults with non-insulin dependent diabetes mellutis. *Behavioral Medicine, 23*(3), 112–120.

Frank, D., Swedmark, J., & Grubbs, L. (2004). Colon cancer screening in African American women. *ABNF Journal, 15*(4), 67–70.

Gerba, C.P., Rose, J.B., & Haas, C.N. (1996). Sensitive populations: Who is at the greatest risk? *International Journal of Food Microbiology, 30,* 113–123.

Glanz, K., Rimer, B.K., & Lewis, F.M. (Eds.). (2002). *Health Behavior and Health Education* (3rd ed.). San Francisco: Jossey-Bass.

Graham, M.E. (2002). Health beliefs and self breast examination in black women. *Journal of Cultural Diversity, 9*(2), 49–54.

Hanson, J.A., & Benedict, J.A. (2002). Use of Health Belief Model to examine older adults' food-handling behaviors. *Journal of Nutrition Education, 34,* S25–S30.

Hochbaum, G.M. (1958). *Public Participation in Medical Screening Programs: A Socio-psychological Study* (Public Health Service Publication No. 572). Washington, DC: Government Printing Office.

Janz, N.K., & Becker, M.H. (1984). The Health Belief Model: A decade later. *Health Education Quarterly, 11*(1), 1–47.

Lamanna, L.M. (2004). College students' knowledge and attitudes about cancer and perceived risks of developing skin cancer. *Dermatology Nursing, 16*(2), 161–176.

Lewis, J.E., & Malow, R.M. (1997). HIV/AIDS risks in heterosexual college students. *Journal of American College Health, 45*(4), 147–155.

Maes, C.A., & Louis, M. (2003). Knowledge of AIDS, perceived risk of AIDS, and at-risk sexual behaviors of older adults. *The Journal of the American Academy of Nurse Practitioners, 15*(11), 509–516.

McCormick-Brown, K. (1999). Health Belief Model. Retrieved September 27, 2005, from http://hsc.usf.edu/~kmbrown/Health_Belief_Model_Overview.htm.

Mullens, A.B., McCaul, K.D., Erickson, S.C., & Sandgren, A.K. (2003). Coping after cancer: Risk perceptions, worry, and health behaviors among colorectal cancer survivors. *Psycho-oncology, 13,* 367–376.

National Cancer Institute. (2003). *Theory at a Glance: A Guide for Health Promotion Practice.* Washington, DC: U.S. Department of Health and Human Services.

National Institute of Neurological Disorders and Stroke. (2007). Transmissible spongiform encephalopathies information page. Retrieved March 29, 2007, from http://www.ninds.nih.gov/disorders/tse/tse.htm.

New York-Presbyterian Hospital. (2006). Colonoscopy promoted during colorectal cancer awareness month. Retrieved April 22, 2007, from http://www.nyp.org/news/health/060322.html.

Rose, M.A. (1995). Knowledge of human immunodeficiency virus and acquired immunodeficiency syndrome, perception of risk, and behaviors among older adults. *Holistic Nursing Practice, 10*(1), 10–17.

Rosenstock, I.M, Strecher, V.J., & Becker, M.H. (1988). Social learning theory and the Health Belief Model. *Health Education Quarterly, 15*(2), 175–183.

Stretcher, V., & Rosenstock, I.M. (1997). The Health Belief Model. In K. Glanz, F.M. Lewis, & B.K. Rimer (Eds.), *Health Behavior and Health Education: Theory, Research and Practice* (2nd ed.). San Francisco: Jossey-Bass.

Umeh, K., & Rogan-Gibson, J. (2001). Perceptions of threat, benefits, and barriers in breast self-examination amongst young asymptomatic women. *British Journal of Health Psychology, 6*(4), 361–673.

Weinrich, S., Hodlford, D., Boyd, M., Creanga, D., Cover, K., Johnson, A., Frank-Stromborg, M., & Weinrich, M. (1998). Prostate cancer education in African American churches. *Public Health Nursing, 15*(3), 188–195.

Weitkunat, R., Pottgieber, C., Meyer, N., Crispin, A., Fischer, R., Schotten, K., Kerr, J., & Uberia, K. (2003). Perceived risk of bovine spongiform encephalopathy and dietary behavior. *Journal of Health Psychology, 8*(3), 373–382.

Wallace, S.L. (2002). Osteoporosis prevention in college women: Application of the Expanded Health Belief Model. *American Journal of Health Behavior, 26*(3), 163–172.

Yep, G.A. (1993). HIV prevention among Asian American college students: Does the Health Belief Model work? *Journal of American College Health, 41*(5), 199–205.

CHAPTER 5

Attribution Theory

Theory Essence Sentence

There is a cause or explanation for things that happen.

STUDENT LEARNING OUTCOMES

After reading this chapter the student will be able to:

1. Explain the concept of Attribution Theory.
2. Discuss the constructs of internal and external locus of control.
3. Explain the construct of stability.
4. Use the theory to explain at least one behavior.

THEORETICAL CONCEPT

Fritz Heider originally conceived Attribution Theory in the late 1950s. Heider, a psychologist by training, had a research interest in the nature of interpersonal relationships. He believed that people strive to understand why others behave the way they do and to determine whether their behavior is caused by internal factors (personality or disposition) or external situations (Strickland, 2006).

As all theories do, Attribution Theory has evolved over time. In the 1970s and 1980s, much of the research with this theory focused on perceived attributional causes of achievement—that is, success or failure relative to a specific behavior and the internal factors or external situations that influ-

ence the outcome (Weiner, 1985; Kearsely, 2006). "Here it is Thanksgiving week, and the Los Angeles Rams are looking like the biggest turkeys in town. Coach Ray Malavasi has eliminated bad luck, biorhythms, and sunspots" as the reason for his team's poor performance (Robert, 1982). Clearly, poor Coach Malavasi was trying to attribute his team's lousy game to some situation in order to explain why they played (behaved) so poorly.

Why is it so important that we attribute a cause to an outcome? Sometimes we need to assign causation to certain behaviors, events, or outcomes to avoid them (if undesirable) or repeat them (if desirable) in the future. Sometimes we want to assign causation just for the sake of having an explanation. Other times, we need to attribute a cause because it helps us psychologically deal with a specific event (Weiner, 1985). A case in point is infection with the human immunodeficiency virus (HIV). Being diagnosed with HIV is traumatic: everything about one's self and the world changes. The challenge is to restore these to some semblance of what they were previous to the diagnosis. Finding a reason or meaning for the adverse situation is one aspect of a readjustment process people need to go through for their own psychological well-being (Clement, 1998; Taylor, 1983). They need to find a reason, an explanation for why they contracted HIV. They need to attribute their situation to something.

Sometimes, it is important for us to understand why certain events happen so we can either repeat the causes (behaviors/actions) to repeat the outcome if it is positive, or change the causes if the outcome is negative (Weiner, 1985). As the saying goes, "If you keep doing the same thing, you'll keep getting the same thing." Now, this is fine if the results are what you want. But if they aren't what you want, then knowing the cause will enable you to change what you are doing so you won't keep getting the same undesirable outcome.

THEORETICAL CONSTRUCTS

Since causality is the basis for this theory, understanding more about the causes helps us better understand why people behave in certain ways. To this end, three aspects of a cause, or causal dimensions, have been identified: locus, stability, and controllability (Weiner, 1985).

Locus of Control

The causal dimension of locus is really referring to the idea of locus of control (Rotter, 1966). Locus of control has to do with the extent to which people believe they have control over events in their lives. Locus of control comes in two flavors, internal and external. A person with an internal locus of control believes events happen as a result of something within himself or herself (e.g., skill, intelligence, desire, commitment, work ethic, values, beliefs), attributes over which the person has control. A person with an external locus of control

FIGURE 5.1 Internal cause for failing a course—sleeping on your notes.

believes events happen because of things outside the realm of personal control or because of things in the environment. External causes are divided into those attributed to fate, luck, or chance and those attributed to powerful others. These powerful others can be significant in health because they are often physicians, dentists, therapists, and other health or medical personnel (Levenson, 1974; Weigmann & Berven, 1998).

Whether someone attributes internal or external causes to a given situation varies from situation to situation (Rotter, 1993). This is typically seen in students. If a student fails a course, the cause for the poor grade is inevitably external and often a powerful other—the professor (she is a tough grader; he didn't like me; his tests are too hard; she didn't teach us anything). However, if a student does really well in a course, then the cause for the good grade is attributed to attending class, taking notes, and studying—internal conditions over which the student has control. It is a rare student who will assign the cause of failure to internal conditions over which he or she had control. How many students do you know fail a course and say, "She was a great professor, but I just didn't care if I learned the information," or "I should have bought the book and read it, taken notes in class, handed in all of the assignments, and not partied as much (Figure 5.1)."

Going back to the person diagnosed with HIV infection, among the many potential causes for this diagnosis is personal behavior (McDonell, 1993)—something the person did or didn't do. The infection may be attributed to internal causes, for example, not using condoms, or sharing unclean needles. On the other hand, the HIV infection may have been the result of external causes not under the person's control, such as luck or fate or the actions of others, as is the case with perinatal transmission or the rare transfusion transmission.

When a poor outcome is attributed to internal causes, as is often the case with HIV infection, it leads to self-blame on the part of the infected individuals and is also seen as their "fault" by others. When people who need the help of others are held responsible for the circumstances that lead to need in the first place, help from others is often not forthcoming (McDonell, 1993). Thus, Attribution Theory helps to explain not only the behavior of the individual affected, but also that of those around him or her.

Stability

There is more to an attributional cause than it simply being internal or external. Causes are also categorized by their stability, that is, how consistent or permanent they are (Wang, 2001).

Although it would be logical to assume that all internal causes of behavior are stable, consistent, and permanent, with no fluctuation in their capacity to cause a particular outcome, this is not necessarily true. For example, let's look at athletic ability as the internal cause of behavior. Athletic ability is pretty stable—it doesn't vary from day to day. Either you have it or you don't. However, other internal causes, such as mood, desire, drive, and effort, do vary. So although these are internal causes, they are not stable, permanent, or consistent (Weiner, 1985). They can fluctuate from day to day, from situation to situation.

The same is true of external causes. The external cause of luck, for instance, is unstable. Luck is inconsistent and certainly not permanent. Sometimes you have it, and unfortunately, sometimes you don't. On the other hand, task difficulty is an external cause, but one that is stable: if a task is difficult, it is difficult (Weiner, 1985). For example, maintaining a vegan lifestyle, even once you get the hang of it, is still difficult in our society.

The idea of cause stability has implications when we are trying to explain health behavior using the Attribution Theory. For instance, when an alcoholic relapses, he or she is more likely to attribute this negative behavior to an external, unstable cause (Seneviratne & Saunders, 2000): "When I wasn't looking, someone switched my soda with champagne, and since everyone was expected to join in the toast, I drank it. I won't ever take my eye off my soda again." The external cause was "someone," and the unstable aspect was that this was a temporary situation that won't happen again. Ah, the devil made me do it!

It is the rare individual who attributes his or her undesirable behavior (relapse) to internal, stable causes (Seneviratne & Saunders, 2000). If the alcoholic from the previous example were to do so, his or her explanation would be something along the lines of "I drank champagne instead of soda because I wanted to get drunk, and the next time I have an opportunity to get drunk on Dom Perignon, I will do it again."

Controllability

In addition to causes being stable or unstable, some causes can be controlled or changed and others cannot. Let's look at the controllability of the internal, *unstable* causes of behavior, effort, and mood (think depression). Effort can be willfully changed at any moment by the person, whereas mood cannot. Although both are internal and unstable, effort is controllable, whereas mood is uncontrollable (Rosenbaum, 1972; Weiner, 1985). When you are in a funk, you can't just change and immediately come out of it. You can, however, decide to put more effort into something right away.

The same issue of controllability is found among the internal, *stable* causes. For example, laziness is internal and stable. Although some people are lazy by nature, they do have control over it—they can change this if they choose to. This is not true of other internal, stable causes such as mathematic or artistic aptitude or physical coordination (Rosenbaum, 1972; Weiner, 1985). Some people have very little innate math ability, can't draw, and are clumsy. No matter how hard these folks try, they will never be math geniuses, famous painters, or Olympic gold medalists. These internal causes are just not changeable at will.

The construct of controllability has a real, practical application. It is the basis of stigmas or stereotypes. In general, people attribute negative outcomes, events, or conditions in other peoples' lives to internal but controllable causes. This is what happens with obesity. Obesity is seen as being the result of internal but controllable causes such as lack of willpower, overeating, laziness, and not exercising (Crandall & Schiffauer, 1998; Puhl & Brownwell, 2001, 2003), which may or may not be causing the increased weight at all. For the person who is genetically predisposed to obesity, this is an internal, uncontrollable cause. Keep in mind those somatotypes of ectoderm, mesoderm, and endoderm. There are internal and uncontrollable causes of body shape, height, and weight. Although these causes should not be used as an excuse for overeating or lack of exercise, not everyone has the genetic blueprint of the ectoderm.

With the stigma of obesity so strong, and blame for it placed within the obese person's control, it is no wonder that people will go to great lengths to avoid this outcome. Couple this with a culture that associates thinness with being "good" and fatness with being "bad" (Puhl & Brownell, 2003), we end up with an increased likelihood of depression and suicidal attempts in the obese (Carpenter et al., 2000) at one extreme and eating disorders and their health consequences at the other.

Dental caries is another example of a health problem that can be attributed to internal, controllable causes of laziness and poor motivation. If the same outcome of dental caries were attributed to dental phobia, the cause would still be internal, but uncontrollable. Another cause could be that the dentist did not remove old fillings. In this case, the cause would be external and uncontrollable (Kneckt & Knuuttila, 2000). This example shows us that in some situations, it is important to identify causality. After all, little would be gained by educating the lazy person if the culprit were the dentist!

Although not all health behaviors can be explained or changed on the basis of causal attribution, it can be a starting point. Assigning causation may not only help explain the behavior but also identify the type of intervention needed to achieve behavior change.

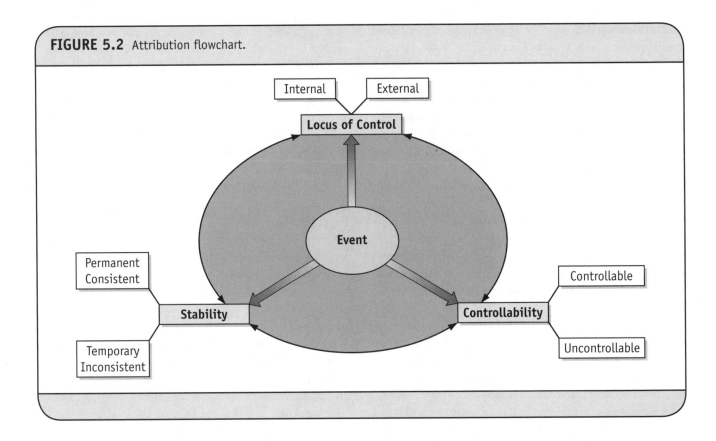

FIGURE 5.2 Attribution flowchart.

In summary, according to Attribution Theory, internal factors, external situations, locus of control, stability, and controllability explain behavior (Figure 5.2).

Attribution Theory Constructs Chart

Locus of control	The extent to which a person has control over life events
Internal	Events happen because of things inside the person, such as skills, intellect, or attitudes
External	Events happen because of things outside the person, such as fate, luck, or other people
Stability	The extent to which a cause is permanent or temporary
Controllability	The extent to which a person can willfully change the cause

Attributing an external, controllable cause to a poor health outcome.

THEORY IN ACTION: CLASS ACTIVITY

Imagine that each day, every day, your job is to sit at a table putting cell phones into boxes. The rate at which you do this is directly related to your rate of pay: the faster you pack the boxes, the more money you make. At the end of each day, you end up with a backache. Using the constructs of Attribution Theory, what might be the reason for your backache? Now read the following article and answer the questions at the end.

Attributions, Stress, and Work-Related Low Back Pain

George Byrns,[1] Jacqueline Agnew,[2] and Barbara Curbow[3]

[1]Department of Health Sciences, Illinois State University, Normal, Illinois; [2]Department of Environmental Health Sciences, Johns Hopkins University, Baltimore, Maryland; [3]Department of Health Policy and Management, Johns Hopkins University, Baltimore, Maryland

Abstract

Occupational low back pain (LBP) is a major cause of morbidity and cost. Efforts to control LBP are largely unsuccessful, and better understanding of risks is needed, especially psychological factors. The purpose of this research was to assess the association between worker attributions and LBP. Attributing LBP to internal causes may increase the worker's perceived control, whereas external attribution may cause distress. A new model was developed to explore these associations.

A cross-sectional design was used in this study of 278 garment workers. Data were gathered by a self-administered questionnaire and through direct observation. Responses to questions on worker attributions of LBP cause and knowledge of back safety were subjected to factor analysis and other psychometric evaluation to develop scales. Six hypotheses were tested using multivariate logistic regression.

Workers who scored high in internal attribution were more likely to be knowledgeable of back safety (OR = 3.7, 95% CI = 2.0–6.7). Workers reporting high demand were more likely to report LBP (OR = 2.3, 95% CI = 1.2–4.4). Workers attributing LBP to job tasks were more likely to report LBP (OR = 3.2, 95% CI = 1.5–6.9), and those reporting high supervisor support were less likely to report LBP (OR = 0.23, 95% CI = 0.08–0.66). Workers with annual incomes above $15,000 were more likely to report LBP in the test of both the Demand-Control-Support and Attribution models (OR = 2.8, 95% CI = 1.2–6.9 and OR = 4.1, 95% CI = 1.5–11.1, respectively).

While both models appeared to be useful for the study of low back pain, the R^2_L of the Demand-Control-Support model equaled only 11.9 percent, whereas the Attribution model equaled 26.2 percent. This study provides evidence that attribution theory is useful in the study of LBP, including in future interventions in the prevention of LBP.

MORBIDITY AND COST OF OCCUPATIONAL LOW BACK PAIN

Work-related low back pain (LBP) is a major contributor to morbidity and workers' compensation costs. Estimates of the cost of occupational back injuries are as high as $49.2 billion annually.[1] Based on 1989 data, Webster and Snook estimated that 16 percent of all workers' compensation claims and 33 percent of all costs were for back injury.[2] The National Occupational Research Agenda lists low back disorders among the priority research areas because they are a significant cause of suffering to working people and a major drain on the economy. To date, occupational LBP has frustrated attempts at prevention and control.[3] The multifactorial nature of risk factors associated with LBP presents considerable challenges to the identification of effective control strategies. The relationships among various risk factors for LBP are complex and need to be better understood, but research suggests that the risk factors for LBP include physical workload, psychosocial, individual, and organizational characteristics.[4–9] To further complicate matters, these factors tend to interact.[10] Knowledge of the relative importance of physical workload and psychosocial or other elements affecting back pain is a critical step in the formulation of effective intervention strategies.

We investigated potential LBP risk factors in a plant making men's suits. Garment making is known to contribute to pain in the neck and upper extremities; however, it has not been identified as a high-risk industry for LBP.[11–13] Since this industry is labor-intensive, often requiring workers to perform mentally demanding tasks while in awkward working postures, it was suspected that LBP could also be a problem. The two main purposes of this study were to determine if garment workers are at high risk for LBP and to determine if workers' attributions of the cause of LBP are associated with self-reports of pain symptoms. Two other purposes of the research were to determine if worker knowledge of back safety and worker perception of job control were related to attributions regarding the cause of LBP.

ATTRIBUTION THEORY

Attributions are a natural human tendency to see patterns or explain events.[14] The study of attributions as presented in the psychology literature has focused on how internal and external factors influence the types of causal determinations individuals make for events. Weiner identified three dimensions of attributions: locus of causation, stability, and controllability. Locus reflects internal characteristics, such as a worker's behavior, and external characteristics, such as performing a task that is perceived to be a requirement of the job. Another type of external locus is attributing the outcome to fate or luck. Stable characteristics are perceived to be permanent, at least in the near future, whereas unstable characteristics are perceived to be temporary. Finally, situations may be perceived as being controllable by the individual; controllable by powerful others, for example, management; or controllable by no one, for example, fate.

Figure 1 is a new model to explore the associations among attributions, degree of perceived control, physical and psychological demands, resources such as social support, knowledge of back safety, and the onset of LBP. In this model, persons may attribute injury causes to internal factors (those intrinsic to and under the control of the injured party) or to external causes (those extrinsic to and not under the control of the injured party). Persons may also attribute responsibility for prevention of the injury internally (to self-protective actions) or externally (to actions by management, supervisors, or others). The associations among variables presented in Figure 1 are complex. Some of the elements are based on the Demand-Control-Support model.[15]

Inclusion of types of attributions for LBP causation and knowledge of back safety in the Attribution model in Figure 1 is unique. According to this new model a worker is expected to attribute the cause of LBP to factors in the work environment, including the availability of resources and the amount of psychological demand created by the job. How a worker attributes the cause of LBP is theorized to affect not just that worker's sense of control but also that worker's knowledge of back safety. The rationale is that unless a worker believes that his or her actions cause LBP, it is unlikely that the worker will see a need to learn safety procedures that may offer protection

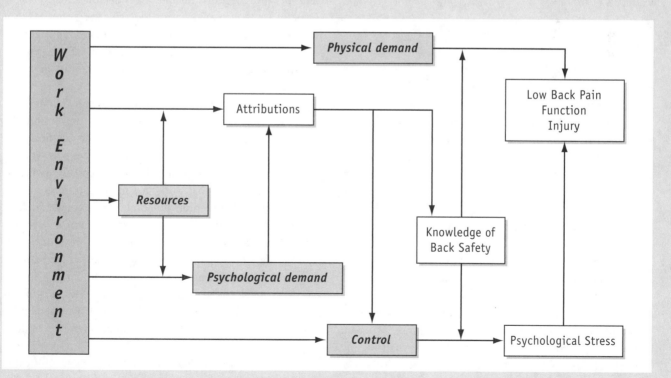

FIGURE 1 Conceptual model for attributions as a risk factor for LBP.

from LBP. Therefore, how one attributes responsibility for injury prevention may also affect how one performs a task, for example, the use of good body mechanics. In turn, the use of proper body mechanics is likely to affect the potential for LBP. Also, if the worker perceives a loss of control because of inadequate or insufficient injury prevention, this may contribute to an increase in workplace stress. This increase in stress may lead to chronic illnesses such as musculoskeletal disorders.[15] Finally, attributions of LBP cause and responsibility for prevention may have long-term implications for the types of interventions attempted and their effectiveness.

The availability of resources is theorized to affect the likelihood that stress will lead to an adverse outcome. Three major sources of resources are individual characteristics, social environment, and the safety climate. Factors such as a person's age, gender, and especially a history of previous LBP may affect the likelihood of having a musculoskeletal disorder.[4,5] The social environment, including support from coworkers, supervisors, family members, or friends, is believed to buffer the negative effects of psychological stress on a worker.[4] A supportive safety climate must have both management support for injury prevention and the worker's perception that the program is being implemented. It is hypothesized that these and other resources would modify the relationship between work stress and health outcomes. See Figure 2 for examples of resources.

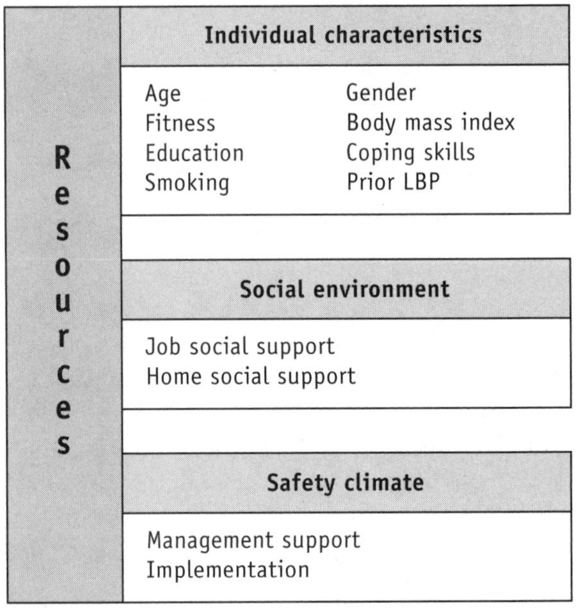

PSYCHOLOGICAL STRESS AND MUSCULOSKELETAL PAIN

There is a substantial body of research that suggests that psychological stress is associated with adverse health effects such as musculoskeletal pain.[4,15–17] A number of theories address psychological stress and LBP. These include an overload of low-threshold motor units and muscle fibers from prolonged muscle contraction or stress-induced tension aggravated by posture.[18,19] Additionally, distressed workers may be more aware of pain or may be more likely to file a report for pain. Other potential mechanisms may be related to the release of stress hormones or the effects of pain on behavior or other individual characteristics.[4]

It is believed that stress and attributions are related, and an understanding of this relationship may be useful in limiting or preventing LBP.[20] Both stress[4,21] and attributions[22] result from exposure to other factors such as physical workload and psychological or environmental stimuli. A person attributing LBP to factors that are external, permanent, and uncontrollable would be expected to have psychological stress. For example, a worker who attributes LBP to a job task may experience psychological strain in addition to physical strain.

FIGURE 2 Examples of resources.

In this example, the situation is external because it deals with a task assigned by management, and it is stable and uncontrollable because the individual perceives that the situation is the result of a management decision requiring the performance of an unsafe task. The worker's perception of job requirements may not be consistent with those of management, who may be unaware that the worker is performing the task in an unsafe manner.

When managers and employees differ in attributions of causes of LBP and responsibility for LBP prevention, the situation is likely to create a mismatch in expectations and a potential source of conflict. Managers may expect workers to change their behaviors in order to prevent LBP, whereas workers may believe that workplace modification is required to prevent LBP. Potential outcomes from a mismatch in expectations are increased stress, increased filing of workers' compensation claims, ineffective interventions, and future episodes of worker pain. Attribution of cause may be independent of assignment of responsibility for prevention.[23] Workers may attribute LBP to their own poor posture or other risk factors, but they may also expect management to make workplace modifications to reduce physical workload or psychological demands.[24]

It was also hypothesized that attributions of LBP cause would affect the worker's knowledge of back safety. For example, workers with internal attribution should be more concerned with self-protective measures and should be more likely to learn them. In addition, these workers characterized by internal attribution should also perceive they are more in control on the job because of their ability to protect themselves from LBP. As mentioned previously, it is reasonable to anticipate that those workers blaming the job tasks for causing LBP may also be more likely to report having LBP.

METHODS

Study Subjects

The associations presented in the model depicted in Figure 1 were tested in a study of garment workers. This was a cross-sectional study at a facility with approximately 417 unionized workers who were predominantly paid by piecework. The garment-making plant operated on three shifts, and the normal workday was eight and one half hours, including two paid 10-minute breaks and a 30-minute unpaid lunch break. Workers were allowed to take brief unscheduled breaks when needed.

There was a joint management and bargaining unit safety and health committee at this facility and a part-time safety officer. At the time of survey, there were 15 supervisors and 29 sections. The 29 sections were primarily involved in fabric cutting, sewing, pressing, examining, altering, ordering and other administrative tasks, and maintenance and cleanup. All currently employed workers, including supervisors and managers, were invited to participate in this study. Participation in any part of the study was strictly voluntary, and there were no repercussions for failure to participate. This research was approved by the Johns Hopkins School of Hygiene and Public Health Committee on Human Research.

Measures

The primary outcome of interest was self-reported LBP. An attempt was made to account for persons who developed LBP from non–work-related causes by classifying as non-cases those who reported "accidents or sudden injuries to the lower back from non-job activities." Unlike other studies that have focused on duration of pain, this study used functional limitation to define case status.[25] Because LBP is subjective, only workers who reported pain that was also linked to a restriction in functional status by limiting movement or by interfering with routine activities (at home or on the job) were considered cases. Functional status was selected instead of persistence because a limitation in movement or other function should be less likely to be subject to recall bias than the specific duration of pain symptoms. Therefore, the definition of a case included any self-reported pain, aching, stiffness, or cramping in the lower back within the last 12 months that limited movement or interfered with work at home or on the job.

Perceptions of job control were assessed separately as dependent (intermediate outcome) and as independent variables. Questions dealing with control were taken from the Job Content Questionnaire.[26] These previously validated questions are used in the "Demand-Control-Support" model. According to this model, workers suffer the most severe psychological strain when their perceived physical and psychological workload is high and their perceived job control and work-related social support is low. A subject's level of perceived job control was determined by using a median split of scaled scores to classify subjects as high or low in control.

Worker knowledge of back safety was also assessed as a dependent variable in one model and as an independent variable in other models. Knowledge scores were generated for subjects based on their responses to questions on LBP prevention. A median split of the scores was used to classify subjects as having high or low levels of LBP knowledge. When perceptions of job control and knowledge of back safety were modeled as dependent variables, their associations with attributions of LBP cause and attributions of responsibility for prevention of LBP were explored. As independent variables, their potential as contributors to LBP was assessed.

Psychological factors were the primary exposures of interest. With the exception of the measure "self-reported stressful life-event," these variables were developed by summing the responses to a series of questions and then classifying subjects as high or low based on a median split. Primary psychological variables were:

- attributions of cause—This category was assessed from responses to a series of questions that measured internal attribution, external attribution to job task, and external attribution to fate/luck. These scales are briefly described in Appendix A.
- job psychological demands, social support, and perceived job control—Each of these variables was based on the Job Content Questionnaire.[27]
- self-reported stressful life event—Subjects were classified as having high stress if they reported having experienced at least one life event with in the past year that was considered to be either very stressful or stressful.

The other primary exposure was physical workload. Job category was assessed as a surrogate of physical workload exposure. Workers were assigned a primary task; however, most also performed secondary tasks. All secondary job assignments were within the same department. A few workers were assigned a utility role that included a variety of jobs. Work table adjustment was determined because it is a potential source of bias for physical workload. If the workstation was recently adjusted, earlier physical exposure may go unnoticed, resulting in misclassification. Shift may be another potential modifier of psychological factors or physical workload; however, the numbers of persons on the second and third shifts were too few to make comparisons. The number of hours worked per week is a surrogate for intensity of workload exposure, since full-time workers would be expected to have more intense exposure than part-time workers. The duration of employment is a surrogate for cumulative exposure to physical workload and is assumed to affect LBP. Information was also collected on break patterns because of the concern that piece-rate workers may feel obligated to skip breaks to increase earnings.

Other factors may confound or modify the association between physical workload or psychological factors and LBP. Age and marital status were assessed because they may also confound associations between the dependent and other independent variables. Education level and income are surrogates for socioeconomic class, another potential confounder. Body Mass Index (BMI) and fitness may be potential modifiers of physical workload exposure factors. BMI, the subject's weight in kg divided by his or her height in m², was classified according to the recently defined categories (Normal < 25, Overweight 25–29.9, and Obese ≥ 30).[28]

Smoking has been identified as a possible risk factor for LBP; however, this association is not well understood.[29,30] Smoking may be a modifier of the effects of both physical workload and psychological risks. While some research suggests that smokers are at an increased risk of back pain, it is conceivable that persons with back pain may increase their smoking as a coping mechanism.[31] There is also convincing evidence that individuals with a prior back injury are at a significant risk of future back pain.[16,30,32] Information about hobbies and exercise was collected because these activities may both serve to improve health (exercising) or may serve as a risk factor (overexertion while exercising).

Procedures

A cross-sectional design was selected for this study because self-reported LBP may not have a clear date of onset. This approach is most appropriate when studying nonfatal diseases and physiological effects.[33] For the variables reported on in this article, data were collected by self-administered questionnaire that included information such as demographics, health and job histories, and perceptions about work, including attributions of the cause of LBP.

A total of 357 questionnaires were administered to garment workers in all sections of the plant, and 305 were returned, for a response rate of 85 percent. Thirteen forms were incomplete, leaving a final sample of 292 participants. Seven supervisors and managers agreed to complete the full questionnaire and nine others answered an abbreviated version that addressed their attributions of the cause of worker LBP and responsibility for prevention. Those who declined to participate cited lack of time, unwillingness to participate in any survey, and other personal reasons. Since only 2.8 percent of employees were males, they were excluded from the analyses. This resulted in a final study population of 278 females.

Data Analysis

Questionnaire data were evaluated using descriptive statistics; for example, frequencies, measures of central tendency, and variance. Relationships between variables were explored using correlation, odds ratios, and other inferential methods. A series of 24 statements attributing different causes of LBP were subjected to factor analysis using principal component analysis and varimax rotation as the basis for item reduction to create three new scales—attribution to fate/luck, attribution to external job tasks, and attribution to internal factors. For each scale, the amount of variance explained was determined, and reliability coefficients were determined. See Appendix A for psychometric characteristics of these scales.

Effects of the independent variables of interest were explored using multivariate logistic regression techniques. Two models for the study of LBP were tested in this analysis, the previously validated Demand-Control-Support[26] model and the Attribution model as depicted in Figure 1. Two additional models were also examined, one model addressing factors associated with back safety knowledge and the other model exploring factors associated with a worker's perception of job control. Logistic regression was used to control for the effects of all other variables and to identify interacting terms.[34] In developing each model, independent variables were included when considered important predictors based on a priori assumptions or when they were found to be associated ($p < 0.05$) with the dependent variable in bivariate analyses. Potential two- and three-way interaction terms were tested using a forward step-wise approach before considering the effect of confounding variables; however, no significant interaction terms were identified. Variables selected for the final model were analyzed in a full logistic regression model. Wald statistic scores, beta values and corresponding odds ratios, and 95 percent confidence intervals of the odds ratios were generated for each of the variables that achieved significance. All analyses were performed with SPSS version 8.0.

Preliminary analyses were performed to identify the presence of exceptional values (outliers) or significant collinearity problems. Outliers were evaluated for possible removal when case "studentized" residuals exceeded 2.5. In the analysis of the Attribution model, one case had a residual exceeding 5.7. This case was removed from the analysis. In the case of potential collinearity, the correlation matrix was examined, and one of the inter-correlated variables was considered for removal; for example, education level but not age was included in the Knowledge model due to collinearity. Finally, R^2_L was evaluated as a measure of association between the independent variables and dependent variables of the LBP models. This statistic, calculated as the model Chi-square divided by (-2 Log Likelihood) is similar to the coefficient of determination, R^2, used in multiple linear regression.[34]

RESULTS

Table I presents the demographics of this study population. The study participants, all female, were predominantly white, and over 95 percent spoke English as their first language. Most were married or were living with a partner. Most participants had completed high school or a GED and reported a total family income of $35,000 or less.

Attribution Scales

Content validity of the newly developed scales was strengthened by careful review of the literature and pilot testing of new questions. Attribution theory and meta-analyses by several researchers on risk factors for LBP served as primary information sources for scale development.[4,7,30] Factor analysis was used to establish construct validity. One measure of construct validity, known-group validity, is the demonstration of expected patterns when applying the instrument to another group with known categorization. For example, studies have shown that managers/supervisors and workers perceive hazards in the workplace differently.[35]

Although the sample size of managers/supervisors in this study was small (n = 16), our results are consistent with these prior studies. While managers tend to overlook hazards in the workplace or discount the significance of the hazard, workers are more likely to see hazards and acknowledge their significance. This was seen in the comparisons of attributions of the causes of LBP by plant managers and supervisors with those of workers. A high percentage of workers (79%) and all of the managers and supervisors (100%) attributed LBP to worker actions. However, an even higher percentage (86%) of workers but only 31 percent of managers attributed LPB to work conditions. When asked which was *most* important, over half (56%) of workers said work conditions were most important

TABLE I Demographic characteristics of study participants

Characteristic	Frequency	Percent
Race		
White	254	91.4
Other	24	8.6
First language		
English	266	95.7
Other	12	4.3
Marital status		
Married	154	55.6
Living with a partner	25	9.0
Widowed	17	6.1
Separated	10	3.6
Divorced	38	13.7
Never married	33	11.9
Education		
Less than grade 12	62	22.5
Grade 12 or GED	155	56.4
More than grade 12	58	21.1
Total	275	100
Annual income		
Below $15,000	49	22.5
$15,001–$35,000	87	39.9
Above $35,000	82	37.6
Total	218	100

compared to only one (6%) manager or supervisor. In each case, the differences between managers and workers were significant, thus demonstrating known group validity. Responses to similar questions about responsibility for preventing LBP, however, did not differ significantly between groups. The validity of the questions on responsibility for prevention was therefore not supported.

LBP Prevalence

Approximately 72 percent of subjects reported having LBP at sometime in their lives and almost 64 percent had more than one episode of LBP within the previous year. One hundred respondents (36%) met the case definition as described in the Methods section. These cases reported having LBP due to occupational causes that was severe enough to limit movement or interfere with work. Only 50 workers had the first onset of pain in the prior 12 months, and 60 subjects failed to report when the onset of LBP occurred.

INDIVIDUAL AND OCCUPATIONAL FACTORS

Prevalence of LBP was examined by age (18–36, 37–51, and > 51 years of age), BMI (normal, overweight, and obese) and income categories (annual family income of $15,000 or less and >$15,000), as well as by other worker characteristics (see Table II). Age, education level, and BMI were not associated with LBP in bivariate analyses. There was a significant linear trend of increased LBP symptoms associated with increased smoking (chi-square for trend = 3.89, p < 0.05). The highest prevalence of LBP reporting was among the heavy smokers, that is, those consuming more than 20 cigarettes per day. (Data not shown.) Although this finding is consistent with those of other studies, there were only 16 heavy smokers in this population, and the results were of borderline statistical significance.(36)

Those workers with family earnings of less than $15,000 per year were significantly less likely to report LBP than those earning more income (chi-square = 7.52, p < 0.01). An odds ratio of 0.36 suggests that lower family earnings were negatively associated with LBP. The only hobby associated with LBP was gardening (Pearson's chi-square test = 4.43, 1 df, p-value < 0.05), although the 95 percent CI of the odds ratio did include 1.0.

Another individual risk factor for LBP is a prior history of back pain. Current LBP was not associated with a prior history of LBP in this study (Pearson's chi-square = 2.18, 1 df, p-value > 0.05). (Data not shown.) Finally, no employment-related factors such as hours worked per week, duration of employment, or job category, were significantly associated with LBP.

Low Back Pain and Stress

Subjects' self-reported stress was investigated. LBP was associated with having a stressful event such as a divorce, family illness, or loss of a spouse (Pearson's chi-square = 4.18, 1 df, p-value < 0.05). The odds of reporting LBP were 1.7 times greater (95% CI = 0.99–3.03) in those persons reporting non-occupational stress in the previous year (data not shown); however, the 95 percent CI included 1.0.

Table III shows the associations between LBP and elements of the Demand-Control-Support model. LBP was significantly associated with reporting high physical demand (OR = 1.8, Pearson's chi-square test = 5.33, 1 df, p-value < 0.05) and high psychological demand (OR = 2.1, Pearson's chi-square test = 8.24, 1 df, p-value < 0.01). High scores in supervisor social support were protective against LBP (OR = 0.39, Pearson's chi-square test = 6.35, 1 df, p-value < 0.05). Neither coworker social support nor perceived job control was associated with LBP in this study.

TABLE II   LBP by individual characteristics and hobby

	LBP symptoms Yes		LBP symptoms No		Odds ratio	95%CI
	n	%	n	%		
Income levels[A]						
≤ $15,000	10	20.4	39	79.6	0.36	0.15–0.80
> $15,000	70	41.9	97	58.1		
	Pearson's chi-square = (7.52, 1), p-value 0.006					
Age levels						
18–37	32	38.6	51	61.4	Ref	NA
38–51	40	43.5	52	56.5	1.23	0.64–2.35
52 or above	24	27.6	63	72.4	0.61	0.30–1.22
	Pearson's chi-square = (5.06, 2), p-value 0.080					
BMI						
Less than 25 (normal)	34	34.3	65	65.7	Ref	NA
25–29.9 (overweight)	34	37.8	56	62.2	1.16	1.61–2.20
30 or above (obese)	28	41.2	40	58.8	1.34	0.67–2.66
	Pearson's chi-square = (0.82, 2), p-value 0.665					
Do gardening						
Yes	37	45.7	44	54.3	1.8	1.00–3.10
No	63	32.3	132	67.7		
	Pearson's chi-square = (4.43, 1), p-value 0.035					

[A]Two individuals did not report LBP status and were excluded from the analysis.

TABLE III   Prevalence of LBP by median split of psychosocial scales

	LBP symptoms Yes		LBP symptoms No		Odds ratio	95%CI
	n	%	n	%		
Worker reports high physical demand						
High	48	44.4	60	55.6	1.8	1.06–3.11
Low	49	30.6	111	69.4		
Pearson's chi-square test = (5.33, 1), p-value = 0.021						
Worker reports high psychological demand						
High	56	44.8	69	55.2		
Low	39	27.9	101	72.1	2.1	2.10–3.62
Pearson's chi-square test = (8.24, 1), p-value = 0.004						
Worker reports high supervisor support						
High	10	20.8	38	79.2		
Low	83	40.3	123	59.7	0.39	0.17–0.87
Pearson's chi-square test = (6.35, 1), p-value = 0.012						
Worker reports high coworker support						
High	15	37.5	25	62.5		
Low	81	36.3	142	63.7	1.1	0.50–2.22
Pearson's chi-square test = (0.02, 1), p-value = 0.887						
Worker reports high job control						
High	40	33.9	78	66.1		
Low	53	39.0	83	61.0	0.80	0.46–1.39
Pearson's chi-square test = (.70, 1), p-value = 0.403						

Table IV displays the associations between LBP and types of attributions. LBP was associated with attribution of LBP to the job task (OR = 2.7, Pearson's chi-square test = 14.02, 1 df, p-value < 0.001). Workers who attributed LBP to the job task were 2.7 times more likely to report LBP than workers who did not attribute it to the job task (95% CI = 1.5–4.6). Neither internal attribution of the cause of LBP nor attribution to fate or luck was associated with LBP.

Multivariate Analysis

Table V shows the results of the logistic regression model for attribution variables and LPB knowledge. Knowledge of back safety was significantly associated with internal attribution of LBP. Workers attributing LBP to their own actions were over 3.6 times more likely to have high levels of knowledge, and those scoring high on attribution of LBP to luck/fate were only half as likely to have high scores on the knowledge scale (OR = 0.49). There was also a positive association between attribution of LBP to the job task and higher scores on back safety (OR = 1.91).

The logistic regression model for perceived job control appears in Table VI. There was a positive association between perceived job control and total social support (OR = 2.91). Age level was inversely related to job control, that is, the youngest workers were more likely to report higher control scores than the middle aged or the oldest workers (OR = 0.41 and 0.27, respectively). Finally, income above $15,000 was positively associated with job control. Workers with family incomes exceeding $15,000 per year were more likely to report high job control than those earning $15,000 or less (OR = 2.65).

Prediction of LBP was assessed using two different models, the Demand-Control-Support model and the Attribution model.

Tables VII and VIII show the results for each model. Age and smoking status, although not significant in bivariate analysis, were included in multivariate analyses because these were risk factors of a priori interest. Total family income was significant in bivariate analysis and was therefore included in both models. Total job demand, perceived job control, and total support were the other variables tested in the Demand-Control-Support model. In the Attribution model, internal

TABLE IV   Prevalence of LBP by attributions of cause

	LBP symptoms Yes		LBP symptoms No		Odds ratio	95%CI
	n	%	n	%		
Worker attributes LBP to internal causes						
High	53	36.1	94	63.9		
Low	43	35.8	77	64.2	1.0	0.58–2.10
Pearson's chi-square test = (0.001, 1), p-value = 0.970						
Worker attributes LBP to job tasks						
High	54	50.5	53	49.5		
Low	43	27.7	112	72.3	2.7	1.53–4.60
Pearson's chi-square test = (14.02, 1), p-value < 0.0001						
Worker attributes LBP to fate/luck						
High	41	32.5	85	67.5		
Low	50	38.5	80	61.5	0.77	0.43–1.33
Pearson's chi-square test = (0.98, 1), p-value = 0.322						

attribution (blaming oneself for LBP), attribution to the job task (blaming the job for LBP), and attribution to fate/luck (blaming LBP on fate or luck) were tested.

Table VII shows that total demand was positively associated with LBP. The odds were 2.25 times greater that subjects reporting a high total demand (physical and psychological) would report LBP. There was also a positive association between income above $15,000 and LBP. Subjects reporting family incomes above $15,000 were more likely to report LBP (OR = 2.83). Table VIII shows that external attribution of LBP cause was significantly associated with LBP, and supervisor support was inversely related to LBP. Subjects blaming the job task were over three times more likely to report LBP, and subjects reporting high supervisor support were less likely to report having LBP (OR = 0.23). As in the Demand-Control-Support model, the odds were greater (OR = 4.13) that subjects reporting a family income greater than $15,000 per year

would be more likely to report LBP. The R^2_L statistic was used to estimate the degree of association between the independent variables and LBP in both the Demand-Control-Support and the Attribution models. For the Demand-Control-Support model, R^2_L equaled only 11.9 percent, compared to 26.2 percent for the Attribution model.

DISCUSSION

This research lends support to the works of several researchers regarding the role of psychosocial factors in musculoskeletal disorders.[4,8,29,37] In addition, our research demonstrates that these garment workers had a relatively high prevalence of LBP that was severe enough to limit movement or interfere with activities. Garment making had not previously been identified as a high-risk occupation for LBP. These results also demonstrate a multitude of risk factors that may contribute to LBP. Unfortunately, our study design does not allow one

TABLE V   Multiple logistic regression model of worker knowledge of back safety

	B	S. E.	Wald	p-value	Odds ratio	95% C. I.
< High school education (ref.)			0.57	0.7508		
High school education	0.22	0.47	0.23	0.6299	1.25	0.50–3.12
> High school education	0.27	0.36	0.57	0.4509	1.31	0.65–2.68
Internal attribution	1.3019	0.31	18.04	0.0000	3.65	2.01–6.65
External fate/luck	−0.71	0.30	5.65	0.0175	0.49	0.28–0.88
External job task	0.68	0.30	5.03	0.0249	1.97	1.09–3.56
Constant	−1.00	0.40	6.28	0.0122		

TABLE VI Multiple logistic regression model of worker perception of job control

	B	S. E.	Wald	p-value	Odds ratio	95% C.I.
Total social support	1.07	0.33	10.62	0.0011	2.91	1.53–5.52
Age 18–36 (reference)			10.40	0.0055		
Age 37–51	−0.89	0.39	5.31	0.0212	0.41	0.19–0.88
Age 52–71	−1.29	0.41	9.72	0.0018	0.27	0.12–0.62
Income > $15,000	0.98	0.41	5.78	0.0182	2.65	1.18–5.96
Internal attribution	0.53	0.33	2.31	0.1284		
Constant	−0.96	0.48	3.99	0.0458		

TABLE VII Multiple logistic regression using the Demand-Control-Support model for LBP

	B	S. E.	Wald	p-value	Odds ratio	95% C.I.
Total demand	0.81	0.34	5.57	0.0183	2.25	1.15–4.40
Income > $15, 000	1.04	0.45	5.32	0.0211	2.83	1.17–6.85
Non- or former smoker (reference)			6.41	0.0933		
Light smoker	−1.75	0.72	5.88	0.0153		
Moderate smoker	−1.51	0.91	2.89	0.0978		
Heavy smoker	−1.31	0.77	2.89	0.0890		
Age 18–36 (reference)				0.0948		
Age 37–51	0.71	0.45	2.48	0.1152		
Age 52–71	0.90	0.42	5.32	0.0327		
Total social support	0.08	0.37	0.05	0.8319		
Control	0.19	0.36	0.28	0.5997		
Constant	0.73	0.80	0.83	0.3634		

TABLE VIII Multiple logistic regression using the Attribution model for LBP

	B	S. E.	Wald	p-value	Odds ratio	95% C. I.
Internal attribution	−0.04	0.39	0.012	0.9123	0.96	0.44–2.06
External fate/luck	−0.56	0.37	2.28	0.1314	0.57	0.27–1.18
External job task	1.17	0.39	9.14	0.0025	3.23	1.51–6.89
Supervisor support	−1.50	0.53	7.51	0.0061	0.23	0.08–0.66
Age18–36 (reference)			5.43	0.0662		
Age 37–51	0.41	0.43	0.93	0.3358	1.51	0.65–3.47
Age 52–71	−0.65	0.46	1.96	0.1618	0.52	0.21–1.30
Income > $15, 000	1.42	0.50	7.99	0.0047	4.13	1.54–11.07
Non- or former smoker (reference)			4.76	0.1899		
Light smoker	0.23	0.66	0.12	0.7242	1.26	0.35–4.59
Moderate smoker	0.57	0.45	1.69	0.1939	1.79	0.74–4.28
Heavy smoker	1.48	0.76	3.84	0.0502	4.40	1.00–19.4
Physical demand	0.47	0.38	1.55	0.2135	1.61	0.76–3.39
Constant	−2.11	0.67	9.89	0.0017		

to evaluate the relative contribution of psychosocial factors such as job stress compared to specific physical factors such as awkward posture.

Nevertheless, this study reveals some interesting findings that may advance the efforts to reduce LBP among workers. First, individuals knowledgeable about the methods of preventing LBP were more likely to have high scores in internal locus of causation, for example, they believed that worker actions contribute to LBP. It was also observed that workers with low knowledge scores were more likely to score low in internal attribution and high in attributing LBP to luck/fate. These results may partially explain why the "back schools" have mixed results in preventing LBP.[38] If the target group receiving training in back injury prevention consists predominantly of those attributing cause of LBP to work conditions or luck, increasing knowledge of proper lifting or good posture may not result in a change in behavior. In order to see a change in behavior, it may be necessary to first convince these workers that their actions can make a difference in preventing LBP. Therefore, before initiating a back safety training program, it may be useful to evaluate workers' beliefs regarding attribution of causation, and those workers scoring low in internal attribution may benefit from attribution retraining, that is, increase their internal locus of causation.[39,40]

A second interesting finding relates to perceived job control. This is important because low scores in job control may contribute to psychological strain. Workers with high scores in job control tended to also have high scores in social support from their supervisors. This finding suggests that workers who perceive that their supervisors support them feel more in control on the job. Encouraging immediate supervisors to be supportive of workers may be an inexpensive but potentially beneficial means of reducing worker stress. Other factors that were associated with high scores in perceived job control were higher family income and younger age. It follows that individuals with higher incomes feel more in control. Also, younger workers may have fewer responsibilities and more job options than their older counterparts, and thus increased sense of control.

The Demand-Control-Support model was partially successful in this study of LBP among garment workers. Increased LBP was associated with high scores in worker perceptions of physical and psychological demand and high family income. The lack of association with perceived job control and total social support may have been related to the pay system. In piecework pay systems, increased income is tightly bound to increased production, thus contributing to a demand for increased workload. Subjects may perceive they have control, but they may be choosing between pay and lower LBP risk.[41] Also, garment making is an assembly line process. Workers' rate of work and pay can depend on the workers who precede them in the assembly process, thus reducing their control.

The Attribution model appeared to be a useful tool for the study of LBP. Multivariate analysis demonstrated a strong association between increased reporting of LBP and attribution of the cause of LBP to the job task. This may have been a reflection of truly elevated levels of physical hazards for the job tasks of those with injuries or may have been related to the retrospective efforts of already injured workers to explain the cause of their own injuries. One factor that appeared to be protective against LBP was a high score in supervisor social support. Another risk factor for increased reporting of LBP was higher income. The finding of more LBP in workers with higher incomes may be influenced by the piecework pay system, in which the measurement of higher pay may be a surrogate for physical workload. The results, including the lack of association between LBP history and LBP, may also be explained by the healthy worker effect that may have occurred because only non-disabled, currently employed workers participated in the study, excluding some workers with LBP.

It is not possible to determine, with a cross-sectional design, whether apparent risk factors contributed to LBP or if the presence of LBP contributed to reporting of risk factors. As mentioned, it may be possible that workers attribute the cause of LBP to the job only after LBP develops. Clarification requires a longitudinal design.

Potential areas for future research include an examination of managers and workers for the presence of mismatch in attributions. For example, if managers attribute LBP solely to worker behavior and workers attribute LBP to the job task, what is the effect of this mismatch in perceptions on psychological stress? More importantly, will the presence of a mismatch interfere with the implementation of effective interventions?

It is also important to use the Attribution model in other occupational groups and with other outcomes to determine its ultimate utility. It would be useful to measure attributions at baseline and to follow workers longitudinally to observe whether attributions remain stable overtime.

CONCLUSIONS

Preventing LBP in the workplace is a complex challenge facing the occupational safety and health professional. The first step in preventing this problem is to define high risk groups and the factors associated with LBP risk. This work suggests that garment workers may be an occupational group at risk for this type of musculoskeletal problem and should therefore be considered for the institution of preventive measures. As previously demonstrated, reports of supervisor support were negatively associated with LBP risk. Approaches that enhance workers' perceptions of supervisor support should therefore be evaluated. Application of attribution theory demonstrated a positive association between LBP and its attribution to job tasks, but the temporal relationship of this observation requires further study. A relationship between internal attribution and knowledge of back safety suggests the need to determine the efficacy of strategies designed to enhance workers' perception that they can prevent LBP through their own actions. LBP prevention must now be pursued through intervention research.

REFERENCES

1. Leigh, J.P.; Markowitz, S.B.; Fahs, M.; Chonggak, S.; Landrigan, P.J.: Occupational Injury and Illness in the United States: Estimates of Costs, Morbidity, and Mortality. Arch Intern Med 157:1557–1568 (1997).

2. Webster, B.S.; Snook, S.H.: The Cost of 1989 Workers' Compensation Low Back Pain Claims. Spine 19:1111–1115 (1994).

3. NIOSH. Low Back Disorders. DHHS (NIOSH) Publication No. 96-115, pp. 18–19. NIOSH, Cincinnati, OH (1996).

4. Bongers, P.M.; deWinter, C.R.; Kompier, M.A.; Hildebrandt, V.H.: Psychosocial Factors at Work and Musculoskeletal Disease. Scand J Work Environ Health 19:297–312 (1993).

5. Burdorf, A.; Rossignol, M.; Fathallah, F.A.; Snook, S.H.; Herrick, R.F.: Challenges in Assessing Risk Factors in Epidemiologic Studies on Back Disorders. Am J Indus Med 32:142–152 (1997).

6. Byrns, G.E.: Attributions, Stress, and Work-Related Low Back Pain. The Johns Hopkins University. Dissertation (1999).

7. NIOSH: Low Back Musculoskeletal Disorders: Evidence for Work-Relatedness. In: Musculoskeletal Disorders and Workplace Factors: A Critical Review of Epidemiologic Evidence for Work Related Musculoskeletal Disorders of the Neck, Upper Extremity, and Low Back, National Institute for Occupational Safety and Health, ed., Cincinnati, pp. 6-1–6-96 (1997).

8. Kerr, M.S.; Frank, J.W.; Shannon, H.S.; et al.: Biomechanical and Psychosocial Risk Factors for Low Back Pain at Work. Am J Pub Health 91:1069–1075 (2001).

9. National Research Council and the Institute of Medicine: Musculoskeletal Disorders and the Workplace: Low Back and Upper Extremities, pp. 1–13. Panel on Musculoskeletal Disorders and the Workplace, National Academy Press, Washington, DC (2001).

10. Josephson, M.; Pernold, G.; Ahlberg-Hulten, G.; et al.: Differences in the Association Between Psychosocial Work Conditions and Physical Work Load in Female- and Male-Dominated Occupations. MUSIC-Norrtalje Study Group. Am Indus Hyg Assoc J 60:673– 678 (1999).

11. Kelly, M.J.; Ortiz, D. J.; Follick, M.J.; Courtney, T. K.: Ergonomic Challenges in Conventional and Advanced Apparel Manufacturing. Int J Hum Factors Manufact 2:39–54(1992).

12. Serratos-Perez, J.N.; Mendiola-Anda, C.: Musculoskeletal Disorders Among Male Sewing Machine Operators in Shoemaking. Ergonomics 36:793–800 (1993).

13. Sokas, R.K.; Spiegelman, D.; Wegman, D.H.: Self-Reported Musculoskeletal Complaints Among Garment Workers. Am J Indus Med 15:197–206 (1989).

14. Weiner, B.: The Structure of Perceived Causality. In: An Attribution Theory of Motivation and Emotion, pp. 43–78. Springer-Verlag, New York (1986).

15. Karasek, R.; Theorell, T.: Health, Productivity, and Work Life. In: Healthy Work: Stress, Productivity, and the Reconstruction of Working Life, pp. 1–30. Basic Books, Inc., New York (1990).

16. Feyer, A.M.; Herbison, P.; Williamson, A.M.; et al.: The Role of Physical and Psychological Factors in Occupational Low Back Pain: A Prospective Cohort Study. Occup Environ Med 57:116–120 (2000).

17. Bigos, S.J.; Battie, M.C.; Spengler, D.M.; et al.: A Prospective Study of Work Perceptions and Psychosocial Factors Affecting the Report of Back Injury [published erratum appears in Spine Jun 16(6):688 (1991)]. Spine 16:1–6 (1991).

18. Caillet, R.: Psychological Aspects of Low Back Pain. In: Low Back Pain Syndrome, pp. 76–93. F. A. Davis, Philadelphia (1995).

19. Ursin, H.; Murison, R.; Knardahl, S.: Conclusion: Sustained Activation and Disease. In: Biological and Psychological Basis of Psychosomatic Disease, pp. 269–277. H. Ursin, R. Murison, eds., Pergamon Press, Oxford (1983).

20. Faller, H.; Schilling, S.; Lang, H.: Causal Attribution and Adaptation Among Lung Cancer Patients. J Psychosom Res 39:619–627 (1995).

21. Klitzman, S.; Stellman, J.M.: The Impact of the Physical Environment on the Psychological Well-Being of Office Workers. Soc Sci Med 29:733–742 (1989).

22. Swartzman, L.C.; Lees, M.C.: Causal Dimensions of College Students' Perceptions of Physical Symptoms. J Behavior Med 19: 95–110 (1996).

23. Brickman, P.; Rabinowitz, V.C.; Karuza, J.; Coates, D.; Cohn, E.; Kidder, L.: Models of Helping and Coping. Am Psychol 37:368–384 (1982).

24. Kanekar, S.; Miranda, J.P.: Attribution as a Function of Agential Distance in a Causal Chain. Genet Soc Gen Psychol Monogr 124:271–282 (1998).

25. Guo, H.R.; Tanaka, S.; Cameron, L.L.; et al.: Back Pain Among Workers in the United States: National Estimates and Workers at High Risk. Am J Indus Med 28:591–602 (1995).

26. Karasek, R.; Kawakami, N.; Brisson, C.; Houtman, I.L.; Bongers, P.M.; Amick, B.: The Job Content Questionnaire (JCQ): An Instrument for Internationally Comparative Assessments of Psychosocial Job Characteristics. J Occup Health Psychol 3:322–355 (1998).

27. Karasek, R.: Job Content Questionnaire. Department of Industrial and Systems Engineering, University of Southern California, Los Angeles (1985).

28. APHA: New Federal Guidelines on Overweight and Obesity. Nation's Health p. 4 (1998).

29. Waddell, G.: Risk Factors for Low Back Pain. In: The Back Pain Revolution, pp. 85–101. Churchill Livingstone, Edinburgh (1998).

30. Burdorf, A.; Sorock, G.: Positive and Negative Evidence of Risk Factors for Back Disorders. Scand J Work Environ Health 23:243–256 (1997).

31. Foppa, I.; Noack, R.H.: The Relation of Self-Reported Back Pain to Psychosocial, Behavioral, and Health-Related Factors in a Working Population in Switzerland. Soc Sci Med 43:1119–1126 (1996).

32. Andersson, G.B.: Factors Important in the Genesis and Prevention of Occupational Back Pain and Disability. J Manipulat Physiol Ther 15:43–46 (1992).

33. Checkoway, H.; Pearce, N.E.; Crawford-Brown, D.J.: Issues of Study Design and Analysis. In: Research Methods in Occupational Epidemiology, pp. 72–102. Oxford University Press, New York (1989).

34. Menard, S.: An Introduction to Logistic Regression Diagnostics. In: Applied Logistic Regression Analysis, pp. 58–79. Sage Publications, Inc., Thousand Oaks, CA (1995).

35. Houtman, I.L.; Goudswaard, A.; Dhondt, S.; van der Grinten, M.P.; Hildebrandt, V.H.; van der Poel, E.G.: Dutch Monitor on Stress and

Physical Load: Risk Factors, Consequences, and Preventive Action. Occup Environ Med 55:73–83 (1998).

36. Waddell, G.: The Epidemiology of Low Back Pain. In: The Back Pain Revolution, pp. 69–84. Churchill Livingstone, Edinburgh (1998).

37. Battie, M.C.; Bigos, S.J.: Industrial Back Pain Complaints. A Broader Perspective. Orthop Clin North Am 22:273–282 (1991).

38. Daltroy, L.H.; Iversen, M.D.; Larson, M.G.; et al.: A Controlled Trial of an Educational Program to Prevent Low Back Injuries. N Engl J Med 337:322–328 (1997).

39. Fosterling, F.: Attributional Retraining: A Review. Psychol Bull 98:495–512 (1985).

40. Weinberg, L.E.; Strain, L.A.: Community-Dwelling Older Adults' Attributions About Falls. Arch Phys Med Rehabil 76:955–960 (1995).

41. Brisson, C.; Vinet, A.; Vezina, M.; Gingras, S.: Effect of Duration of Employment in Piecework on Severe Disability Among Female Garment Workers. Scand J Work Environ Health 15:329–334 (1989).

APPENDIX A—NEWLY DEVELOPED SCALES

1. Worker Attributions scales:

   Respondents rated items listed below according to levels of importance for causes of low back pain (LBP). Response format was in a Likert scale where: not important = 1, somewhat important = 2, important = 3, and very important = 4.

   a) Lifting something too heavy
   b) Fate
   c) Being physically out of shape
   d) Not following proper procedures
   e) Lack of training
   f) Being careless
   g) Smoking cigarettes
   h) Jobs that require sitting too long in one place
   i) Chance
   j) Jobs that require standing too long in one place
   k) Bad luck
   l) Jobs that require twisting the back
   m) Jobs that require doing too many tasks at once
   n) Act of God
   o) Jobs that require working in an awkward position
   p) Using the wrong body motion in doing a job
   q) Jobs that require working too quickly
   r) Tripping on an object
   s) Coming to work tired
   t) Jobs that are tiring
   u) Unsafe equipment
   v) Getting older
   w) Having an old back injury
   x) Jobs that require holding the same position too long

   Three components were created using factor analysis with principal components and varimax rotations.

1) External fate/luck scale (using items b, i, k, and n)
2) External job tasks scale (using items h, j, q, and x)
3) Internal attribution scale (using items d, e, and f)

Analyses were conducted using the three scales as dichotomous variables split at their median values into high versus low attributers. The total variance explained by the factor analysis was 68.9 percent (component 1 = 29.8 percent, component 2 = 22. 4 percent, and component 3 = 16.6 percent). Mean inter-item correlations were 0.59 for component 1, 0.51 for component 2, and 0.60 for component 3, and Cronbach's alphas were 0.85 for component 1, 0.81 for component 2, and 0.82 for component 3.

The descriptive statistics for the attribution scores were as follows:

Attribution scores

Characteristic	N	Mean	Std. Dev.	Range of values Actual	Possible
Internal attribution	269	9.8	2.1	3–12	3–12
External—job task	264	12.0	2.8	4–16	4–16
External—fate/luck	258	6.5	2.9	4–16	4–16

2. Worker Knowledge Scale

   A knowledge-of-back-safety scale was also developed using 20 questions that described possible methods of preventing back injury. For example, "changing the workplace to reduce the need to move materials," should be rated as very likely to prevent LBP, but "adjusting the humidity of the air," should be rated as not likely to prevent LBP. Questions on design or operations were based on the literature. (3) Items were rated by subjects as: not likely = 1, somewhat likely = 2, likely = 3, or very likely = 4 to prevent LBP. In some cases, questions were scored in reverse order or omitted. See below.

   a) Changing the workplace to reduce the need to move materials
   b) Reducing the weight of materials
   c) Adjusting the humidity of the air (scored in reverse order)
   d) Staying in shape by exercising (not scored)
   e) Reducing the size of materials
   f) Keeping the back straight while lifting
   g) Eating a proper diet (not scored)

h) Using handles on containers

i) Keeping the back bent (or rounded) while lifting (scored in reverse order)

j) Reducing the distance to carry materials

k) Lifting with the legs bent

l) Holding materials away from the body while carrying (scored in reverse order)

m) Using pushcarts instead of carrying materials

n) Using back supports (belts) while lifting (not scored)

o) Using adjustable worktables

p) Using adjustable chairs

q) Lifting with the legs straight (scored in reverse order)

r) Following the supervisor's directions in doing a job (not scored)

s) Holding materials close to the body while carrying

t) Not smoking (not scored)

APPENDIX B—JOB CATEGORIES

The 29 sections were combined into one of nine categories

Task	Number of workers	Percent
Machine sewing	105	37.8
Pressing/ironing	28	10.1
Manual cutting	24	8.6
Automatic cutting	19	6.8
Other standing jobs (inspection, etc.)	35	12.6
Hand sewing	14	5.0
Alterations	8	2.9
Office workers	37	13.3
Misc/unknown	8	2.9
Total	278	100

Article Source: Burns, G., Agnew, J., & Curbow, B. (2002). Attributions, stress and work-related low back pain. *Applied Occupational and Environmental Hygiene*, *17*(11), 752–764. Copyright 2002. ACGIH®, Cincinnati, OH. Reprinted with permission.

QUESTIONS

1. How does knowledge affect locus of causality?

2. Why would it be important to know the locus of causality before planning an educational intervention to reduce the risk of lower back injury?

3. To what did the managers attribute lower back pain, and how did this differ for the workers?

4. Why would the difference in lower back pain attribution between the managers and workers affect the success of an intervention to address this health problem?

CHAPTER REFERENCES

Carpenter, K.M., Hasin, D.S., Allsion, D.B., & Faith, M.S. (2000). Relationships between obesity and DSM-IV major depressive disorder, suicide ideation, and suicide attempts: Results from a general population study. *American Journal of Public Health*, *90*(2), 251–257.

Clement, U. (1998). Subjective HIV attribution theories, coping and psychological functioning among homosexual men. *AIDS Care*, *10*(3), 355–364.

Crandall, C.S., & Schiffauer, K.L. (1998). Anti-fat prejudice: Beliefs, values and American culture. *Obesity Research*, 6, 458–460.

Kearsley, G. (2006). Attribution Theory. In *Explorations in Learning & Instruction: The Theory into Practice Database*. Retrieved December 8, 2007, from http://tip.psychology.org/weiner.html.

Kneckt, M.C., & Knuuttila, M.L.E. (2000). Attributions to dental and diabetes health outcomes. *Journal of Clinical Periodontics*, *27*, 205–211.

Levenson, H. (1974). Activism and powerful others: Distinctions within the concept of internal-external control. *Journal of Personality Assessment*, *38*, 377–383.

McDonell, J.R. (1993). Judgments of personal responsibility for HIV infection: An attributional analysis. *Social Work*, *38*(4), 403–410.

Puhl, R., & Brownell, K.D. (2001). Obesity, bias and discrimination. *Obesity Research*, *9*, 788–805.

Puhl, R., & Brownell, K.D. (2003). Psychosocial origins of obesity stigma: Toward changing a powerful and pervasive bias. *Obesity Reviews*, *4*, 213–227.

Robert, R. (1982, November 24). Malavasi questions character of some, says coaching is tough. *Los Angeles Times*, Pt. 3, p. 3.

Rosenbaum, R.M. (1972). *A Dimensional Analysis of the Perceived Causes of Success and Failure*. Doctoral dissertation, University of California, Los Angeles.

Rotter, J.B. (1966). Generalized expectancies for internal versus external control of reinforcement. *Psychological Monograph*, *80*, 1–28.

Rotter, J.B. (1993). Expectancies. In C.E. Walker (Ed.), *The History of Clinical Psychology in Autobiography* (Vol. II, pp. 273–284). Pacific Grove, CA: Brooks/Cole.

Seneviratne, H., & Saunders, B. (2000). An investigation of alcohol dependent respondents' attributions for their own and "others" relapses. *Addiction Research*, *8*(5), 439–453.

Strickland, B.R. (Ed.). (2006). Fritz Heider. In *Encyclopedia of Psychology* (2nd ed.). Retrieved December 7, 2007, from http://www.enotes.com/gale-psychology-encyclopedia/fritz-heider.

Taylor, S.E. (1983). Adjusting to threatening events—a theory of cognitive adaptation. *American Psychologist, 41,* 1161–1173.

Wang, S. (2001). Motivation: General overview of theories. In M. Orey (Ed.), *Emerging Perspectives on Learning, Teaching, and Technology.* Retrieved November 27, 2005, from http://www.coe.uga.edu/epltt/Motivation .htm.

Weiner, B. (1985). An attributional theory of achievement motivation and emotion. *Psychological Review, 92,* (4), 548–573.

Wiegmann, S.M., & Berven, N.L. (1998). Health locus-of-control beliefs and improvement in physical functioning in a work-hardening, return-to-work program. *Rehabilitation Psychology, 43*(2), 83–100.

CHAPTER 6

Transtheoretical Model

Theory Essence Sentence

Behavior change is a process that occurs in stages.

STUDENT LEARNING OUTCOMES

At the end of this chapter the student will be able to:

1. Explain the conceptual basis of the Transtheoretical Model.
2. Describe the five different stages of change.
3. Explain the 10 processes of change.
4. Analyze decisional balance.
5. Use the theory to explain the adoption of a common health behavior.

THEORETICAL CONCEPT

The Transtheoretical Model (TTM) was developed in the early 1980s as a way to understand behavior change, in particular, change associated with addictive behaviors (Prochaska, DiClemente, & Norcross, 1992). TTM proposes that behavior change is a process that occurs in stages, with people moving through these stages in a very specific sequence as they change. Thus, the theory is also known as Stages of Change.

THEORETICAL CONSTRUCTS

The constructs of the theory include not only the stages of change, but also the processes of change and self-efficacy.

Analyzing behavior change from these perspectives is helpful when trying to understand why some people are successful at changing behavior and others are not.

Stages of Change

There are five stages of change: pre-contemplation, contemplation, preparation, action, and maintenance. Each has its own distinct characteristics and timeframe and builds upon the preceding stage.

Pre-contemplation

The first stage of change is pre-contemplation. People are in this stage from 6 months prior to the point they begin thinking about making a change in their behavior to when they actually begin thinking about changing. People in this "pre-thinking stage" either don't recognize they have a behavior needing change or are just not ready to change a behavior they know they should (Prochaska, DiClemente, & Norcross, 1992).

Among the possible reasons for people being in the pre-contemplation stage are being uninformed or underinformed about the negative consequence of continuing a behavior or about the benefits of changing the behavior (Cancer Prevention Research Center [CPRC], n.d.; Velicer et al., 1998). We see this with older adults and exercise behavior. Some older adults view exercise as a behavior for the young and believe it is not good for people with certain health conditions (Lach et al., 2004). Clearly, this is a case where being uninformed explains why change to a healthy behavior, exercise, is avoided. A change in this behavior will not begin until the uninformed are informed that exercise is beneficial at any age and is not restricted by most health conditions.

Another reason why people are in the pre-contemplation stage is past experience. People who have tried in the past but failed to change a behavior give no thought to changing the behavior again. This is often the case with cigarette smokers, who say, "Quitting is easy, I've done it a million times before," or with people who have lost weight only to regain it.

Knowing why people might be in the pre-contemplation stage is useful when trying to understand why unhealthy behaviors are not changed. The goal is to take this information and assist them in moving forward from not thinking about changing their behavior to contemplating, or thinking about, changing.

Contemplation

When people move from pre-contemplation to contemplation it means they recognize there is a problem and they are starting to think about changing. A myriad of things can get people to start thinking about changing their behavior. Examples include the same cues to action discussed in the Health Belief Model, such as newspapers, magazines, TV, news reports, family, friends, health care professionals, and so on.

In order to move out of the "thinking" mode, a decision has to be made to either proceed with the change or not. This is *decisional balance*, the process of weighing the perceived pros and cons or costs and benefits of the new behavior against the old (Prochaska, 1994). Since the weight or strength of the pros and cons is determined by individual assessment, the length of time needed to make a decision varies, and can be prolonged. In the case of cigarette smokers, for instance, some remain in this decisional stage for as long as 2 years (DiClemente & Prochaska, 1985; Prochaska & DiClemente, 1984). When it takes more than 6 months to make a decision, this is behavioral procrastination or chronic contemplation (CPRC, n.d.; Velicer et al., 1998).

In the case of domestic abuse, decisional balance can result in a woman deciding to remain in the abusive situation. This happens when the cons of leaving are stronger than the pros (Burke et al., 2004). The cons, or reasons for not leaving, may include not wanting to lose the relationship (even though it is abusive), financial dependency, emotional need, or low self-esteem. Often, it is only after the safety of her children is factored in as a reason for leaving (pro) that the woman is able to leave (Burke et al., 2004).

Typically, once people start thinking about changing their behavior, they usually make a decision and plan to make the change within the following 6 months. However, this does not hold true for everyone in all situations. Some people stay in this "thinking" mode for extended periods of time—some for

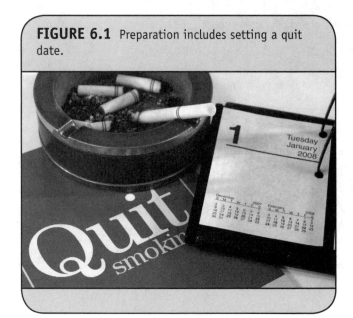

FIGURE 6.1 Preparation includes setting a quit date.

years (DiClemente, Schlundt, & Gemmell, 2004; Prochaska, DiClemente, & Norcross, 1992).

Preparation

The preparation stage begins once the decision to change the behavior is made. Preparation is a short stage, lasting only about 1 month, since once people decide to change a behavior, they are often anxious to get started. This preparation time is used to make a plan, obtain any tools needed, learn new skills (CPRC, n.d.; Velicer et al., 1998), acquire resources of money or support, housing, and whatever else is necessary for the change to occur.

In the case of a smoker, preparation may mean setting a quit date, obtaining a prescription for a nicotine patch, or signing up for a smoking cessation program (Figure 6.1). For a woman at risk of osteoporosis, preparation may mean learning exercises to prevent bone loss, attending a lecture on new treatments (Lach et al., 2004), buying weights or new sneakers, or developing an exercise plan. For the student who wants to eat healthier, it may mean buying a cookbook, developing a weekly menu, and going grocery shopping.

Action

Once preparation is complete, the action stage begins. This is when the plan is put into action. However, just because there is action does not necessarily mean the behavior will change. Action and change are not the same thing (Prochaska, DiClemente, & Norcross, 1992). Action is when people are in the active process of modifying their behavior to address the problem they identified in earlier stages. These modifications tend to be observable changes and to be recognized and rewarded by others (Prochaska, DiClemente, & Norcross, 1992).

In order for action to be successful, it needs to be measured against criteria previously determined to reduce the risk of disease. For example, in the case of the smoker, the change that needs to be accomplished is quitting; switching to a low-tar cigarette or cutting down by half is not enough (CPRC, n.d.; Prochaska, DiClemente, & Norcross, 1992). For the woman at risk of osteoporosis, the change that needs to be accomplished is improvements in bone density measurements. For the student who wants to eat healthier, it is the daily consumption of meals that follow the food pyramid recommendations.

Maintenance

Maintenance is the final stage of change. During this stage, people work (and sometimes struggle) to prevent relapsing to the old behavior. In general, maintenance begins after 6 months of being in the active stage of changing and continues for at least 6 months. With some behavior changes, maintenance goes on for years (Prochaska, DiClemente, & Norcross, 1992), as is the case with recovering alcoholics.

For some behaviors, such as diet and exercise changes implemented for weight loss, maintaining change is extremely difficult. Although most people who participate in a weight loss program are successful in losing weight (i.e., they make it through the action), almost all regain the weight lost within 5 years (Thomas, 1995); that is, they relapse to their old diet and sedentary behaviors. Therefore, while changing may be difficult, permanently incorporating the new behavior, or the change, into one's lifestyle is the most difficult phase.

Self-Efficacy

The second construct of the TTM is self-efficacy. Self-efficacy plays a major role in how successful people are in changing their behavior and maintaining the change. Remember, self-efficacy is one's confidence in one's own ability to do something (see Chapter 2). In the context of maintaining a behavior change, it has to do with one's confidence in coping with situations in which there is a high risk of relapse. For example, an ex-smoker would need a great deal of self-efficacy to avoid relapsing to smoking in social situations where alcohol is served or when under financial stress (Borland, 1990; Dijkstra & Borland, 2003; Siahpush & Carlin, 2006). For a disabled person who wants to maintain a change to an active lifestyle, self-efficacy means having confidence in the ability to overcome barriers to physical activity (Kosma et al., 2006),

which may include negotiating public transportation to an exercise facility or park, for example, or wheelchair-inaccessible dressing rooms. For elderly women wanting to maintain physical activity, self-efficacy may mean having confidence in their ability to overcome a lack of energy, motivation, or discomfort with body image (Aubertin-Leheudre et al., 2005).

Among college students, self-efficacy is predictive of successful exercise behavior change. It seems that students with greater levels of self-efficacy at the start of an exercise change process are able to maintain their increased exercise levels, while students with less self-efficacy relapse to their old sedentary ways (Sullum, Clark, & King, 2000).

Processes of Change

While the stages of change help us understand *when* people change their behavior, the processes of change help us understand *how* change occurs (Prochaska & DiClemente, 1982). There are 10 processes of change: consciousness raising, dramatic relief or emotional arousal, environmental reevaluation, social liberation, self-reevaluation, stimulus control, helping relationships, counter conditioning, reinforcement management, and self-liberation (Prochaska & DiClemente, 1983; Prochaska et al., 1988; Velicer et al., 1998).

The 10 processes are divided into two groups: cognitive processes and behavioral processes. Consciousness raising, dramatic relief, self-reevaluation, environmental reevaluation, and social liberation are cognitive and stimulus control, helping relationships, counter conditioning, reinforcement management, and self-liberation are behavioral (Prochaska et al., 1988).

Consciousness Raising

Consciousness raising is the process whereby people obtain information about themselves and the problem behavior. It is the process of becoming aware of the problem and the causes and consequences of continuing a particular behavior (Prochaska, DiClemente, & Norcross, 1992; Velicer et al., 1998). Using fast food as an example, consciousness raising might be evidenced by a person saying, "I didn't realize fast food was so bad for me until I saw *Super Size Me* and *Fast Food Nation*." This awareness may help move a person from pre-contemplation to contemplation. Or, it may have been the nutrition course a student took that provided new insight into his or her poor eating habits.

Dramatic Relief

Dramatic relief, also referred to as emotional arousal, is being able to express feelings about or react emotionally to the behavior in question (Prochaska, DiClemente, & Norcross,

1992; Velicer et al., 1998). For the smoker, this process may mean talking about how much one loathes quitting (Andersen & Keller, 2002); for the fast food junkie, it might be getting upset with fast food commercials on TV.

Environmental Reevaluation

The process of environmental reevaluation is looking at the behavior in light of its impact or effect on the physical environment (Prochaska, DiClemente, & Norcross, 1992; Velicer et al., 1998). Examples of this process are understanding the environmental effects of secondhand smoke (Andersen & Keller, 2002) or the environmental damage caused by pesticide use.

Social Liberation

Social liberation is the process whereby options or alternatives are sought that support the new behavior (Prochaska, DiClemente, & Norcross, 1992; Velicer et al., 1998). For the smoker trying to quit, social liberation would be sitting in the nonsmoking section of a restaurant (Andersen & Keller, 2002). For the recovering junk food addict, it would mean ordering a salad at a fast food restaurant or, for the former couch potato, planning a vacation at a resort with a gym.

Self-Reevaluation

Self-reevaluation is the process in which people look at themselves with and without the problem behavior and assess the differences in their self-esteem (Prochaska, DiClemente, & Norcross, 1992; Velicer et al., 1998). For smokers, this process means thinking about themselves as smokers and comparing

FIGURE 6.2 Stimulus control may mean avoiding fast food restaurants.

it to how they feel about themselves as nonsmokers (Andersen & Keller, 2002). For fast food junkies, it means asking "If I stopped eating fast foods, would I be healthier and happier, and would I like myself better?"

Stimulus Control

Stimulus control is when people remove the cues or triggers for the problem behavior from their environment (Prochaska, DiClemente & Norcross, 1992; Velicer et al., 1998). The fast food junkie might drive to work on back roads rather than the highway in order to avoid passing fast food restaurants (Figure 6.2). The smoker might avoid drinking coffee after dinner and switch to drinking tea, since coffee is a trigger for many smokers. The overeater might stop buying the half-gallon carton of ice cream and switch to the pint-size fruit sorbet instead.

Helping Relationships

Helping relationships are relationships with people who act as a support system for changing the unwanted, unhealthy behavior (Prochaska, DiClemente, & Norcross, 1992; Velicer et al., 1998). This might be the roommate who agrees to keep only fruit to snack on in the room, or the sponsor in a 12-step program for alcoholics who is there whenever the urge for a drink hits. It can be a neighbor who calls another neighbor at 7 a.m. to confirm they are meeting for their morning walk.

Counter Conditioning

In counter conditioning, a healthier behavior is substituted for the unhealthy one (Prochaska, DiClemente, & Norcross, 1992; Velicer et al., 1998). Using this process, the person trying to change fast food consumption might bring fruit to eat in the car on the way home from work, instead of stopping for fries and a soda. The smoker might doodle when talking on the phone rather than smoke a cigarette. The person wanting to add more activity to his or her daily routine might use the stairs rather than the elevator whenever possible.

Reinforcement Management

The process of reinforcement management has to do with rewards and punishments. Although unwanted behavior can be changed through the fear of punishment or negative consequences (as any child will tell you), rewards for engaging in the targeted behavior are more natural. The reward can be from the person to himself or herself, or from someone else (Prochaska, DiClemente, & Norcross, 1992; Velicer et al., 1998). For example, a reward for not eating fast food during the week might be dinner at a nice restaurant with friends. For the woman who quits smoking, a reward from a significant other might be a bouquet of fresh flowers at the end of every week she doesn't smoke. For the exerciser, it might be a new exercise outfit or sneakers.

Self-Liberation

When using the process of self-liberation, people choose to change their behavior, believe they can, and commit to making the change (Andersen & Keller, 2002; Burke et al., 2004; Prochaska, DiClemente, & Norcross, 1992). In self-liberation, people free themselves from a behavior in which they no longer choose to engage.

This process is what enables women in abusive relationships to do something about changing their situation. The behavior they choose to change is remaining in an abusive relationship. The commitment they make is to a different lifestyle, one that does not rely on violence as an expression of love (Burke et al., 2004). For the person with chronic obstructive pulmonary disease (COPD), self-liberation is frequently used to change from being inactive to exercising (walking) (Yang & Chen, 2005). For a college student, self-liberation might mean choosing not to drink every night.

Stages of Change and Processes of Change

The processes of change help move people through the stages of change. Thus, different processes are used during different stages (Table 6-1). The research to identify the processes used in each stage was originally conducted on smokers and may or may not hold true for all behavior changes (DiClemente et al., 1991; Prochaska, DiClemente, & Norcross, 1992; Fava, Velicer, & Prochaska, 1995).

People in pre-contemplation use processes of change the least as they move from pre-contemplation to contemplation (DiClemente et al., 1991). When processes of change are used, consciousness raising, dramatic relief, and environmental reevaluation (Prochaska, DiClemente, & Norcross, 1992), social liberation (Andersen & Keller, 2002; Marcus et al., 1992), and counter conditioning (Andersen & Keller, 2002) are used more than the others. These processes increase awareness of a behavior as being a problem, including talking about the behavior as a problem and looking at how the behavior affects others in the environment.

All of the processes are used as people move through contemplation to preparation, although helping relationships, self-reevaluation, social liberation, and dramatic relief are the ones most associated with this stage (Andersen & Keller, 2002; DiClemente et al., 1991). Using these processes helps people talk with others and express feelings about the change, to look at themselves with respect to the problem behavior, and to

---

TABLE 6.1 Moving Through the Stages of Change

Transition Between Stages	Processes Used
From pre-contemplation to contemplation	Consciousness raising
	Dramatic relief
	Environmental reevaluation
	Social liberation
	Counter conditioning
From contemplation to preparation	Helping relationships
	Self-reevaluation
	Social liberation
	Dramatic relief
From preparation to action	Self-liberation
Maintenance	Counter conditioning
	Helping relationships
	Reinforcement management
	Stimulus control

Transtheoretical Model Constructs Chart

Stages of change	Pre-contemplation, contemplation, preparation, action, maintenance
Decisional balance	Weighting the pros and cons of the change
Processes of change	Consciousness raising, dramatic relief or emotional arousal, environmental reevaluation, social liberation, self-reevaluation, stimulus control, helping relationships, counter conditioning, reinforcement management, and self-liberation
Self-efficacy	One's belief in one's own ability to do something

look at or evaluate the types of support they have available in their social environments.

In moving from preparation to action, self-liberation is the most important process (Andersen & Keller, 2002; DiClemente et al., 1991; Marcus et al., 1992). Self-liberation makes sense in this stage because this is the point at which people are ready to actually do something about changing their behavior. Logically, they need to make a commitment to act before they take action.

In maintenance, the processes of counter conditioning, helping relationships, reinforcement management, and stimulus control are used most often (DiClemente et al., 1991). These enable people to sustain the new behaviors, have supportive people available, avoid triggers for the problem behavior that may cause relapse, and be rewarded for changing.

In summary, according to the Transtheoretical Model, behavior change occurs in stages with specific processes moving the change along.

Behavior change happens in stages over time.

THEORY IN ACTION: CLASS ACTIVITY

Brainstorm ways your campus can begin to move students through the stages of change to eventually become an alcohol-free campus. Develop a list of the pros of your campus being alcohol free, and then a list of the cons. Now think about actions that could be taken to support the processes of change. Once you have completed this, read the accompanying article and answer the questions that follow.

The Transtheoretical Model of Change for Multi-Level Interventions for Alcohol Abuse on Campus

JANICE M. PROCHASKA, MSW, PH.D
Pro-Change Behavior Systems, Inc. President & CEO
JAMES O. PROCHASKA, PH.D
FRANCES C. COHEN, MA
SUSAN O. GOMES, MA
ROBERT G. LAFORGE, ScD
ANDREA L. EASTWOOD, BS
University of Rhode Island

ABSTRACT

This paper brings together the pressing problem of alcohol abuse on college campuses on one of the most promising solution—stage-based interventions applied at multiple levels. The interventions fit the Transtheoretical Model, which construes behavior change as a process that unfolds over time and involves progress through a series of stages. Unique to the paper is how the stage paradigm can be applied at four levels of the university (leadership, faculty and staff, students, and alumni) and into the community. This approach to change can produce impressive impacts on alcohol abuse and its serious consequences.

Alcohol abuse is considered by college presidents and administrators to be the number one health problem on campuses (Presidents Leadership Group, 1997). One of the most promising approaches to this problem on a population basis is to apply the Transtheoretical Model of Change (TTM) at multiple levels of a campus. TTM construes behavior change as a process that unfolds over time and involves progress through a series of changes: Precontemplation, Contemplation, Preparation, Action and Maintenance (Prochaska, Diclemente, & Norcross, 1992). The TTM is a comprehensive model that integrates ideas from several different theories and approaches to change to explain and predict how and when individuals end high-risk behaviors or adopt health ones. This paper will describe TTM and how it can be applied at four levels (leadership, faculty and staff, students, and alumni). Practical examples will be presented, drawing primarily from experiences at a state university in the northwest that has been part of Weschsler and colleagues' (2002) studies since 1993. Finally, results will demonstrate how an organization and population approach to change can produce impressive impacts on alcohol abuse and its serious consequences.

Alcohol abuse is a major contributing factor to individual and social problems on campuses throughout the United States (Carnegie Foundation for the Advancement of Teaching, 1990; Presley, Meilman, & Lyerla, 1995; U.S. Department of Education Safe and Drug-Free Schools Program, 2000). The first two years of college is a time of transition to independent adulthood for many students, and offers new opportunities to experiment with lifestyles and behaviors that place students at high risk for alcohol abuse. While most traditional college age students cannot drink legally, Wechsler's 2002 Harvard School of Public Health study at 119 nationally representative colleges reported that 44.4 percent of college students admitted binge drinking (five or more drinks in one sitting for males, four for females) in the previous two weeks. Moreover, this percentage remained relatively unchanged from similar Harvard studies by Wechsler and colleagues (Wechsler, Davenport, Dowdall, Moeykens, & Castillo, 1994; Weshsler, Dowdall, Maenner, Gledhill-Hoyt, & Lee, 1998; Wechsler, Lee, Kuo, & Lee, 2000).

Heavy drinking by college students has been consistently associated with higher rates of property damage, driving under influence, injury, behaviors that are regretted, missed classes, interpersonal relationship difficulties, and unprotected or unplanned sex (Johnson, O'Malley, & Bachman, 1996). Wechsler and colleague's (1994) national college study reported that students who binged were at higher risk for experiencing a variety of alcohol related problems than those who drank but did not binge. In that study heavy drinkers were five times more likely than non-binge drinkers to report that they had experienced five or more of twelve alcohol-related problems. A dose response relationship has also been observed, with more frequent bingers experiencing substantially higher risks than less frequent bingers (Johnston et al., 1996). In 1996, the northeastern university reported that approximately 80% of violations of community standards involved substance use, primarily alcohol abuse (Cohen & Rogers, 1997).

Alcohol abuse is an issue that has concerned the northeast university for many years. For three years during the 90's the Princeton Review college guide listed the university as the nation's top party school. Sixty-seven percent of the students reported that they were binge drinkers, compared to 44% nationally (Wechsler et al., 1994). Healthy people 2010 reports a 1998 baseline rate of 39% for binge drinking among college students with a 2010 target of 20% (U.S. Department of Health and Human Services (USDHHS), 2000). Given the problem on this campus, the President recognized that he needed an intervention strategy that could be applied on a population basis and at multiple levels. As (Wechsler, Nelson, & Weitzman, 2000) encourage, colleges need to move beyond a simple didactic model of education interventions. Some of the strategies that developed over time were based a priori on the Transtheoretical Model, while others will be analyzed post hoc from a Transtheoretical perspective.

The Transtheoretical Model (TTM) is one of the leading intervention models for behavior change (O'Donnell, 1997). It offers a promising approach to behavior change on college campuses. The model systematically integrates four theoretical concepts central to change: (1) Stages of Change (readiness to act); (2) Processes of Change (10 cognitive, affective, behavioral activities that facilitate change); (3) Self-Efficacy (confidence to make and sustain changes in difficult situations); (4) Decisional Balance (pros and cons of changing).

The TTM has been shown to be robust in explaining and facilitating change across a broad range of health behaviors, including smoking cessation, and dietary change (Prochaska, Diclemente, Velicer, & Rossi, 1993; Greene, Rossi, Rossi, Velicer, Fava, & Prochaska, 1999). The model has been applied to organizational change efforts including collaborative service delivery, time-limited therapy, and continuous quality improvement in healthcare (Levesque, Prochaska, & Prochaska, 1999; Prochaska, 2000; Levesque, Prochaska, Dewart, Hornby, & Weeks, 2001).

Stage of Change represents the temporal and motivational dimensions of the change process. Longitudinal studies found that people move through a series of five stages (Prochaska & Diclemente, 1983). In the *Precontemplation Stage*, individuals deny the problem, are unaware of the negative consequences of their behavior, believe the consequences are insignificant, or have given up on changing because they are demoralized. They are not intending to take action in the next months. Individuals in the *Contemplation Stage* are likely to recognize more of the pros of changing. However, they overestimate the cons of changing and, therefore, experience ambivalence. They are intending to act within the next six months. Individuals in the *Preparation Stage* have decided to take action in the next 30 days, and have begun to take small steps toward that goal. Individuals in the *Action Stage* are overtly engaged in modifying their problem behaviors. Individuals in the *Maintenance Stage* have been able to sustain action for at least six months, and are striving to prevent relapse. For most people, the change process is not linear, but spiral, with several relapses to earlier stages before they attain permanent behavior change (Prochaska & Diclemente, 1986). The importance of a stage approach can be illustrated by data from the northeast university. A survey that included TTM assessment of stage of change for alcohol abuse was given to approximately 1500 freshman and sophomores and found that about 70% are in the Precontemplation stage and less than 10% were in the Preparation stage for stopping abusing alcohol (Laforge, 2001). If only 10% of students are prepared to take action, it should come as no surprise that many organizational change initiatives fail. Individuals in Precontemplation and Contemplation are likely to see change as imposed, and can become resistant and defensive if forced to take action before they are ready.

PROCESSES OF CHANGE

In comparison of 24 systems of therapy, 10 change processes were identified (Prochaska, 1984). Table 1 illustrates how the processes could be applied in interventions for an alcohol free campus.

Research on a variety of health behaviors has identified strategies or processes of change that are employed in each stage to facilitate change. Individuals in the early stages rely more on cognitive, affective and evaluative strategies to change. Individuals in the later stages rely more on behav-

TABLE 1   Processes of Change for Becoming an Alcohol Free Campus

Processes	Illustrations
1. Consciousness Raising	Communicating information about the goals and benefits of making a campus alcohol free.
2. Dramatic Relief	Generating inspiration for the change and anxiety about the status quo.
3. Self-Reevaluation	Encouraging students to imagine how they will think and feel about themselves as members of a campus that treats alcohol seriously.
4. Environmental Reevaluation	Encouraging students to imagine how an alcohol free campus will produce a healthier environment for the entire campus community.
5. Self-Liberation	Expressing a firm commitment to act and encouraging others to do so.
6. Helping Relationships	Offering social support for the healthy behavioral change and encouraging students to seek support.
7. Counter Conditioning	Creating conditions that will counter alcohol use on campus and will substitute healthier alternatives (e.g., wellness dorms).
8. Stimulus Control	Removing cues that encourage drinking (e.g., alcohol ads and alcohol in dorms) and providing cues that encourage a healthy alternative (e.g., ads about alcohol free events).
9. Social Liberation	Helping students realize that the social norms are changing in ways that will help students be free from alcohol on campus.
10. Contingency Management	Reinforcing students and staff for supporting the alcohol free campus (articles about improvement) and punishing students for violating the policies (expulsion after three violations).

ioral strategies including social support, reinforcement, commitments, and environmental management techniques. For example, the data show that individuals in the Precontemplation stage emphasize Consciousness Raising, Dramatic Relief, and Environmental Reevaluation; individuals in Contemplation emphasize Self-Reevaluation; individuals in Preparation emphasize Self-Liberation; and individuals in Action emphasize Reinforcement Management, Helping Relationships, Counter Conditioning, and Stimulus Control to sustain changes (Prochaska et al., 1992).

Self-efficacy is the confidence to change in challenging situations, such as resistance from students, faculty or alumni. Self-efficacy has been found to increase as people process through the stages of change, with the greatest increases occurring in Action and Maintenance. One way to increase self-efficacy is to apply a stage-based approach that increases confidence as populations progress from one stage to the next.

DECISIONAL BALANCE

The decision to move towards action is based on the relative weight given to the pros and cons of changing. Across 12 problem behaviors consistent patterns emerged that generate principles for producing progress (Prochaska et al., 1994). In Precontemplation, the cons always outweigh the pros. From Precontemplation to Contemation the pros always increase and the cons consistently decrease from Contemplation to Action. The pros begin to outweigh the cons of changing prior to action being taken. From Precontemplation to Action the pros increase about one standard deviation while the cons decrease one-half standard deviation from Contemplation to Action (Prochaska et al., 1994). Therefore, twice as much emphasis should be placed on increasing appreciation on campus of the pros of changing to an alcohol free campus. The functional relationships of pros and cons across the stages of change have been replicated in separate studies of alcohol abuse among college students, high school students and adults in an HMO population (Prochaska, 2002). Table 2 lists some of the pros and cons that could occur as a result of intervening on alcohol abuse on campus. Cons like a decline in admissions are less likely to occur if the leadership takes care to communicate the way the pros are outweighing the cons.

At the leadership level, considerable time is usually taken debating the pros and cons of adopting a program for reducing alcohol abuse. When the leaders become convinced that the pros clearly outweigh the cons, they are ready to take action. The problem is that other levels of the organization have not gone through this process and are not likely to be prepared to take action. If the leaders launch an action intervention when staff, faculty and students are in Precontemplation, they are highly likely to encounter resistance and their program is likely to fail.

Stage-Matched Versus Action-Oriented Interventions

Research has shown that stage-matched interventions can have greater impacts than action-oriented programs. First, stage-matched interventions can allow *all* individuals to participate in the change process, even if they are not prepared to take action. The impact of a program equals participation rate

TABLE 2   Pros and Cons for Intervening on Alcohol Abuse on Campus

Pros
Reduce hangovers, nausea, blackouts
Reduce injuries and alcohol poisonings
Reduce legal suits
Reduce unplanned sex
Reduce unwanted pregnancies
Reduce drop-outs
Reduce crime and violence
Increase academic performance
Improve community image
Bring in resources through grants
Become a national leader
Bring SAT scores up
Reduce property damage
Improve town/gown relations
Reduce negative publicity

Cons
Decline in applications for admission
Can lose students at orientation
Risk alienating alumni
Risk conflict with parents
Takes more effort and time
Can hurt athletic teams
Can have lawsuits

times the efficacy rate (percent of students who take action). Therefore, the more at risk students who are at risk for alcohol who participate the greater the impact the program can be. Second, stage-matched interventions can increase the likelihood that individuals will take action. Stage-matched interventions for smokers more than doubled the efficacy on cessation rates of one of the best action oriented interventions available (Prochaska et al., 1993). Stage-matched interventions have been out-performed one-size-fits-all interventions for exercise acquisition, dietary behavior, and other health behaviors in population-based studies (Diclemente & Hughes, 1990); (Campbell et al., 1994). These findings have important implications for alcohol elimination on campuses. Interventions should be individualized and matched to students' readiness to change to reduce resistance, reduce stress, and reduce the time needed to implement the change by accelerating movement toward the Action stage.

In most TTM research, stage-matched interventions are delivered directly to individuals via counselors, computer-based expert systems, and/or manuals or other tailored communications (Velicer, Prochaska, Fava, Laforge, & Rossi,

1999). However, *organizations* also can become powerful change agents by creating more optimal conditions for change. If a majority of students are in the Precontemplation stage, universities can facilitate early-stage processes like Consciousness Raising (e.g., by communicating about the change at orientation, convocation, and in the student newspaper) and Dramatic Relief (e.g., by giving examples about the consequences of not changing) to help students progress to the Contemplation stage. If a majority of students are already in Action, universities can facilitate behavioral processes like Counter Conditioning and Stimulus Control (e.g., providing resources like alcohol free events to support the change) and Helping Relationships (e.g., by providing R.A.'s and counselors) to help students make and sustain the changes. Students who are asked to change without adequate information, inspiration, resources, or assistance are more likely to become apathetic, resistant, or resentful.

LEADERSHIP LEVEL

The TTM can be applied to better understand interventions that were applied at each level of the northeast university—leadership, faculty and staff, and alumni. The change initiative began at the leadership level with the President. The President was leading a campus that received national recognition for being the number one party school in the country. Alcohol abuse was deeply embedded in its history and identity, but this cultural context did not keep this President from declaring at the 1995 convocation ceremonies that "it was time to take a stand" and henceforth "the university would be a university in recovery" (Carothers, 1995). One of the first challenges at the leadership level is to decide on the action criteria for the campus. Unfortunately, there is no consensus about what represents optimum action for a campus. This is not like changing smoking behavior on an individual level, where there is a scientific consensus that abstinence is the appropriate goal. Leaders must debate the pros and cons of alternative goals for their campus. Leadership at the northwest university set an action criteria by adopting a policy of an alcohol free campus. For those who might see an alcohol free campus as regressive like prohibition, there are other action criteria that could be applied. Policies that are being instituted at other campuses include no illegal drinking and no drinking of three or more drinks on any occasion. Further research will need to determine which of the criteria help produce better outcomes. As will be shown, several policies flowed from this first policy of no alcohol on campus. They include such areas as an increase in alcohol free alternative activities, Friday classes, longer library and recreation hours, and the prohibition of alcohol product ads.

To begin to move the faculty staff and students from the Precontemplation stage to Contemplation, the President, who knows TTM well, raised awareness (Consciousness Raising) of the pros of change at all parent/student orientation sessions. This was measured in part by the percent of students aware of alcohol policies (97%). The President also provided inspiration for the change and raised anxiety about the status quo (Dramatic Relief). Then leadership encouraged the faculty, staff and students to imagine how they might think and feel about themselves as part of an alcohol free campus that could become a leader in the field of substance abuse prevention. It was described how an alcohol free campus would produce a healthier environment for the entire campus community. Being a party school and abusing alcohol was shown as inconsistent with having a positive learning setting (Self and Environmental Reevaluation). To demonstrate his commitment the President accepted an appointment to the Higher Education Center for Alcohol Prevention Leadership Group that compiled a report, *Be Vocal, Be Visible, Be Visionary*. He also joined the NIAAA Advisory Committee on College Drinking where he assumed a leadership role in bringing together leading researchers and university Presidents to evaluate the quality of research on college drinking and to establish the agenda for future research. He helped others realize that social norms were changing in ways to support alcohol risk reduction (Self-Liberation and Social Liberation).

For those students in Preparation, the behavioral processes were used to help them progress to Action. Stimulus Control was applied through the prohibition of alcohol product ads in University publications; the non-availability of alcohol at any campus function; date of birth was placed on student ID cards; and substance free wellness residence halls were created. Contingency Management strategies included reinforcing those who supported an alcohol free campus, discipline and fines for minor infractions with a "three strikes you're out" policy, a judicial system to hear problem cases, and letters sent to students and parents if arrested. A hotline was established to report problems and a Substance Abuse Prevention Director was hired (Helping Relationship). Counter Conditioning was supported through increased non-alcohol entertainment options for students.

FACULTY AND STAFF

While the President provided the leadership, faculty and staff became involved in delivering Consciousness Raising by providing substance abuse educators as guest speakers in academic courses, offering a three credit course to train peer educators, and giving an interactive social norms correction class for freshmen funded by the U.S. Department of Education. In this intervention based on social norms theory, data are collected during a class presentation and correct norm information is fed back to the students in the same period. The class intervention encourages Consciousness Raising, Dramatic Relief and Self-Reevaluation to new students on campus who primarily are in Precontemplation or Contemplation for reducing high risk drinking. Faculty also schedule classes on Fridays to emphasize the importance of academics and discourage the alcohol fueled partying that may occur on Thursday nights if students do not need to attend class on Fridays (Counter Conditioning). Staff keeps the library and recreation facilities open longer (Stimulus Control).

In an effort to provide Helping Relationships to at risk students more ready to take action, the Counseling Center and Substance Abuse Services offer short-term treatment for alcohol abuse and referrals for long-term treatment. Individuals in violation of the alcohol policy are required after two violations to attend an educational meeting to examine their current patterns of alcohol use and to work on strategies for risk reduction. Motivational interviewing based on the TTM is used in the session. Motivational interviewing is a directive, client-centered counseling style of eliciting behavior change by helping clients to explore and resolve ambivalence (Rollnick & Miller, 1995).

An Alcohol Team was formed to apply a range of change strategies and processes. The Alcohol Team's goals are to build a unified campus-wide collaborative approach to alcohol abuse prevention and research, reduce harm from abusive use of alcohol, and apply research in its interventions. Team meetings serve as a mechanism for: communication and collaboration between researchers and practitioners, a sounding board for policy revision and implementation, an exchange of information about research and resources, an avoidance of duplication, and pooling budget and space for team efforts. Members are from the Psychology Department, the Cancer Prevention Research Center, marketing, communications, the Counseling Center, Research & Grants, Health Services, Housing and Residential Life, and Student Life.

To create conditions to counter alcohol abuse and substitute healthier alternatives, the faculty has several grants in progress. A five-year project based on social cognitive theory works with approximately 400 students to examine the effects of individualized normative feedback and alcohol expectancy challenges in reducing alcohol abuse. The program is designed to correct first-year students' misperceptions of high risk drinking. The intervention group receives statistics about alcohol intake, thereby debunking the myth that everyone drinks. Among students who learn about their misperceptions, drinking levels decreased about half a drink per week (Caliri, 2001). Those who did not receive the normative correction substantially increased their weekly drinking over the course of the first semester.

A three year program to create peer athlete mentors for athletic teams is underway as well as a three year project on the applicability of TTM tailored communications to college student alcohol abuse. The TTM study is designed to test the efficacy of a low cost and readily disseminable computerized expert system intervention program for college students to reduce high-risk alcohol behaviors and minimize alcohol related problems. The proactive harm reduction intervention consists of three telephone survey assessments at three-month intervals, each followed by mail delivery of an individualized intervention feedback report. Over sixteen hundred students are participating—78% of all eligible freshmen and sophomores. The participation rates are particularly encouraging given that population surveys have indicated that about 70% of at risk students are in the Precontemplation stage and less than 10% are in Preparation (Laforge, 2001).

STUDENTS

Students serve as peer educators and provide Consciousness Raising and other processes through workshops on risk reduction to their peers. A Student Against Drunk Driving chapter was formed and helps provide change processes like Dramatic Relief by emphasizing some of the terrible tragedies that could be prevented by zero tolerance for drink driving. To express a firm commitment to act and to encourage others to do so (Self-Liberation) and to help students realize that social norms are changing in ways that help students be free from alcohol on campus (Social Liberation), undergraduate and graduate student interns have initiated and advance abuse prevention and research activities throughout the campus. Counseling, pharmacy, public relations, and public speaking students are all involved in developing prevention programs, creating alternative approaches, and working in the above-mentioned research grants.

For those more ready to change to an alcohol free campus, students are available to provide Helping Relationships and other processes through AA meetings on campus. To substitute healthier alternatives (Counter Conditioning) at the beginning of every academic year, student teams offer "Same Planet, Different World" programs designed to get new students off to a safe start with a variety of non-alcohol entertainment and social options. A month-long series of events aimed at providing "fun without the buzz" include scavenger hunts and Hawaiian luaus on the quad.

ALUMNI

In comparison to the leadership, faculty, staff, and students, the alumni appear to be primarily in Precontemplation for being alcohol free on any of the University's campuses. For the first time in the summer of 2001, the alumni magazine included an article on reducing alcohol abuse on the campus. While the intention was to raise the consciousness level of the alumni this was not assessed. Soon after an action plan was mandated. Until 2001, alcohol was tolerated on campus at tailgating activities at Homecoming. When alcohol tailgating was banned in 2001 there was an angry alumni reaction. Being primarily in Precontemplation, the alumni saw the change as imposed and became resistant and defensive. They were not ready to take action to have an alcohol free campus.

COMMUNITY

Student alcohol use and abuse is a problem of the campus and the entire surrounding community. What is required is community-level action, including the local government, law enforcement, community prevention advocates, owners of local bars and restaurants, realtors, and high schools (Gebhardt, Kaphingst, & DeJong, 2000). In this case study the local town council came to the university President and demanded action. The President quickly responded. Regular town/gown meetings have resulted in enhanced and publicized police enforcement of the age 21 drinking and drunk driving laws, the local police stepping up bar checks, the Realtors Association creating model leases that the university distributes, landlords now being responsible for tenants disturbing the peace, the university listing where students can volunteer in the community, the Neighborhood Associations hosting brunches in September to welcome students who live in their communities. In addition, at college fairs at high schools, university representatives emphasize the university's alcohol policy of no alcohol use on campus.

The university also has three federally funded population based research trials that reach out to all ninth graders in 14 Rhode Island schools, their parents at home, and members of a New England HMO. The adolescent and parents project will intervene on six major behavioral risk factors including alcohol abuse. The HMO project intervenes only on alcohol abuse. Besides reaching the community, these projects have the potential to help the university reduce alcohol abuse by having more high school students, their parents and community members participating in alcohol abuse programs. These populations should provide increasing support for campus-based programs designed to combat alcohol abuse.

OUTCOMES OR IMPACTS

Leaders at the northeast university knew it was not enough to distribute its alcohol policy printed in the back of a handbook, host a one session alcohol awareness program, offer counseling programs for those who sought them, and expect the alcohol abuse problem to go away. Instead, the university President brought together administrators, faculty and staff, students, parents, alumni and local community members to develop and implement effective policies and programs. The university deceased the availability of alcohol, increased the number and variety of alcohol-free activities, and created a climate that discourages high-risk drinking and reinforces students to abstain or drink legally and moderately. To facilitate change, TTM and other models of behavior change were used at multiple levels. To evaluate how the interventions were working the university leaders needed to look at outcomes from multi levels and multi perspectives. For example, did the decline in binge drinking on campus at the same time increase problem drinking in nearby towns? Among the findings, the following demonstrate that was not the case:

- a 13% decline in binge-drinking (Wechsler, 2002)
- a 39% decline in town police complaints from 1999 to 2000 (Narragansett, 2001)
- fewer alcohol poisonings at Health Services and a local hospital (except Homecoming Day prior to 2001) (Cohen, 1999)
- a rise in simple violations (underage possession or consumption) from 70 to 267 (Cohen, 1999)
- a decline in complex violations (vandalism or endangerment) from 155 to 63 (Cohen, 1999)
- an increased voluntary attendance at drug awareness workshops from 25% to 50% (University of Rhode Island, 1999)
- only 10% of students cited a second time for violations (University of Rhode Island, 1999)
- 97% of students aware of alcohol policies (73% nationwide) (University of Rhode Island, 1999)
- an increase in SAT scores by 140 points (University of Rhode Island, 1999)
- an increase number of faculty and staff committed to alcohol abuse reduction (University of Rhode Island, 1999)
- an increase in research grants and monies (Cohen, 1999).

CONCLUSION

Current theory is consistent with the lessons that can be learned from this case study. Maximum impacts of major problems like alcohol abuse on campuses can best be accomplished when intervention strategies apply principles and processes that can produce change at each stage of change. An eclectic approach that drives interventions from across a variety of theories is one way of applying multiple principles and processes. In many ways, the case study was more eclectic than systematic. A more systematic and integrative approach would be to consistently use a model, like TTM, that is designed to tailor change principles and processes to individuals at each stage of change.

Other universities and colleges will need to experiment with applying TTM more systematically versus eclectically. They will need to experiment with what action criteria fit their campus, e.g., alcohol free versus responsible drinking. They will also need to assess their campus for students' readiness to adopt action criteria for drinking. The more their students are in Precontemplation the more resources they will need to dedicate. With such replication across different campuses we can better learn which approaches to population-based interventions work best for universities and colleges.

Maximum impacts on major problems like alcohol abuse can best be accomplished when principles and processes are applied at multiple levels of change (Institute of Medicine, 2001). While more controlled research to support this conclusion is needed, there is a consensus amongst leaders in behavior change that a multiple level approach is most promising. In the case of the northeast university, the President knew what all Presidents learn: they do not have enough power or influence to transform an organization without bringing on board as many faculty, staff, students and alumni as possible. Some levels of the university will be further along in the stages of change, such at the leaders and the Alcohol Team at this university, while some will be much more in Precontemplation stage, such as the students and the alumni. By applying TTM principles and resources that can be inclusive for people at each stage and each level, interventions of alcohol abuse can maximize participation at each level which can maximize impacts across the organization. This is not to say that the northeast university has recovered. As the President diagnosed it, it is a university in recovery. But it is also a case where many more people at each level of change are participating in the change process and are pulling together to help the university progress toward its goal of being an alcohol free campus.

REFERENCES

Caliri, M. (2001). Out of harm's way. *Quad Angles*, 8, 20–21.

Campbell M.K., DeVellis B.M., Strecher V.J., Ammerman A.S., DeVellis R.F., & Sandler R.S. (1994). Improving dietary behavior: the effectiveness of tailored messages in primary care settings. *American Journal of Public Health, 85*, 783-878.

Carnegie Foundation for the Advancement of Teaching (1990). *Campus Life: In search of Community.* Princeton, NJ.

Carothers, R. Convocation Speech; University of Rhode Island. 1995. Ref Type: Personal Communication

Cohen, F. The University of Rhode Island addresses substance abuse. 1999. Ref Type: Unpublished Work

Cohen, F. & Rogers, D. (1997). Effects of Alcohol Policy Change. *Journal of Alcohol and Drug Education, 42,* 69.

Diclemente, C.C. & Hughes, S.O. (1990). Stages of change profiles in outpatient alcoholism treatment. *Journal of Substance Abuse, 2,* 217–235.

Gebhardt, T.L., Kaphingst, K., & DeJong, W. (2000). A campus-community coalition to control alcohol-related problems off campus: an environmental management case study. *Journal of American College Health, 48,* 211–215.

Greene G.W., Rossi, S.R., Rossie, J.S., Velicer, W.F., Fava, J.L., & Prochaska, J.O. (1999). Dietary applications of the stages of change model. *Journal of the American Dietetic Association, 99,* 673–678.

Johnston, L.D., O'Malley, P.M., & Bachman, J.G. (1996). *National Survey on Drug Use from Monitoring the Future; Volume II: College Students and Young Adults.*

Laforge, R. Preliminary report describing research in progess. 2000. Ref Type: Personal Communication

Levesque, D.A., Prochaska, J.M., & Prochaska, J.O. (1999). Stage of change and integrated service delivery. *Consulting Psychology Journal. Practice and Research, 51*(4), 226–241.

Levesque, D.A., Prochaska, J.M., Prochaska, J.O., Dewart, S.R., Hornby, L.S., & Weeks, W.B. (2001). Organizational stages and processes of change for continuous quality improvement. *Consulting Psychology Journal: Practice and Research, 53,* 139–153.

Narragansett (2001). *Rhode Island Police Department Annual Report.*

O'Donnell, M.P. (1997). Editorial: The anatomy of stages of change. *American Journal of Health Promotion, 12,* 8–10.

Presidents Leadership Group (1997). *Be vocal, be visible, be visionary.*

Presley, C.A., Meilman, P.W., & Lyerla, R. (1995). *Alcohol and Drugs on American College Campuses. Use, Consequences, and Perceptions of the Campus Environment. Volume II: 1990–1992.* Carbondale, IL: Southern Illinois University at Carbondale.

Prochaska, J.M. (2000). A transtheoretical model for assessing organizational change: A study of family service agencies' movement to time-limited therapy. *Families in Society, 81,* 76–84.

Prochaska, J.O. (1984). *Systems of Psychotherapy: A transtheoretical approach.* Homewood, IL: Doe Jones Irwin.

Prochaska, J.O. Early findings from unpublished works. 2002. Ref Type: Unpublished Work

Prochaska, J.O., & Diclemente, C.C. (1983). Stages and processes of self-change of smoking: toward an integrative model of change. *Journal of Consulting and Clinical Psychology, 51,* 390–395.

Prochaska, J.O. & Diclemente, C.C. (1986). Toward a comprehensive model of behavior change. In W.R. Miller & N. Heather (Eds.) *Treating addictive behaviors: Processes of change.* (pp. 3–27). New York: Plenum Press.

Prochaska, J.O., Diclemente, C.C. & Norcross, J.C. (1992). In search of how people change. Applications to addictive behaviors. *American Psychologist, 47,* 1102–1114.

Prochaska, J.O., Diclemente, C.C., Velicer, W.F., & Rossi, J.S. (1993). Standardized, individualized, interactive, and personalized self-help programs for smoking cessation. *Health Psychology, 12,* 399–405.

Prochaska, J.O., W.F., Rossi, J.S., Goldstein, M.G., Marcus, B.H., Rakowski, W., Fiore, C., Harlow, L. L., Redding. C.A., Rosenbloom, D., & Rossi, S.R. (1994). Stages of change and decisional balance for 12 problem behaviors. *Health Psychology, 13,* 39–46.

U.S. Department of Education Safe and Drug-Free Schools Programs (2000). *Alcohol and Other Drug Prevention on College Campuses (Model Programs 1999 AND 2000).* Washington, DC: Author.

U.S. Department of Health and Human Services. (2000). *Healthy People 2010.* Washington DC: Government Printing Office.

University of Rhode Island. *Campus Climate Check-Up: Improving Campus Health.* (1999). University of Rhode Island, Substance Abuse Prevention Services.

Velicer, W., Prochaska, J.O., Fava, J.L., Laforge, R.G., & Rossi, J.S. (1999). Interactive versus Non-interactive Interventions and Dose-Response Relationships for Stage Matched Smoking Cessation Programs in a Managed Care Setting. *Health Psychology, 18,* 21–28.

Wechsler, H. (2002). *Private report to Case Study University for 1997 study.*

Wechsler, H., Davenport, A. Dowdall, G., Moeykens, B., & Castillo, S. (1994). Health and behavioral consequences of binge drinking in college. A national survey of students at 140 campuses. *Journal of the American Medical Association, 272,* 1672–1677.

Wechsler, H., Dowdall, G.W., Maenner, G., Gledhill-Hoyt, J., & Lee, H. (1998). Changes in binge drinking and related problems among American college students between 1993 and 1997. Results of the Harvard School of Public Health College Alcohol Study. *Journal of American College Health, 47,* 57–68.

Wechsler, H., Lee, J.E., Kuo, M., & Lee, H. (2000). College binge drinking in the 1900's: a continuing problem. Results of the Harvard School of Public Health 1999 College Alcohol Study. *Journal of American College Health, 48,* 199–210.

Wechsler, H., Nelson, T.F., and Weitzman, E. (2000). From knowledge to action: How Harvard's college alcohol study can help your campus design a campaign against student alcohol abuse. *Change,* 38–43.

Article Source: Prochaska, J.M., Prochaska, J.O., Cohen, F.C., Gomes, S.O., LaForge, R.G., & Eastwood, A.L. (2004). The Transtheoretical Model of Change for multi-level interventions for alcohol abuse on campus. *Journal of Alcohol and Drug Education, 47*(3), 34–50. Reprinted with permission.

QUESTIONS

1. What was done in the article to move students through the stages of change that you didn't think of?

2. How were the actions suggested to support the processes of change different from what you identified? How likely would it be that these suggestions would work on your campus?

3. What pros and cons did you identify that were different from those presented in the article? Do you think the pros in the article would be strong enough to result in a decision to give up drinking?

CHAPTER REFERENCES

Andersen, S., & Keller, C. (2002). Examination of the Transtheoretical Model in current smokers. *Western Journal of Nursing Research, 24*(3), 282–294.

Aubertin-Leheudre, M., Rousseau, S., Melancon, M.O., Chaput, J., & Dionne, I.J. (2005). Barriers to physical activity participation in North American elderly women: A literature review. *American Journal of Recreation Therapy, 4*(1), 21–30.

Borland, R. (1990). Slips-ups, and relapse in attempts to quit smoking. *Addictive Behavior, 15*(3), 235–245.

Burke, J.G., Denison, J.A., Gielen, A.C., McDonnell, K.A., & O'Campo, P. (2004). Ending intimate partner violence: An application of the Transtheoretical Model. *American Journal of Health Behavior, 28*(2), 122–133.

Cancer Prevention Research Center. (n.d.) Transtheoretical Model. Retrieved March 27, 2006, from http://www.uri.edu/research/cprc/TTM/detailedoverview.htm.

DiClemente, C.C., & Prochaska, J.O. (1985). Processes and stages of change: Coping and competence in smoking behavior change. In S. Shiffman & T.A. Wills (Eds.), *Coping and Substance Abuse* (pp. 319–343). San Diego: Academic Press.

DiClemente, C.C., Prochaska, J.O., Fairhurst, S.K., Velicer, W.F., Velasquez, M.M., & Rossi, J.S. (1991). The process of smoking cessation: An analysis of precontemplation, contemplation, and preparation stages of change. *Journal of Consulting and Clinical Psychology, 59*(2), 295–304.

DiClemente, C.C., Schlundt, D., & Gemmell, L. (2004). Readiness and stages of change in addiction treatment. *American Journal of Addiction, 13*, 103–119.

Dijkstra, A., & Borland, R. (2003). Residual outcome expectations and relapse in ex-smokers. *Health Psychology, 23*(4), 340–346.

Fava, J.L., Velicer, W.F., & Prochaska, J.O. (1995). Applying the transtheoretical model to a representative sample of smokers. *Addictive Behaviors, 20*(2), 189–201.

Kosma, M., Gardner, R.E., Cardinal, B.J., Bauer, J.J., & McCubbin, J.A. (2006). Psychosocial determinants of stages of change and physical activity among adults with physical disabilities. *Adapted Physical Activity Quarterly, 23*, 49–64.

Lach, H.W., Everard, K.M., Highstein, G., & Brownson, C.A. (2004). Application of the Transtheoretical Model to health education for older adults. *Health Promotion Practice, 5*(1), 88–93.

Marcus, H., Ross, J., Selby, V., Niaura, R., & Abrams, D. (1992). The stages and processes of exercise adoption and maintenance in a worksite sample. *Health Psychology, 11*(6), 386–395.

Prochaska, J.O. (1994). Strong and weak principles for progressing from precontemplation to action on the basis of twelve problem behaviors. *Health Psychology, 13*, 47–51.

Prochaska, J.O., & DiClemente, C.C. (1982). Transtheoretical therapy: Toward a more integrative model of change. *Psychotherapy: Theory, Research and Practice, 20*, 161–173.

Prochaska, J.O., & DiClemente, C.C. (1983). Stages and processes of self-change of smoking: Toward an integrative model of change. *Journal of Consulting and Clinical Psychology, 51*, 390–395.

Prochaska, J.O., & DiClemente, C.C. (1984). *The Transtheoretical Approach: Crossing Traditional Boundaries of Change.* Homewood, IL: Dorsey Press.

Prochaska, J.O., DiClemente, C.C., & Norcross, J.C. (1992). In search of how people change: Applications to addictive behaviors. *American Psychologist, 47*(9), 1102–1114.

Prochaska, J.O., Velicer, W.F., DiClemente, C.C., & Fava, J.L. (1988). Measuring the processes of change: Applications to the cessation of smoking. *Journal of Consulting and Clinical Psychology, 56*, 520–528.

Siahpush, M., & Carlin, J. (2006). Financial stress, smoking cessation and relapse: Results from a prospective study of Australian national sample. *Addiction, 101*(1), 121–127.

Sullum, J., Clark, M.M., & King, T.K. (2000). Predictors of exercise relapse in a college population. *American Journal of College Health, 48*(4), 175–180.

Thomas, P.R. (Ed), Committee to Develop Criteria for Evaluating the Outcomes of Approaches to Prevent and Treat Obesity. (1995). *Weighing the options: Criteria for evaluating the weight-management programs.* Institute of Medicine. Retrieved February 19, 2008, from www.nap.edu/catalog/4756.htmlluating.

Velicer, W.F, Prochaska, J.O., Fava, J.L., Norman, G.J., & Redding, C.A. (1998). Smoking cessation and stress management: Applications of the Transtheoretical Model of behavior change. *Homeostasis, 38*, 216–233.

Yang, P., & Chen, C. (2005). Exercise and process of change in patients with chronic obstructive pulmonary disease. *Journal of Nursing Research, 13*(2), 97–104.

CHAPTER 7

Social Cognitive Theory

Theory Essence Sentence

Behavior, personal factors, and environmental factors interact with each other, and changing one changes them all.

STUDENT LEARNING OUTCOMES

After reading this chapter the student will be able to:

1. Explain the concept of reciprocal determinism.
2. Differentiate among the many constructs of the Social Cognitive Theory.
3. Explain how each of the constructs influences health behavior.
4. Use the theory to analyze at least one behavior.

THEORETICAL CONCEPT

Social Cognitive Theory (SCT) was developed by Albert Bandura in the 1970s. It is based on the concept of *reciprocal determinism*, which is the dynamic interplay among personal factors (knowledge, skills, experience, culture, etc.), the environment, and behavior (Bandura, 1977). It proposes that changing one of these factors will change them all.

An example of this interaction can be seen when we look at the food pyramid. First introduced in the 1990s, it recommended that no more than 30% of our calories each day should come from fat. Based on this new information, the food industry flooded the marketplace with low-fat versions of every conceivable food. Everyone started buying and eating low-fat versions of their favorite foods. Thus, there was a change in personal factors (knowledge), which fueled a change in the environment (a marketplace chock-full of low-fat foods) that led people to a change in behavior (eating low-fat food).

THEORETICAL CONSTRUCTS

The factors of reciprocal determinism—personal, environmental, and behavioral—are affected by the many constructs of SCT. These include self-efficacy, observational learning (modeling), expectations, expectancies, emotional arousal, behavioral capability, reinforcement, and locus of control.

Self-Efficacy

Of all the constructs of SCT, self-efficacy is probably the single most important determinant of behavior (National Cancer Institute [NCI], 2003). This construct forms the basis of Self-Efficacy Theory, as was discussed in detail in Chapter 2, and plays a role in the Health Belief Model and the Transtheoretical Model as well. As we know, even when people have the skills and knowledge to accomplish a task, it is their belief in their ability to use them that enables people to actually perform the task (Bandura, 1993).

Observational Learning

Observational learning (or modeling) is learning by watching others and copying their behavior. Think back to when you were a child. How did you learn to brush your teeth, tie your shoes, ride a bike, color within the lines, bake cookies, hammer a nail, and get dressed? In addition to learning basic life skills through observation, we adopt observed mannerisms, interpersonal communication style, leadership style, and health practices, to name a few. So much of our behavior results from observational learning that the list might be endless.

As a result, the construct of observational learning can be very useful in explaining why people behave the way they do. Unfortunately, it does not always lead to healthy behaviors. For example, we have known for some time that if a parent (role model) smokes, it is more likely that the child will also smoke. Children learn and do what they see.

The strength of observational learning depends on how much attention is given to the person who is modeling the behavior. This degree of attention is influenced by a number of things, among them the attractiveness of the model, the circumstances under which the model is being observed, what is motivating the person to learn the behavior, how important it is that the behavior be learned, and the complexity of the behavior (Bandura, 1977, 1986; Grusec, 1992).

Observational learning is most useful when the model is considered to be a powerful person, is well respected, or is someone to whom the observer can relate (NCI, 2003). This is why companies use celebrity endorsements to sell their products. Think of the athlete who makes it onto the cereal box. An Olympic gold medalist is a role model for many children. Having this person's picture on the cereal box implies that the athlete eats the cereal in the box. If the child eats the cereal, he or she will be like this athlete. The child's desire to be like the role model may be one explanation for why he or she eats the cereal, which is what the food company hopes.

We pay more attention to a model when we need to learn the behavior and when the behavior is complex. For example, the person newly diagnosed with Type I diabetes needs to learn how to inject insulin, a complex task that is essential for survival. This person is likely to be more attentive when observing how to inject insulin than he or she is when observing how to measure a cup of food.

Expectations

Behavior is influenced by expectations. This construct suggests that people behave in certain ways because of the results they expect. A man uses a condom because he expects to be protected from sexually transmitted infections and fatherhood. An obese woman begins exercising because she expects to lose weight. Students drink because they expect to be accepted as part of the group.

Our expectations of the outcome of a behavior can also cause us to avoid the behavior. For example, women who worry that cancer will be found if they have a mammogram tend not to have mammograms (Rawl et al., 2000). It is the expectation of worry that deters them from having this important screening test done.

Similar behavior is seen relative to influenza vaccination. People who expect to get sick from the flu vaccine won't be vaccinated. This same avoidance is also found with digital rectal examinations for prostate cancer. If a man expects that he will be embarrassed having this examination performed, then he probably will not go for the screening (Shelton, Weinrich, & Reynolds, 1999).

Our expectations of outcomes are influenced by any number of things, including our past experiences in similar situations, observing others or hearing about others in a similar situation, and by the emotional or physical response that occurs as a result of the behavior. For example, because of my past experience playing badminton, there is an expectation that I can play tennis. Because the women's figure skating champions are the same age as me, there is an expectation that I can also skate. Because quitting smoking increases appetite, I expect to gain weight.

Expectancies

While expectations are the anticipated or expected outcomes of a particular behavior, *expectancies* are the values we place on those outcomes. A certain behavior is more likely to occur when the expectancy, or value placed on its outcome, maximizes a positive result and minimizes a negative one. Returning to the mammogram example used earlier, for the woman who worries that the mammogram will show cancer, the outcome (expectation) of the behavior (having a mammogram) is seen as being negative, something to be avoided. In this case, the negative expectancy (diagnosis of cancer) is another way to explain why she avoids having the mammogram in the first place. On the other hand, if a woman viewed early diagnosis of breast cancer as something that would increase her chance of cure (positive expectancy), this could explain why she *would* have an annual mammogram.

Emotional Arousal

The construct of emotional arousal suggests that in certain situations people become fearful and, when this happens, their behavior becomes defensive in an effort to reduce the fear (Bandura, 1977; Glanz, Rimer, & Lewis, 2002). The possibility of having unprotected sex with a new partner leads to the fear of contracting the human immunodeficiency virus

(HIV). To reduce the fear, abstinence is practiced until HIV testing is done or condoms are used, or both. In this situation, emotional arousal leads to a more positive health behavior, namely, HIV risk reduction.

However, emotional arousal may also hinder good health practices. For some people, going to the dentist causes intense fear and anxiety. To reduce the fear and anxiety, people avoid going to the dentist. Thus, their dental health is compromised.

Behavioral Capability

The construct of behavioral capability tells us that if people are to perform a certain behavior, they must have knowledge of the behavior and the skills to perform it. Simply put, before doing something, you have to know what it is you're going to do and know how to do it.

When we look at the 2005 Dietary Guidelines for Americans, one of the recommendations is for people to choose carbohydrates wisely (U.S. Department of Health and Human Services & U.S. Department of Agriculture, 2005) (Figure 7.1). According to the construct of behavioral capability, in order for people to choose wisely, they must know what wise choices are, and have the ability (skill) to make the better choices.

Reinforcement

Reinforcement is a construct in the SCT with which you may be familiar, because it is also the basis for operant conditioning and behavior modification. In general, reinforcement is a system of rewards (positive reinforcement) and punishments (negative reinforcements) in response to behavior. Behavior occurs because people either want the reward or want to avoid the punishment.

FIGURE 7.1 Dietary guidelines for Americans.

A common example of this can be found with children. If a child eats all of the vegetables on his plate, he is rewarded with a favorite dessert; thus, the behavior (eating vegetables) is repeated so the reward (dessert) can be obtained again.

Behavior resulting in a negative reinforcement or punishment tends not to be repeated. A child who refuses to eat her vegetables is denied dessert, and watches as everyone else eats. To avoid this punishment, she eats her vegetables the next time, unless, of course, she doesn't like what is being served for dessert.

Locus of Control

Although most of the constructs in the SCT explain behavior by the influence of external or social forces, the construct of locus of control is a bit different. This construct explains behavior based on the idea that people have varying degrees of belief in their ability to control what happens to them. This belief in the extent of personal control has an impact on health decisions, and thus on health behavior. This construct is also found in Attribution Theory, which was discussed in detail in Chapter 5.

Locus of control works on a continuum from internal to external. Internally controlled people believe that everything that happens to them is a result of their own decisions and behaviors. They believe they have control over all aspects of their lives and their destiny. Externally controlled people believe that forces outside of their control, such as fate, God's will, or important or powerful others, govern all aspects of their lives (Levenson, 1974).

Internality or externality has a strong influence on our health decision making. In the case of breast cancer, for example, women who are more externally controlled are not likely to have mammograms unless their physicians (important or powerful others) tell them to have one. In contrast, women who are more internally controlled will have mammograms regardless of whether their physicians recommend them or not (Borrayo & Guarnaccia, 2002). In young adults, internality is associated with greater odds of engaging in healthy behaviors, specifically, eating fiber, exercising, and low salt and fat consumption (Steptoe & Wardle, 2001).

Where people fall on the continuum of internality and externality may change depending upon the situation. Some people are very internal when it comes to changing unhealthy behaviors, such as weight loss or stress management, for example. Yet these same people do not wear seatbelts, for instance, because "What will be, will be" or "If it's my time to go, there is nothing I can do about it."

In summary, according to Social Cognitive Theory, personal factors, the environment, and behavior interact with each other; therefore, changing one of them changes all of them (Figure 7.2).

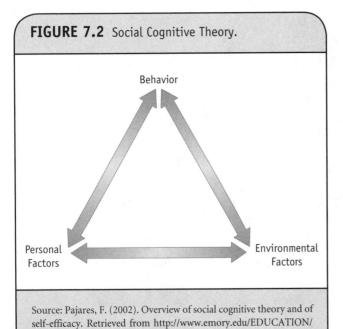

FIGURE 7.2 Social Cognitive Theory.

Behavior

Personal Factors

Environmental Factors

Source: Pajares, F. (2002). Overview of social cognitive theory and of self-efficacy. Retrieved from http://www.emory.edu/EDUCATION/mfp/eff.html. Reprinted with permission.

Social Cognitive Theory Constructs Chart

Self-efficacy	One's own estimation of one's personal ability to do something
Observational learning (modeling)	Learning by watching others
Expectations	The likely outcome of a particular behavior
Expectancies	The value placed on the outcome of the behavior
Emotional arousal	The emotional reaction to a situation and its resulting behavior
Behavioral capability	The knowledge and skills needed to engage in a particular behavior
Reinforcement	The rewards or punishments for doing something
Locus of control	One's belief regarding one's personal power over life events

Learning by watching others.

Influences on Fruit and Vegetable Consumption by Low-Income Black American Adolescents

Elaine Fontenot Molaison, PhD, RD[1]; Carol L. Connell, PhD, RD[2]; Janice E. Stuff, PhD, RD[3]; M. Kathleen Yadrick, PhD, RD[4]; Margaret Bogle, PhD, RD[5]

[1]Department of Nutrition and Food Systems, University of Southern Mississippi, Hattiesburg, Mississippi;

[2]Delta Nutrition Intervention Research Initiative, University of Southern Mississippi, Hattiesburg, Mississippi;

[3]Agricultural Research Service/US Department of Agriculture—Children's Nutrition Research Center, Baylor College of Medicine, Houston, TX;

[4]Department of Nutrition and Food Systems, Delta Nutrition Intervention Research Initiative, University of Southern Mississippi, Hattiesburg, Mississippi;

[5]Delta Nutrition Intervention Research Initiative, Agricultural Research Service/ US Department of Agriculture, Southern Plains Area, Little Rock, Arkansas

ABSTRACT

Objective: The purpose of this study was to identify personal, behavioral, and environmental factors influencing fruit and vegetable consumption among 10- to 13-year-old low-income black American youth in the lower Mississippi Delta Region. Social Cognitive Theory, along with other theoretical constructs, guided focus group questions and analysis.

Design: A qualitative study using focus group methodology.

Setting: Enrichment program of a sports summer camp for low-income youth.

Participants: Forty-two adolescents (21 female, 21 male) participated in 6 focus groups.

Main Outcome Measures: Personal, behavioral, and environmental influences on fruit and vegetable consumption.

Analysis: Content analysis methods were used by 3 independent reviewers to identify themes within the focus group transcripts. Themes were summarized and then categorized into the 3 domains of Social Cognitive Theory.

Results: The major themes were taste, availability, extended family influence, visual proof of the benefits of fruit and vegetable consumption, and the need for gender-specific behavioral skills.

Conclusions and Implications: This formative research will aid in the development of a culturally relevant nutrition intervention for low-income black American adolescents in the lower Mississippi Delta region. The results indicate that this group is more likely to respond to interventions that use role models who can provide proof that fruit and vegetable consumption is related to improved health.

INTRODUCTION

Current national recommendations for health promotion and disease prevention advise increased consumption of fruits and vegetables.[1,2] At the national level, 20% or less of children and adolescents eat the recommended 5 or more servings of fruits and vegetables per day.[3] Regional studies indicate even higher rates of inadequate fruit and vegetable consumption among children and adolescents from low socioeconomic backgrounds or from minority ethnic groups.[4-6] One of the initial steps in planning an intervention to improve fruit and vegetable intake among adolescents is to identify environmental, personal, and behavioral factors that mediate their consumption. Theoretical behavior models aid in identifying and understanding these factors.

Social Cognitive Theory (SCT) postulates that behavior is the result of environmental and personal factors and that behavior, in turn, affects these environmental and personal factors in constant reciprocal relationships.[7] SCT has been used to identify factors predictive of fruit and vegetable consumption among middle-income elementary school children (grades 3–5) and to develop interventions to modify those eating behaviors.[8–15] However, only recently have studies assessing SCT constructs associated with fruit and vegetable consumption among adolescents been published.[6,15–17] Although these studies included ethnically and racially diverse samples, little information is available regarding the personal, environmental, and behavioral constructs operating in the fruit and vegetable choices of low-income black American adolescents. Cultural factors, such as the influence of the historical effects of slavery on establishing dietary patterns, or socioeconomic factors, such as the food resource constraints associated with food insecurity and their sequiturs, may impact on fruit and vegetable choices in this group in ways that are not likely to occur in other groups.[18,19] Therefore, the purpose of this qualitative study was to use a framework of SCT to explore environmental, personal, and behavioral factors among 10- to 13-year-old southern, low-income black American adolescents that mediate fruit and vegetable selection and may aid the planning of an intervention aimed at increasing fruit and vegetable consumption in this group.

DESCRIPTION OF PARTICIPANTS AND PROCEDURES

As part of the formative research phase of a pilot intervention to increase fruit and vegetable consumption among low-income black American adolescents, we used focus group methodology to elicit personal, behavioral, and environmental factors influencing fruit and vegetable consumption in this target group. The research was approved by the Institutional Review Board at the University of Southern Mississippi. Participants were recruited from adolescents enrolled in the National Youth Sports Program (NYSP) during the summer of 2000. The NYSP is a 5-week program that incorporates athletic skills training with life skills training by providing a minimum of 15 hours of educational activities emphasizing substance abuse prevention, career planning and education, nutrition, and an active lifestyle. Ninety percent of the participants in the program must meet federal poverty guidelines.[20] Since NYSP participants were recruited from schools and housing projects with high rates of poverty among their students/residents, income data were not collected from participants. However, the program participants were drawn from a black American adolescent population in a 2-county area. For this population, median household income ranged from $18 903 to $21 365, 46% of children 6 to 11 years old were from households below the poverty level, and 40% to 42% of 12 to 14 year olds were from households below the poverty level.[21] During registration for the NYSP, parents gave consent for their children to participate in the focus groups.

Focus group questions were developed following standard procedures.[22] Constructs from SCT identified from the literature as salient factors influencing fruit and vegetable consumption among children were used to develop the initial questions (Table 1).[6,8–11,14,15,23] Environmental constructs included family and peer social support and fruit and vegetable availability. Personal constructs included outcome expectancies and self-efficacy. The behavioral construct was behavioral capability to prepare meals and snacks. Other questions were developed to assess influences on fruit and vegetable consumption likely associated with the developmental stages of adolescence (locus of control and benefits and barriers to fruit and vegetable consumption), to explore factors that might motivate low-income black American adolescents to consume more fruits and vegetables, and to identify places outside the home where fruits and vegetables were eaten. These constructs could also be classified into 1 of the 3 primary domains of SCT. A researcher knowledgeable of SCT, who had not developed the questions, reviewed them, and changes were made to the questions as needed. However, owing to time constraints within the NYSP, questions were not pretested with children prior to conducting the focus groups.

Graduate students and research staff who conducted the focus groups were trained in standardized focus group methods during a 3-day workshop.[24] Moderators and group participants were of the same ethnic or racial background. Research staff served as the recorders during each session. During enrichment classes of the NYSP, volunteers were recruited from each class to participate in focus groups held in a separate room. Prior to the start of the focus group session, children signed consent forms. Each of 6 focus groups (3 female, 3 male groups) included 5 to 7 participants who were of similar age. Discussions were tape-recorded, and notes were taken by the recorders. Following the sessions, all tapes were transcribed verbatim by a single recorder.

Focus group data were then analyzed using content analysis methods.[25] Three separate reviewers, 2 of whom were recorders, evaluated response content from each focus group and identified themes in each. In the final step, 1 reviewer summarized themes and developed a narrative summary of the findings for each question. Responses in the focus groups were summarized by theme, and, in turn, the themes were assigned to SCT domains. The 3 reviewers who coded the data reviewed the final themes to ensure that they were appropriate and adequately reflected responses gathered during the focus group sessions.

QUALITATIVE FINDINGS

Forty-two low-income black American adolescents (21 males, 21 females) participated in 6 focus groups, which were segmented by gender and age to include 10 to 11 year olds, 12 year olds, and 13 year olds. Despite a lack of pretesting of the focus group questions, children did not voice problems comprehending the intent of the questions, nor did their answers indicate that the questions were misinterpreted. Table 2 shows major themes grouped by personal, behavioral, and environmental constructs.

Taste emerged as a major limiting factor related to consumption. The taste of vegetables produced more negative reactions than the taste of fruits. Common terms used to describe the taste of vegetables included "nasty" and "yucky." Another barrier expressed by adolescents was the type of preparation. Many of the participants said that vegetables had to be prepared with sugar if they were going to eat them. Vegetables prepared with cheese were also preferred, suggesting that these preparation methods directly affected taste. Statements made by participants related to this factor included "If they ain't got no sugar, I ain't gonna eat no vegetables" and "I like fruits, but vegetables gotta have some sugar." Other barriers mentioned included dislike of the form of the fruits

and vegetables (canned fruits and vegetables from the store), boredom with the same vegetables, and allergies.

In addition to being a barrier to consumption, taste also emerged as a positive outcome expectancy; several adolescents reported that they ate fruit merely for the sweet taste: "I like fruits the best 'cause they're sweet . . . ." Another positive outcome expectancy expressed was eating fruits and vegetables for general health or for specific nutrients or benefits, such as potassium, vitamins, energy, and improved skin appearance.

In response to questions about eating fruits and vegetables in a variety of situations (self-efficacy), a majority of the participants believed that they could. Both genders and most age groups indicated high levels of self-efficacy for fruit and vegetable consumption. The only group that did not express a high level of self-efficacy was the 13-year-old males. One comment related to the low level of self-efficacy in this group was ". . . because my parents don't teach me to eat . . . you know, different types of fruits and vegetables." Participants verbally affirmed that their self-efficacy in the presence of peers would be high. However, the recorder noted that the tone of the group changed during this question, with some participants hesitating before speaking and others "boasting" about their ability to do what they wanted despite the opinion

TABLE 1. Question Guide and Social Cognitive Theory Construct Related to Each Question

Question	SCT Construct
Home	
If you looked in the refrigerator or the kitchen cabinet at your home right now, what kinds of fruits would you find?	Environmental
If you looked in the refrigerator or the kitchen cabinet at your home right now, what kinds of vegetables would you find?	Environmental
Do you ever eat fruit away from home? What are some other places that you eat fruit?	Environmental
Do you ever eat vegetables away from home? What are some other places that you eat vegetables?	Environmental
Do you help prepare the meals and snacks in your home?	Behavioral
Personal Belief	
What do you think will happen if you don't eat fruit? Vegetables?	Personal
What are some reasons you don't eat fruit? Vegetables?	Personal
Do you make the decisions about what you eat? If not, who decides what you will eat?	Personal
If you wanted to eat more fruits or vegetables, would you be able to? Why or why not? How would you get them?	Personal
What would make you eat more fruit? Vegetables?	Personal
Family and Friends	
Do you think that your friends would help you eat more fruits and vegetables?	Environmental
How could they help you eat more fruit? Vegetables?	
Is there any member of your family who you feel would help you eat more fruits and vegetables?	Environmental
How could they help you eat more fruit? Vegetables?	
What are some reasons you and your friends eat fruit? What are some reasons you and your friends eat vegetables?	Personal
What would you do if no one is eating fruits or vegetables, but you would like to eat fruits or vegetables?	Personal

SCT indicates Social Cognitive Theory.

of their friends: "I don't care what they're doin'; I'd get me some [fruit/vegetable]."

To evaluate behavioral capability, we asked about involvement in preparation of meals and snacks containing fruits and vegetables. The majority indicated that they at least helped with preparation of meals and snacks. There appeared to be gender differences related to this construct. For example, helping with prepreparation of foods, such as chopping onions and celery, cutting potatoes or cabbage, or cooking simple dishes such as "noodles," were mentioned by the females. Males either did not cook or were involved only in very simple food-associated tasks.

An environmental factor impacting fruit and vegetable consumption was a lack of availability. Some participants expressed that they did not have fruits and vegetables available at home. For example, one participant stated, "Most of the time, we don't have them at home … 'cause fruit is not something that parents just buy, just to be buying." Other children expressed that the grocery store where parents shopped did not sell fruits and vegetables. One participant indicated a lack of refrigeration as a barrier to fruit and vegetable consumption.

Responses related to the construct of locus of control indicated that few adolescents made decisions about what they ate (internal locus of control) at home. Rather, external locus of control, classified as a personal factor in our schema, appeared to be the predominant theme related to eating fruits and vegetables in this context. A mother or grandmother was most often mentioned as making the decision about what the participants ate at home. A representative statement here was "because my momma does the cooking, and she chooses." Some older adolescents indicated that they did not choose what they ate at home if their mother or grandmother was present but did make their own decisions in their absence: "mine makes me eat what she wants, but when she's gone, I eat what I want."

Participants identified several locations where they were likely to eat fruits and vegetables outside the home; the 3 most common locations included the homes of other family members, restaurants, and school. Some responded that they obtained fruits and vegetables at the grocery store, and one participant ate fruits and vegetables at the hospital, where he visited during the summer.

There were 2 dimensions to social support: family and peer social support. Generally, participants expressed that they had support from family members to increase fruit and vegetable consumption. Again, mothers and grandmothers were named as the primary support for the consumption of fruits and vegetables. One participant noted, "[Momma] takes

TABLE 2. Themes Identified During Focus Groups by Construct

Personal
Barriers to F&V consumption
Taste
Preparation method
Form (canned vs fresh)
Outcome expectancies
Sweet taste of fruit
General health
Cosmetic benefits
Sports performance
Self-efficacy
Positive (with exception of 13-year-old males)
Locus of control
External locus of control at home
Mothers and grandmothers are primary decision-makers at home
Preference
Sweet taste
Fruits preferred over vegetables
Behavioral
Behavioral capability
Males, simple food preparation tasks
Females, more complex food preparation tasks
Environmental
Barriers to F&V consumption
Lack of availability at home
Lack of availability at neighborhood grocery store
Locations to eat F&Vs outside home
Extended family
Restaurants
School
Social support
Family, positive support
Peers, negative support

F&V indicates fruit and vegetable.

away the junk food." One 12-year-old female explained about eating vegetables, "At my grandma's house, that's all you eat." Only 3 participants, all 13-year-old males, believed that their families would not encourage fruit and vegetable consumption. Peer support was perceived as negative. Most respondents believed that their peers would not support them in consuming more fruits and vegetables because most of their peers ate "junk." A statement embodying this concept was "my friend got a lot of junk food, and he be eatin' it a lot."

Only a few adolescents indicated that friends would encourage them to eat fruits and vegetables.

DISCUSSION

The purpose of this qualitative study was to explore psychosocial factors from SCT that might mediate the consumption of fruits and vegetable among low-income black American adolescents. Previous research has primarily focused on middle-income children. The responses of focus group participants could be categorized into themes in each of the 3 domains of SCT. Within the personal domain, taste appeared to be a major theme or factor influencing fruit and vegetable consumption among these low-income black American adolescents, appearing in 3 of 4 constructs in this domain (see Table 2). This is in agreement with others who have studied the food choices of children.[13,14,23] In our study, taste could be a negative factor (barrier) and a positive factor (preference and outcome expectancy) of fruit and vegetable consumption. In particular, the sweet flavor of fruit or adding sugar to vegetables was mentioned numerous times and with great emphasis by the focus group participants. Adding sugar to vegetables during preparation was mentioned frequently in the focus groups and anecdotally has been a common practice in many southern households. Future research should further explore this practice because it has not been well documented in the literature.

Self-efficacy for eating fruits and vegetables was generally positive among participants, with the exception of the 13-year-old males. This group indicated that their apparent lack of self-efficacy was related to the absence of family social support at home. Corwin et al reported that children (predominantly middle-income white) with the highest levels of self-efficacy to improve eating behaviors were more likely to consume recommended dietary intakes.[9] The expressed influence of mothers and grandmothers on fruit and vegetable consumption is similar to the findings of Young et al, who reported that parents influenced fruit and vegetable consumption,[26] but contrasts with those of Cullen et al, who reported that black parents did not prepare or encourage consumption of fruits and vegetables.[14] Some of the participants in our study talked about family members, grandparents in particular, who grew vegetables, and this may partially explain why grandmothers in our study were identified as having a strong positive influence on fruit and vegetable consumption. Although our participants expressed self-efficacy for choosing fruits and vegetables among peers, we suspect that peer pressure within groups may have prompted responses to impress other group members and the moderator. Cullen et al also reported that adolescents in their study said that peer influ-

ence would not affect their intake of fruits and vegetables, yet peers were the strongest influence not to eat fruits and vegetables.[14] Further exploration of self-efficacy and its interaction with family and peer social support in this group could help clarify our findings.

In our study, a lack of availability was identified as a barrier to fruit and vegetable consumption by a small number of the participants. Most research showing a relationship between availability and children's food consumption has focused on availability at home or at school.[10,12] We probed for locations where fruits and vegetables are eaten outside of the home, assuming that adolescents might be more independent in selecting places to eat and thus have potentially greater exposure to fruit and vegetable availability than elementary children. Participants identified other relatives' homes, particularly their grandmother's house, and restaurants, in addition to school and home, although restaurants were more frequently mentioned as a source of vegetables than fruits. Determining the locations where fruits and vegetables are available may potentially provide information for intervention planning in the future. Other researchers have found that fruits and vegetables are only occasionally consumed by children when dining out.[14]

We also probed for more information on the role that motivation plays in low-income adolescents' consumption of fruits and vegetables; however, factors that comprise their motivation are not fully known. We asked what would influence participants to eat more fruits and vegetables. The majority discussed improved health or sports performance, which we categorized as positive outcome expectancies. For example, one 12 year old stated, "'Cause we be havin' to play baseball, you know what I'm sayin'? If you ain't in shape, you gonna ride that pine [sit the bench].... I gotta stay in shape 'cause I run that 100, and I run the 200 too." A theme on the need to have visual proof that eating fruits and vegetables would result in a healthy body also emerged in relation to motivation to eat fruits and vegetables ("... if I see their body get better ..."). Since focus groups were held during a sports camp, it is possible that the groups were already more conscious of a diet–health connection. However, we are not aware of previous literature that has reported adolescents' need to see visual evidence of the benefits of eating fruits and vegetables.

In summary, our study identified important and unique aspects of personal, environmental, and behavior factors related to fruit and vegetable intake of low-income black American adolescents in a southern rural state. Although our study shared perspectives with previous investigations using SCT factors related to fruit and vegetable consumption by children, there were subtleties expressed for this sample. We found that taste, availability, extended family influence, visual proof of the benefits of fruits and vegetables, and the need for gender-specific behavioral skills are important areas to include in an intervention designed for this target group. The limitations of this study include a small convenience sample of children selected for ethnic or racial and socioeconomic backgrounds. As with any qualitative research, the ability to generalize to a larger population is limited. However, the purpose of our research was to explore factors influencing low-income southern black American adolescents' fruit and vegetable choices for the purpose of developing culturally relevant interventions and measurement tools for a comparable group. In addition, responses were similar and consistent over the 6 focus groups. According to Morgan, when themes across the groups become repetitive, conducting additional focus groups is unnecessary.[27] Therefore, these results provide valuable information for the formative phase of a pilot intervention to increase fruit and vegetable consumption among similar black American adolescents. As part of the focus group process, all participants were assured that all comments would remain confidential. Therefore, the researchers assumed that the comments made were honest and based on reality. However, children varied in their ability to verbally express their thoughts, which may have resulted in some comments that seem unusual or unbelievable. In addition, peer influence may have affected responses in some of the groups, with some of the adolescents making comments that would enhance their acceptance within the group.

IMPLICATIONS FOR RESEARCH AND PRACTICE

Our research has implications for planning a culturally appropriate intervention and for developing measurement instruments for low-income black American adolescents. From a practitioner's standpoint, an intervention should allow hands-on activities to help incorporate fruits and vegetables into meals and snacks, as well as provide interaction with individuals who demonstrate good health as it relates to fruit and vegetable consumption. The lack of availability of fruits and vegetables in the homes is a primary concern, indicating the need to involve family members in intervention activities. In addition, our research indicates a need for gender-specific educational materials and gender-segregated educational groups for children at this age. The strong role of extended family, particularly grandmothers, in promoting fruit and vegetable intake also suggests that they be considered a channel for increasing fruit and vegetable intake with this population. It is interesting to note that seeing physical proof of the benefits of fruit and vegetable consumption was

suggested as a way to help improve intake. This suggests that interventions with this group may be more effective if physically fit and culturally appropriate role models are involved in providing nutrition education. From a policy standpoint, summer programs for children, such as the NYSP, may be vehicles for delivery of nutrition education or reinforcement of nutrition messages provided through child nutrition programs. The possible lack of fruits and vegetables at grocery stores in local neighborhoods also needs further investigation. It was not a primary focus of this study but would certainly impact any intervention aimed at increasing fruit and vegetable consumption in the home.

ACKNOWLEDGMENT

Funding for this research was provided by Agricultural Research Service/US Department of Agriculture project number 6251-530000-0020-OOD.

REFERENCES

1. US Dept of Health and Human Services. *Healthy People 2010.* 2nd ed. 2000.
2. US Dept of Agriculture and US Dept of Health and Human Services. *Dietary Guidelines for Americans.* 6th ed. 2005.
3. Krebs-Smith SM, Cook A, Subar AF, et al. Fruit and vegetable intakes of children and adolescents in the United States. *Arch Pediatr Adolesc Med.* 1996;150:81-86.
4. Neumark-Sztainer D, Story M, Resnick MD, et al. Correlates of inadequate fruit and vegetable consumption among adolescents. *Prev Med.* 1996;25:497-505.
5. Champagne CM, Bogle ML, McGee BB, et al. Dietary intake in the lower Mississippi Delta region: results from the Foods of Our Delta Study. *J Am Diet Assoc.* 2004; 104:199-207.
6. Rafiroiu AC, Anderson EP, Sargent RG, et al. Dietary practices of South Carolina adolescents and their parents. *Am J Health Behav.* 2002;26:200-212.
7. Baranowski T, Perry CL, Parcel GS. How individuals, environments, and health behavior interact. In: Glanz K, Lewis FM, Rimer BK, eds. *Health Behavior and Health Education: Theory, Research, and Practice.* San Francisco, Calif: Jossey-Bass; 1997:153-178.
8. Resnicow K, Davis-Hearn M, Smith M, et al. Social-cognitive predictors of fruit and vegetable intake in children. *Health Psychol.* 1997; 16:272-276.
9. Corwin SJ, Sargent RG, Rheaume GE, et al. Dietary behaviors among fourth graders: a social cognitive theory study approach. *Am J Health Behav.* 1999;23:182-197.
10. Kratt P, Reynolds K, Shewchuk R. The role of availability as a moderator of family fruit and vegetable consumption. *Health Educ Behav.* 2000;27:471-482.
11. Cullen KW, Baranowski T, Rittenberry L, et al. Child-reported family and peer influences on fruit, juice and vegetable consumption: reliability and validity of measures. *Health Educ Res.* 2001; 16:187-200.
12. Reynolds KD, Franklin, FA, Binkley D, et al. Increasing the fruit and vegetable consumption of 4th-graders: results from the High 5 Project. *Prev Med.* 2000:30:309-319.
13. Thompson VJ, Baranowski T, Gullen K, et al. Influences on diet and physical activity among middle-class black American 8- to 10-year-old girls at risk of becoming obese. *J Nutr Educ Behav.* 2003;35:115-123.

14. Cullen KW, Baranowski L, Olvera N. Social-environmental influences on children's diets: results from focus groups with African-, Euro- and Mexican-American children and their parents. *Health Educ Res.* 2000;5:581-590.

15. Neumark-Sztainer D, Wall M, Perry C, Story M. Correlates of fruit and vegetable intake among adolescents. Findings from Project EAT. *Prev Med.* 2003:37:198-208.

16. Lytle LA, Barnell S, Murray DM, et al. Predicting adolescents' intake of fruits and vegetables. *J Nutr Educ Behav.* 2003;35:170-178.

17. Granner ML, Sargent RG, Calderon KS, Hussey JR, Evans AE, Watkins KW. Factors of fruit and vegetable intake by race, gender and age among young adolescents. *J Nutr Educ Behav.* 2004;36:173-180.

18. Airhihenbuwa GO, Kumanyika S, Agurs TD, Lowe A, Saunders D, Morssink GB. Cultural aspects of African American eating patterns. *Ethn Health.* 1996; 1:245-260.

19. Connell CL, Nord M, Lofton KL, Yadrick K. Food security of older children can be assessed using a standardized survey instrument. *J Nutr.* 2004:134:2566-2572.

20. National Youth Sports Corporation. National Youth Sports Program: summer program statistics for 2002 National Youth Sports Corporation [on-line]. Available at: http://www.nyscorp.org/nysp_statistics.htm. Accessed November 12, 2002.

21. US Census Bureau. Census 2000 summary file 4 (SF-4) - sample data [on-line]. Available at: http://factfinder.census.gov. Accessed September 28, 2004.

22. Krueger RA. *Developing Questions for Focus Groups.* Thousand Oaks, Calif: Sage; 1997.

23. Neumark-Sztainer D, Story M, Perry G, et al. Factors influencing food choices of adolescents: findings from focus-group discussions with adolescents. *J Am Diet Assoc.* 1999;99:929-934, 937.

24. Krueger RA. *Moderating Focus Groups.* Thousand Oaks, Calif: Sage; 1997.

25. Krueger RA. *Analyzing and Reporting Focus Group Results.* Thousand Oaks, Calif: Sage; 1997.

26. Young EM, Fors SW, Hayes DM. Associations between perceived parent behaviors and middle school student fruit and vegetable consumption. *J Nutr Educ Behav.* 2004;36:2-12.

27. Morgan DL. *Planning Focus Groups.* Thousand Oaks, Calif: Sage; 1997.

Funding for this research was provided by Agricultural Research Service/US Department of Agriculture project number 6251-530000-0020-OOD. Work was completed at the University of Southern Mississippi.

QUESTIONS

1. How did the constructs identified as personal factors influence the fruit and vegetable consumption of the 10- to 13-year-olds in the study? How similar is this to how your own personal factors influence your fruit and vegetable consumption?

2. How did the constructs identified as environmental factors influence fruit and vegetable consumption? How similar or different was this from the effect of these factors on your own consumption?

3. What was the behavioral factor that influenced fruit and vegetable consumption in the study? To what extent do you feel this factor affects your own fruit and vegetable intake?

4. Taken all together, how do you think you could use this information to change your own intake of fruits and vegetables?

CHAPTER REFERENCES

Bandura, A. (1977). *Social Learning Theory.* Englewood Cliffs, NJ: Prentice-Hall.

Bandura, A. (1986). *Social Foundations of Thought and Action: A Social Cognitive Theory.* Englewood Cliffs, NJ: Prentice-Hall.

Bandura, A. (1993). Perceived self-efficacy in cognitive development and functioning. *Educational Psychologist, 28*(2), 117–148.

Borrayo, E.A., & Guarnaccia, C.A. (2002). Differences in Mexican-born and U.S.-born women of Mexican descent regarding factors related to breast cancer screening behaviors. *Health Care for Women International, 21*(7), 599–614.

Glanz, K., Rimer, B.K., & Lewis, F.M. (Eds.). (2002). *Health Behavior and Health Education* (3rd ed.). San Francisco: Jossey-Bass.

Grusec, J.E. (1992). Social learning theory and developmental psychology: The legacies of Robert Sears and Albert Bandura. *Developmental Psychology, 28*(5), 776–786.

Levenson, H. (1974). Activism and powerful others: Distinctions within the concept of internal-external control. *Journal of Personality Assessment, 38,* 377–383.

National Cancer Institute. (2003). *Theory at a Glance: A Guide for Health Promotion Practice.* Washington, DC: U.S. Department of Health and Human Services.

Rawl, S.M., Champion, V.L., Menon, U., & Foster, J.L. (2000). The impact of age and race on mammography practices. *Health Care for Women International, 21*(7), 583–598.

Shelton, P., Weinrich, S., & Reynolds, W.A. (1999). Barriers to prostate cancer screening in African-American men. *Journal of National Black Nurses Association, 10*(2), 14–28.

Steptoe, A., & Wardle, J. (2001). Locus of control and health behaviour revisited: A multivariate analysis of young adults from 18 countries. *British Journal of Psychology, 92,* 659–672.

U.S. Department of Health and Human Services & U.S. Department of Agriculture. (2005). *Dietary Guidelines for Americans 2005.* Washington, DC: U.S. Government Printing Office.

CHAPTER 8

Diffusion of Innovation

Theory Essence Sentence

Behavior changes as innovations are adopted.

After reading this chapter the student will be able to:

1. Explain the concepts of Diffusion Theory.
2. Discuss the characteristics of an innovation.
3. Discuss the components of time relative to innovation adoption.
4. Identify communication channels used in diffusion.
5. Identify social systems through which innovations diffuse.
6. Use the theory to explain the adoption of one health behavior.

THEORETICAL CONCEPT

Diffusion of Innovation is the means by which a new idea is disseminated and adopted by a society. The theory was originally used in the 1950s to understand how farmers in Iowa adopted hybrid corn seed. Since hybrid seed increased crop yield and produced hardier, drought-resistant corn, farmers were expected to quickly switch to this new seed. However, this is not what happened. On average, it took 7 years for a farmer to go from trying the hybrid seed to planting 100% of his land with it. Obviously, something other than economics was at the root of this seemingly irrational behavior (Rogers, 2004; Ryan & Gross, 1943). Diffusion of Innovation provided the explanation for the farmers' slow adoption of the new type of seed.

THEORETICAL CONSTRUCTS

How a new idea (innovation) spreads through a society, and why some become part of the social fabric and others do not, can be explained by the four main constructs of this theory: the innovation, the channels through which it is communicated, time, and the social system. Diffusion is the process by which this takes place (Rogers, 2003).

Innovation

An innovation is something new, or novel, whether it is a device, a practice, or an idea (National Cancer Institute [NCI], 2003). Diffusion and ultimate adoption (or rejection) of an innovation is affected by certain characteristics of the innovation itself. These characteristics include having an advantage over what is already available, compatibility with social norms and values, trial on a limited basis, ease of use, and having observable results. Innovations with these characteristics will be adopted more rapidly than those without these characteristics (Rogers, 2003; Rogers & Scott, 1997).

Relative Advantage

An innovation has a greater chance of being adopted if it is better than what is already out there, or if it fills a void where nothing else similar exists. In either case, the innovation has a relative advantage over what is currently available.

An example of a product having a relative advantage is the female condom. When this product was introduced in 1993, it had a decided advantage over what was already available because no other product like it existed. Although its adoption has not been as great as anticipated for a number of reasons, relative advantage is not one of them.

Another example is "candy" calcium supplements. Standard calcium supplements are relatively large pills that must be taken, on average, two to three times a day. Changing the calcium delivery system from a large pill to a candy-like formulation was an innovation with a relative advantage. Eating a piece of chocolate "candy" twice a day is much more appealing than swallowing a bunch of large pills.

Mobile mammography is yet another example of an innovation with a relative advantage. A mobile mammography unit provides the same services as a radiology office or hospital, but is more convenient and saves the time and cost of transportation (NCI, 2003). These are certainly all advantages when compared with the alternative of having a mammogram done at a radiology office or hospital.

Trialability

It is advantageous if an innovation can be used on a trial basis or limited scale. If people can try something new without making a major commitment to it in terms of time, money, or effort, there is a better chance of it being adopted. This is why companies make trial sizes of new products.

Take vision correction, for example. If you decide to switch from glasses to contact lenses, there is a trial period before you make a commitment to using contacts and buy a supply of them. Even then, you can switch back and forth between the contacts and glasses. On the other hand, Lasik vision correction cannot be tried or used on a limited scale because Lasik is corrective surgery that permanently changes the shape of the cornea (Food and Drug Administration [FDA], 2004).

A classic example of trialability is the practice of pharmaceutical companies giving physicians free samples. Free samples promote physician adoption of medication, and, when samples are given to patients, it promotes their adoption as well (Kane & Mittman, 2002).

Complexity

An innovation's complexity will also affect its likelihood of adoption. The more complex it is to understand and use, the less likely it is to be adopted or even tried. For example, female condoms are not easy to use the first time (Piot, 1998). They require proper placement before and during sex and careful removal afterwards. Unless a woman feels she can insert the condom, keep it in place, and remove it correctly, the odds of her using it again after the first time are not good nor are the chances of it being adopted (Hollander, 2004).

In contrast, the nicotine patch is relatively simple to use. Choose an area of skin on the upper body that is free from hair, intact, and dry. Open the package, peel the protective covering off the patch, and apply it to the skin. Pretty simple.

Recently, a movement was started to have people adopt an innovative technique to reduce disease transmission through droplet infection. It calls for people to sneeze and cough into their upper sleeve instead of into their hands or into the air (Centers for Disease Control and Prevention [CDC], 2007; Lounsbury, 2006). This is an easy-to-use innovation that anyone can adopt. It requires no special training, equipment, or practice.

Compatibility

To be adopted, an innovation needs to be compatible with the existing values and needs of the people, culture, or social environment (Rogers, 2003). Certainly in the case of the female condom, its adoption would not likely occur among women whose culture considers touching one's own genitals taboo or whose religious beliefs prohibit contraception.

Incompatibility with social norms is one of the issues at the heart of HIV/AIDS prevention in Tanzania, a country with one of the highest rates of AIDS in the world. Although most infections are transmitted horizontally (adult to adult) through heterosexual intercourse, a substantial number of infants are infected through vertical transmission (from infected mother to child). Consequently, one of the interventions being tried is aimed at preventing transmission of HIV through breast milk.

Although the solution to this problem seems obvious—just have mothers use formula—it is not that easy. The majority of Tanzanian women breastfeed their children until 2 years of age because it is expected of them. Even HIV-positive women are expected to breastfeed. Consequently, women who do not breastfeed are stigmatized. However, there is a way to reduce the risk of HIV transmission in breast milk, namely, by heat treating. Heat treating destroys HIV in breast milk without significantly changing its nutrient content (Burke, 2004; Israel-Ballard et al., 2005). But heat treating breast milk requires the mother to express her milk and then heat it using one of two simple methods. Although heat treating is effective, simple to do, and still allows the mother to feed her child breast milk, expressing breast milk is taboo and incompatible with local practices and beliefs (Burke, 2004).

Although originally introduced in the 1980s, hand sanitizers were not considered socially acceptable at the time. If a business provided them for its customers, questions were raised about the cleanliness of the establishment. Times have changed, and people are now more germ phobic. Today, if a business offers hand sanitizers, customers are grateful (Yee, 2007). Hand sanitizers are now available in a host of places—from supermarkets (to wipe off cart handles) to fast food restaurants and children's playgrounds. People are carrying small, personal-size containers of sanitizer in their purses, briefcases, and backpacks. It is almost to the point now where *not* using a hand sanitizer is socially unacceptable.

Observability

If the results of using an innovation can be seen by other people, it is more likely to be adopted. Think about the rate of adoption of breast augmentation, tattoos, and body piercing. Observability may explain why these have become so widely adopted. Observability drives the diet industry. People try new diets because, if they work, the results are noticeable.

Observability has affected health care as well. Early on, chiropractic care was something novel, an innovation. It was a different way to treat illness. Its adoption was largely based on word of mouth and the improvement observed by others (McCarthy & Milus, 2000). The same situation occurred with acupuncture. While it was first seen as something novel (although it dates back 2,500 years in China), it is now an accepted treatment option, especially for chronic pain man-

FIGURE 8.1 Friends talking with friends is an effective means of diffusing information about an innovation.

agement. Its results are observable (Eshkevari & Heath, 2005) in that many people who had limited mobility prior to treatment are active after.

Communication Channel

Diffusion is the active sharing or communication of information among people. It is a social process: people talking to one another about a new idea, product, tool, food, or so on (Haider & Kreps, 2004; Rogers, 2003). The communication channel is how word of an innovation spreads.

The most effective and rapid means of communicating something new is through mass media—the television, newspapers, radio, and now, the Internet. Mass media channels can reach a huge audience very quickly, making a large portion of a society readily aware of a new product or idea.

As appealing as this method is to get the message out, it is often not the best means of ensuring adoption of an innovation. Sometimes, one-on-one conversation is more effective. For example, one person tries a new product, and she talks with a friend about it, who then talks to another friend, and so on. This is demonstrative of diffusion as a social process that relies on interpersonal communication (Rogers, 2003).

Interpersonal communication and the transfer of information about ideas occur most frequently between two people who are the same, *homophilius*, meaning they share the same beliefs, education level, or socioeconomic level, to name but a few characteristics (Rogers, 2003). A friend talking to friends would have a greater impact on the latter trying something new that the former has already tried (Figure 8.1). Thus, the likelihood of an innovation being adopted also depends on how people find out about it, and from whom.

Time

The adoption or rejection of an innovation is the result of the innovation-decision process. This process takes time because it follows a sequence of steps that includes knowledge, persuasion, decision, implementation, and confirmation (Rogers, 2003). (In the past, these steps were identified as awareness, interest, trial, decision, and adoption.)

The Innovation-Decision Process

KNOWLEDGE

Common sense tells us that before people can adopt an innovation, they have to know it exists. Knowledge of an innovation is where the communication channels come into play, as discussed previously. Think about how the general public was made aware of the pharmaceutical innovation for erectile dysfunction. Advertisements in magazines, newspapers, TV, direct mail, and disclosure by well-known public figures were all used to inform us about a pharmaceutical innovation to treat a problem many people didn't even know existed.

In 2006, a vaccine against human papillomavirus (HPV) that protects against cervical cancer was introduced for girls and young women aged 9 to 26. Prior to its release, the pharmaceutical company that developed the vaccine began a multimedia "Tell Someone" disease awareness campaign. The campaign was designed to raise awareness of the relationship between HPV and cervical cancer, preparing the U.S. market for the vaccine's release (O'Malley, 2006). Once parents, teens, and young women were made aware of the vaccine's availability, they were able to decide if they would adopt the innovation, that is, be vaccinated. (Unfortunately, the campaign failed to mention that HPV is a sexually transmitted infection and that there are other ways to prevent or reduce infection [O'Malley, 2006].)

PERSUASION

During the persuasion stage, people develop an attitude (either positive or negative) about the innovation (Haider & Kreps, 2004; Rogers, 2003). This comes from having knowledge of or information about the innovation and then mentally applying it to a present or future situation. It is a thought process people go through that helps them formulate a perception of the innovation (Rogers, 2003). It's like trying the innovation on, so to speak.

Persuasion was used when a hospital administration tried to implement an innovative screening program for domestic violence in a postpartum clinic. The clinic staff had to be persuaded of the benefits and appropriateness of the program. They had to be given information that would help them develop a positive attitude toward asking new mothers questions about domestic violence right after they delivered their babies. This was accomplished by having staff engage in training activities that made domestic violence real to them through dialogue with survivors, sharing their own stories, and clinical storytelling (Janssen, Holt, & Sugg, 2002).

Sometimes, opinion leaders are the ones who need to be persuaded about the benefits of an innovation in order to gain access to the people who would be helped most by the innovation. This is what happened in rural Haiti when HIV/AIDS education was introduced. The trusted, influential opinion leaders among this population were voodoo practitioners. They had to be persuaded that preventing HIV/AIDS was easier than trying to cure it. Once these influential people adopted the idea of prevention, they made people in the rural villages accessible, and the message of HIV/AIDS prevention was passed along. (Unfortunately, funding for this project was terminated because "the U.S. government objected to the involvement of voodoo practitioners in the project" [Barker, 2004, p. 133].)

DECISION

Once people have knowledge of an innovation and have developed an attitude toward it, they are ready to make a decision about using it. It is during this stage that people engage in activities that result in a decision to adopt or reject an innovation (Rogers, 2003). This is similar to decisional balance in the Transtheoretical Model.

To support adoption of the postpartum violence program discussed earlier, the program developers provided opportunities for the staff to observe assessments being conducted. Watching new mothers respond in a positive, nonjudgmental way to questions about domestic violence (Janssen, Holt & Sugg, 2002) helped the staff decide to adopt the violence assessment.

Let's look at the "candy" calcium supplements again. Before this method of delivery can be adopted, people need to know about this innovative way to take a mineral supplement and they need a good attitude about eating candy. Trying the supplements would be the activity that would result in the decision to adopt or reject the innovation.

Sometimes, however, even if people decide that an innovation is a good idea, they still decide not to adopt it. Reasons for rejection of an innovation that clearly is beneficial might be cost, conflict with values and beliefs, logistics, or lack of skill needed to use the innovation. For example, even though taking calcium in candy form might be seen as a terrific idea, especially after trying it, it still may not be adopted because it is much more expensive than taking calcium in pill form.

IMPLEMENTATION

The implementation stage occurs when the innovation is tried. Obviously, before people adopt something new, they have to try it to see if they like it. You may have decided that a hybrid car is a terrific innovation, and that you'd like one. But, before you buy a hybrid, you'll take one for a test drive.

Sometimes, even though people decide an innovation is good, they don't try it and consequently don't adopt it. For example, Internet-based cardiac recovery (rehabilitation) interventions are a new way to serve the needs of those who cannot, or who choose not to, attend in-person programs. However, some cardiac clients will not try it, even though they may have decided the idea is good. The reasons are many, including lack of access to the necessary computer equipment, inability to operate a keyboard, and inadequate health literacy (Nguygen et al., 2004).

The implementation stage results in the adoption, rejection, or reinvention of the innovation. If the trial implementation results are positive, adoption takes place, which means the innovation becomes integrated into the individual's lifestyle.

If the trial implementation results in unacceptable outcomes or the innovation is too costly, culturally inconsistent, or logistically not feasible, it will be rejected. In the example of HIV/AIDS in rural Haiti discussed earlier, if the voodoo practitioners had not been persuaded that prevention was easier than curing, then promoting HIV/AIDS prevention in the villages would not have been possible.

However, sometimes the trial implementation results in the need to modify the innovation before it can be adopted. In the domestic violence program discussed previously, a modification would have been to have the new mothers complete a questionnaire rather than be interviewed (Rogers, 2003).

Confirmation

Sometimes the innovation-decision process is completed once the decision is made to either adopt or reject the innovation. Other times, when the decision is made to adopt, people need reinforcement or confirmation from others that it was a good decision. Conflicting messages about the goodness of their decision causes dissonance, or an uncomfortable state of mind (Rogers, 2003) that comes from having made a decision that continues to be questioned or evaluated. We have all done this at one time or another: we make a decision and then continue to question ourselves and others as to whether the decision was a good one or not.

There are times when the decision to adopt is not supported by others, leading to discontinuance or rejection of the innovation. People also discontinue the use of something that was previously adopted when a better "something" comes along to replace it, or if they are dissatisfied with its performance or outcome (Rogers, 2003). Sometimes, instead of discontinuing use of the innovation in these situations, the innovation is reinvented or modified.

A prime example of discontinuance or rejection of a previously adopted innovation is Project DARE (Drug Abuse Resistance Education). Project DARE was implemented in the late 1980s as a way to decrease or eliminate drug use among children and adolescents. Its innovation was having uniformed police officers teach children about the perils of drug use. There was tremendous interest in and adoption of this way to address a growing drug problem. As it turned out, the program was not effective (Dukes, Ullman, & Stein, 1996; Dukes, Stein, & Ullman, 1997; Lynam et al., 1999). Consequently, some schools have modified (reinvented) the program by having only certain lessons taught by a uniformed police officer, whereas others have discontinued its use altogether (Roger, 2003).

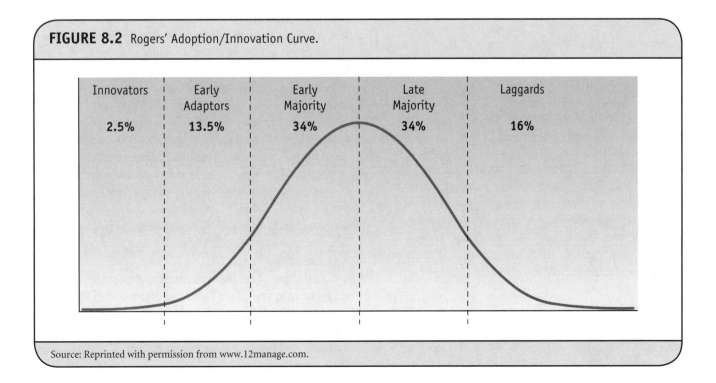

FIGURE 8.2 Rogers' Adoption/Innovation Curve.

Innovators	Early Adaptors	Early Majority	Late Majority	Laggards
2.5%	13.5%	34%	34%	16%

Source: Reprinted with permission from www.12manage.com.

Adoption Curve

In addition to the innovation-decision process, adoption occurs at different rates by different segments of the population. The rate of adoption follows an adoption curve, a bell-shaped curve that sorts people into the following five categories or segments: innovators, early adopters, early majority, late majority, and laggards (Figure 8.2). These segments reflect the amount of time it takes to adopt an innovation. Placement on the curve depends on a number of characteristics, such as comfort with risk taking, socioeconomic status, extent of social networks, and leadership. Where one falls on the adoption curve may differ depending on the innovation.

INNOVATORS

People in the first segment on the curve are the innovators. Innovators represent that small fraction of the population who like to take chances. Innovators are risk takers. They have the financial resources to absorb possible loss from an unprofitable innovation. They are technologically savvy in that they understand and can apply complex technical knowledge, and they can cope with the unpredictability of an innovation (Rogers, 2003).

Innovators are the people who try everything as soon as it is available. They were the first ones to buy an iPod and plasma screen TV, to drive a hybrid, have acupuncture, use solar power, recycle, and eat organic. Innovators tend to be independent, change-oriented risk takers who are inclined to interact with others like themselves rather than a broad cross section of the population. In fact, going back to the Lasik example used earlier, people who are risk takers are considered good candidates for this procedure (FDA, 2004).

EARLY ADOPTERS

Early adopters make up the next segment on the adoption curve. They represent a slightly larger portion of the population than do the innovators. Early adopters tend to be the opinion leaders in a community. They are well respected and are often seen as role models. They have a powerful influence over others because they are often the people others like to emulate. They usually have high self-esteem and complex communication networks. They talk to and know a lot of different people and therefore have a broad influence in the community (Rogers, 2003).

EARLY MAJORITY

The early majority represents one of the largest segments of the population. On the bell curve, they are part of the inclin-

ing side of the bell. They are greatly influenced by opinion leaders and mass media. Although they do adopt new things, they do so over time. But, given their sheer number, when they begin to adopt, the innovation becomes mainstream (Rogers, 2003).

LATE MAJORITY

The late majority is on the downward side of the bell curve. These people tend to question change, choosing to wait until an innovation is an established norm or for it to become a social or economic necessity. They tend to have more modest financial resources and to be greatly influenced by their peers (Rogers, 2003). These are the people who only recently bought a cell phone and a DVD player.

LAGGARDS

The last group on the curve is the laggards. Laggards tend to be conservative and traditional, have lower self-esteem, have less education, are suspicious of innovation, and are adverse to risk taking. They also tend to be geographically mobile and detached from the social environment. Laggards are the last group of people to adopt an innovation. They wait until very late, even when it's obvious that the innovation is advantageous (Rogers, 2003). These would be the people who just bought their first computer.

Social System

The fourth construct in Diffusion of Innovation is the social system. A social system can be individuals, an informal or formal group of people, or organizations that are interrelated and engaged in solving a joint problem to accomplish a goal (Backer & Rogers, 1998; Rogers, 2003). Examples of social systems are the physicians in a hospital, the families in a community, or consumers in the United States. All units in a social system, whether they are individuals (such as the physicians in the hospital) or a collective entity (such as each family in a community), cooperate with each other to reach a common goal. It is the common goal that holds them together (Rogers, 2003). Social systems are essentially different groupings of people. As such, they also include the norms, values, beliefs, attitudes, and other common characteristics of the people who comprise the system. Diffusion takes place within these social systems (Rogers, 2003).

Diffusion of an innovation through a social system is exemplified by the CDC's Business Responds to AIDS (BRTA) program. BRTA was a way to bring HIV/AIDS prevention education to the workplace and, through this effort, prevent discrimination against people with HIV/AIDS at work.

FIGURE 8.3 Diffusion of Innovation.

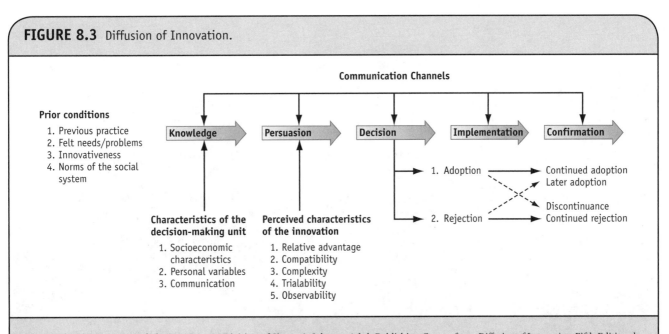

The social system through which this program was diffused included all private companies in the United States (Backer & Rogers, 1998).

The Kitchen Garden Project in the South Central Asian country of Nepal is another example of diffusion of an innovation through a social system. The social system used here was neighborhoods. The project was implemented to combat the country's high infant and maternal mortality rates, which were due mostly to inadequate vitamin A intake. The innovation was to have individual households in neighborhoods plant gardens to grow their own high vitamin A–containing fruits and vegetables (Barker, 2004).

In summary, according to Diffusion of Innovation, the characteristics of an innovation—how it is made known, how long it takes for a decision to be made about it, and the group structure into which it is being introduced—all affect its adoption and, therefore, behavior (Figure 8.3).

Diffusion of Innovation Constructs Chart

Innovation	The new idea, product, process, etc.
Communication channels	Methods through which the innovation is made known to the members of the social system
Time	How much time it takes for the innovation-decision process to occur, and the rate at which different segments of the social system adopt the innovation
Social system	The group structure into which the innovation is being introduced

Innovators spread the word about an innovation through interpersonal communication channels.

Diffusion of Innovations and HIV/AIDS

JANE T. BERTRAND

Bloomberg School of Public Health, Center for Communication Programs,
Johns Hopkins University, Baltimore, Maryland, USA

ABSTRACT

As the HIV/AIDS epidemic continues its relentless spread in many parts of the world, DOI provides a useful framework for analyzing the difficulties in achieving behavior change necessary to reduce HIV rates. The DOI concepts most relevant to this question include communication channels, the innovation-decision process, homophily, the attributes of the innovation, adopter categories, and opinion leaders. The preventive measures needed to halt the transmission of HIV constitute a "preventive innovation." This article describes the attributes of this preventive innovation in terms of relative advantage, compatibility, complexity, trialability, and observability. It reviews studies that incorporated DOI into HIV/AIDS behavior change interventions, both in Western countries and in the developing world. Finally, it discusses possible reasons that the use of DOI has been fairly limited to date in HIV/AIDS prevention interventions in developing countries.

THE CHALLENGE OF HIV/AIDS

HIV/AIDS has emerged as the greatest public health challenge in contemporary times. Given the lack of a vaccine or cure, behavior change is the only means to curb the further spread of this epidemic. In the vast majority of afflicted countries, the primary route of transmission is sexual. In response, many countries have instituted prevention efforts focused on the ABCs: abstinence, being faithful, and condom use. However, transmission by injection drug use has fueled the epidemic in other parts of the world, especially in the former Soviet Union and parts of Asia, including India and China. Needle exchange programs—to avoid the reuse of infected needles—are the response of choice to reduce the rate of infection in such countries. The epidemic initially spreads within subgroups of the population with high-risk behaviors, including commercial sex workers, migrant workers, truck drivers, and injec-tion drug users. As HIV rates increase among these groups, the epidemic slowly progresses into the general population through sexual transmission from these groups to spouses, casual partners, and others. Indeed, once the HIV prevalence rate reaches five percent in a given country, the epidemic has generalized into the larger population and becomes much more difficult to contain.

The HIV/AIDS epidemic continues to advance at a relentless pace. Over 40 million persons were infected with the HIV virus as of 2002; over 70% live in sub-Saharan Africa. Five African countries have an HIV prevalence of over 20%. The two demographic giants in Asia—China and India—have relatively low prevalence rates, but the number of persons infected runs into the millions (UNAIDS, 2002). Eastern Europe and Central Asia have the fastest growing regional epidemics, with the number skyrocketing from an estimated 5000 cases in 1990 to 1 million in 2001 (Lamptey, Wigley, Carr, Colleymore, 2002).

San Francisco was one of the first communities to recognize the threat of the HIV/AIDS epidemic, and in the early 1980s members of the gay community mobilized to educate and persuade others to practice safer sex. The results were dramatic, and demonstrated the potential of political advocacy and community mobilization to halt the spread of HIV/AIDS.

In the developing world, only four countries to date have successfully reduced HIV rates or blocked the spread of the virus into the general population. Thailand and Uganda dramatically reduced levels of HIV/AIDS in the 1990s, and descriptions of these successes are frequent in the HIV/AIDS literature (Hogle et al., 2002; Singhal and Rogers, 2003; Stein-fatt, 2002). Cambodia has shown more modest reductions, but appears to be following the Thai model. And Senegal, with an HIV prevalence less than 1%, has been successful in blocking the entry of HIV into the general population. However, these countries represent the exception to the rule. Despite millions of dollars that have gone into prevention programs, the majority of developing countries have not been able to curb the spread of the epidemic.

Why has HIV/AIDS been so difficult to stop? The public health community has had dramatic success in other areas of public health requiring behavior change, such as family planning, control of diarrhea through oral rehydration salts, use of Vitamin B, and immunization. However, behavior change for HIV/AIDS has proven far more problematic.

Diffusion of Innovations (DOI) Theory provides useful insight into the difficulty of achieving the behavior change necessary to curb the HIV/AIDS epidemic in developing countries. This paper uses elements of DOI to examine both the lack of success in changing behavior that has resulted in the continued spread of HIV/AIDS in much of the developing world, and in the successful programmatic initiatives that have come to be known as the San Francisco model. Finally, we address the question: why is DOI generally absent from the vast literature on HIV/AIDS prevention in developing countries, with a few notable exceptions described below?

DIFFUSION OF INNOVATIONS CONCEPTS RELEVANT TO HIV/AIDS PREVENTION

The Diffusion of Innovations is characterized by four elements: an innovation, communicated via certain channels, over a period of time, to members of a social system (Rogers, 1995). The innovation refers to an idea, practice, or object that is perceived as new to an individual. The DOI literature is replete with examples of successful innovations: hybrid corn, modern math, new prescription drugs, and family planning, to name a few. However, the changes in behavior needed to halt the HIV/AIDS epidemic constitute what Rogers has labeled a "preventive innovation," defined as "an idea that an individual adopts at one point in time in order to lower the probability that some future unwanted event may occur" (Rogers, 2003). In countries where HIV transmission occurs primarily through sexual relations, the specific behaviors include abstinence, being faithful (to an uninfected partner), or condom use—known as the "ABCs." In countries with a high level of injection drug use, the behavior change intervention includes both needle exchange for injection drug users and adherence to the ABCs. For the sake of brevity, this paper will focus on the ABCs only.

Although the theory of DOI is very comprehensive, Rao and Svenkerud (1998) have identified the six DOI concepts that are most relevant to HIV/AIDS prevention:

- **Communication** channels are the means by which a message is transmitted from one person to another.
- **The innovation-decision** process is an over-time sequence through which a target audience member passes. This sequence has five stages:
  1. awareness,
  2. knowledge,
  3. persuasion,
  4. adoption, and
  5. implementation.
- **Homophily** is the extent to which two or more people who communicate perceive that they are similar to one another.
- An **attribute** is a characteristic of the innovation that may be perceived either positively or negatively; these include:
  - relative advantage
  - comparability
  - complexity
  - trialability
  - observability
- **Adopter categories** or classifications of individual groups on the basis of relative time at which they adopted a new idea, technique, or process.
- **Opinion leaders** are people who are respected for their knowledge and reputation on some particular topic.

These concepts provide a useful framework for analyzing the effectiveness of programs in the handful of countries that have been successful, as well as the failure of prevention efforts to halt the epidemic in the majority of afflicted countries.

USE OF DOI AS A FRAMEWORK FOR HIV/AIDS PREVENTION

There is no single theory that informs or guides the development of HIV/AIDS prevention programs. Indeed, many different theories have emerged, both to design programs and to evaluate their effectiveness (King, 1999; McKee et al., forthcoming). King (1999) classifies these different theories in one of three categories:

1. focus on individual change,
2. social theories and models, and
3. structural and environmental.

DOI corresponds to the second category, given that it explains how a new practice can diffuse through a given social system to the point it becomes a social norm. As Rogers explained (1995), when "trend setters" in a social group begin to model a new behavior to others, they alter the perception of what is normative. Subsequently, others will begin to adopt the new behavior. Ultimately, community members, regardless of whether they have had contact with the original trendsetters, are expected to adopt the new behavior as it diffuses throughout the community's social networks. Members of the social system in question pass through the stages of the innovation-decision process (awareness, knowledge, persuasion, adoption, and implementation) at different rates, leading to the well-known categories of acceptors: from innovators to laggards.

The early experience with HIV/AIDS in the United States lends credence to this theory. DOI was central to one of the most effective HIV/AIDS prevention programs to date: STOP AIDS in San Francisco. The intervention program drew on Kurt Lewin's small Group Communication Theory and the Diffusion of Innovation Theory (Singhal & Rogers, 2003). In the early 1980s, gay men in San Francisco took action to combat this deadly disease that had hit their community with brutal force. STOP AIDS began by conducting focus groups to learn how much gay men already knew about HIV/AIDS (Wohlfeiler, 1998) as a basis for designing effective interventions. However, the founders soon realized that the focus groups were having a strong educational effect, as men shared information about HIV prevention. STOP AIDS then employed a group of outreach workers from the gay community to conduct small group meeting in homes and apartments throughout the gay neighborhoods, which launched the diffusion process. From 1985 to 1987, STOP AIDS reached 30,000 men through its various outreach activities (Singhal & Rogers, 2003).

According to DOI and as shown in San Francisco, only those early adopters, who make up a relatively small segment of the population, need to initiate a new behavior for it to spread throughout the population (Wohlfeiler, 1998). In the case of STOP AIDS, a well-respected individual who was seropositive led the session attended by other gay and bi-sexual men. He would explain how the virus spreads and encourage participants to either use condoms or seek monogamous relationships. At the end of each session, participants were asked to make a pledge to safer sex, and to volunteer to organize and lead future small group meetings with gay men. Concurrently with the small group meetings, media campaigns helped to increase awareness and knowledge of HIV/AIDS among the gay community. The rate of new infections dropped precipitously by the mid-1980s. Curiously, attendance at the STOP AIDS meetings fell off, and STOP AIDS found it difficult to recruit new volunteers. The program had reached the critical mass of early adopters of safer sex. In 1987, STOP AIDS declared victory and discontinued its local operation, only to reopen in 1990 for new cohorts of younger gay men migrating to the city (Singhal & Rogers, 2003).

Unquestionably, the San Francisco experience demonstrated the power of diffusion and the importance of DOI concepts such as homophily and opinion leaders. STOP AIDS had effectively recruited staff who were part of the community to serve as outreach workers. The opinion leaders within the gay community championed the cause, despite the fear of negative publicity it could bring to the gay community.

One cannot attribute the success of the San Francisco program exclusively to DOI. Indeed, it relied heavily on the epidemiological concept of targeting a group at high risk of spreading the disease, and it utilized other strategies such as Lewin's theories of the social psychology of individual behavior change. However, the experience of San Francisco was sufficiently compelling to lead Kelly and colleagues to study other interventions among gay men in different U.S. communities.

Kelly and his colleagues adapted the San Francisco model to reach gay men in small U.S. cities through bars that served as a major congregating point for this group in these cities. The model called for identifying the natural opinion leaders in the community and enlisting them to endorse behavior change. The intervention consisted of four steps:

1. bar staff were trained to identify natural "opinion leaders" among bar patrons;
2. patrons who had been independently nominated by several bar staff were recruited into the project as opinion leaders;
3. opinion leaders were trained in basic communication skills; and
4. contracts were made with opinion leaders to have a specified number of conversations with peers following the training sessions.

Researchers surveyed bar patrons in both intervention and comparison cities, before and after the intervention. These bar-based opinion leader interventions produced community-level adoption of condom use in two-city and three-city comparison group studies (Kelly, St. Lawrence, Diaz, et al., 1991; Kelly, St. Lawrence, Stevenson, et al., 1992) and in a multi-city randomized field trial (Kelly, Winett et al., 1993). Kelly et al.'s work (1991, 1992, 1993) underscores that the nature of urban gay male bar networks provides a particularly powerful place in which diffusion might occur. It also acknowledges the important role that perceived peer norms play in influencing individuals' behavior (Miller et al., 1998).

Inspired by the Kelly et al. research and by Diffusion of Innovation Theory, Miller et al. (1998) attempted to replicate and adapt the bar-based intervention with male prostitutes and other patrons in New York City "hustler" bars. Moreover, these researchers were more systematic in establishing and testing the underlying theoretical model for the intervention. As with the Kelly et al. (1991, 1992, 1993) studies, they sought to alter peer norms to encourage safer sexual behavior by having opinion leaders endorse these behaviors with their peers. Analysis of data on a sample of 1741 male prostitutes and bar patrons indicated significant reductions in paid, unprotected sexual intercourse and oral sex following the intervention. The changes were generally small, though statistically significant. However, the study failed to demonstrate that peer norms mediated the relationship between intervention and behavior.

DOI was also used in the design and evaluation of a study among gay men in London. Elford et al. (2002) noted that the most rigorous studies to date on HIV/AIDS prevention among gay men were all U.S.-based, and they set out to replicate the work for gays in London. However, instead of bars, Elford et al. (2002) tested the design in gyms that gay men frequented. However, they were not able to replicate the significant change in behavior found in the earlier studies among gay men, possibly because the peer educators found it difficult to approach clients and discuss HIV/AIDS in the atmosphere of the gym.

If HIV/AIDS prevention proved so effective in San Francisco in the early 1980s, why then has the epidemic continued to spread so virulently in many countries around the world, infecting over a third of the population in the most extreme cases? Unquestionably, numerous factors favored the intervention in San Francisco: the gay men were highly educated, had a very cohesive sense of community, and had pre-established media channels that targeted the gay community. Moreover, they could focus high levels of energy on this one problem, in contrast to persons in developing countries who must simultaneously struggle with hunger, unemployment, inadequate housing, and other consequences of poverty.

DOI provides useful insights into the failure of prevention efforts in many developing countries worldwide, as outlined below.

WHY HAS BEHAVIOR CHANGE (THE ABCS) BEEN SO DIFFICULT IN DEVELOPING COUNTRIES?

As mentioned above, a handful of countries in the developing world have been successful in curbing the spread of HIV/AIDS: Thailand, Uganda, Senegal, and, to a lesser extent, Cambodia. Zambia appears to be making progress as well. Yet in contrast to these few nations, the vast majority of developing countries affected by HIV/AIDS have been unsuccessful in reducing their HIV rates.

DOI theory provides a compelling rationale for the failure of prevention efforts throughout much of the developing world. According to DOI, the pace of diffusion relates directly to the five attributes (characteristics) of the innovation, described earlier. If we consider these five attributes in relation to the ABCs, it becomes clear why this "preventive innovation" has been slow to diffuse in the large majority of developing countries.

Relative advantage is the degree to which an innovation is perceived as better than the idea it supersedes. In the case of HIV/AIDS, we are asking sexually active individuals to adopt safer sex practices or forgo sex for a period of time. To do so requires foregoing (or reducing) the pleasure associated with a fundamental biological drive. Adoption of innovations is more rapid when the innovation confers prestige, convenience, or satisfaction. Safer sex confers none of these. Indeed, for a young woman struggling to survive or feed her children, risky transactional sex (*not* abstinence) offers the greater advantage, at least in the short term.

Compatibility is the degree to which an innovation is perceived as being consistent with the existing values, past experiences, and needs of potential adopters. By contrast, the practice of safer sex (or no sex) often challenges the existing value structure. For example, a woman's negotiating for condom use would be taken as a direct affront to the male's position of dominance in sexual decision-making in many societies. Remaining faithful or limiting the number of partners is contrary to "past experience" in societies that condone multiple sexual partners for males, including visits to commercial sex workers, as well as for females in some societies. By contrast, in many societies it is high-risk behaviors—including multiple sexual partners, visits to commercial sex workers, dry sex, unprotected sex, and transactional sex—that fulfill the immediate needs of the population in question.

Complexity is the degree to which an innovation is perceived as difficult to understand and use. Whereas the behaviors that comprise the ABCs are not particularly complex, they are difficult to sustain over an extended period. Young, sexually active adults must maintain constant vigilance over a 30–50 year period if they are to avoid HIV infection. The burden is onerous and for many of those buying condoms, expensive.

Trialability is the degree to which an innovation may be experimented with on a limited basis. Of the five attributes of an innovation, trialability is perhaps the least problematic. A person can experiment with the ABCs on a trial basis. Young people can attempt to delay sexual debut; spouses can commit to being faithful; those who are unable to abstain or remain monogamous can try to use the condom and decide whether it works for them. Thus, the ABCs do offer trialability. Yet trialability is closely linked to observability, on which the ABCs score low.

Observability is the degree to which the results of an innovation are visible to others. In contrast to the early diffusion experiments with hybrid corn in rural Iowa, in which farmers could readily observe the improvements available from adopting a new type of corn, the ABCs do not produce a readily observable outcome. Indeed, the ultimate goal (avoiding HIV infection) is a non-event that is highly desired but low on immediate, tangible rewards. It is particularly difficult to convince sexually active individuals that practicing safer sex is worth the sacrifice, given that they may not get infected anyway. Moreover, the problem itself is not observable; and if they do contract HIV, the symptoms of AIDS may not surface for years to come.

In short, HIV/AIDS prevention provides a textbook example of how the attributes of the innovation can affect its rate of diffusion. The handful of success stories indicates that it is possible to overcome the obstacles outlined above, but the challenge is immense.

USE OF DOI FOR THE DESIGN AND IMPLEMENTATION OF HIV/AIDS INTERVENTIONS IN DEVELOPING COUNTRIES

Despite the utility of DOI in explaining the slow diffusion of the ABCs in developing countries, DOI Theory has played a relatively small role in prevention programs in developing countries. It is often cited as one of the theories that underscores the design or evaluation of HIV/AIDS prevention efforts (King, 1999; McKee et al., forth-coming). Yet there are surprisingly few citations to DOI in the vast literature of HIV/AIDS prevention in the developing world.

One exception is the study by Rao and Svenkerud (1998), who analyzed the extent to which relatively more effective and relatively less effective HIV/AIDS prevention programs in San Francisco and Bangkok used Diffusion of Innovations Theory and Social Marketing Theory in reaching culturally unique populations. In Bangkok, as in San Francisco, the programs recruited members of unique populations (e.g., commercial sex workers in the case of Thailand) to reach peers with life-saving information about HIV/AIDS and condom use. With respect to DOI, the authors concluded that program administrators should use outreach workers who are either homophilous with the intended audience or are opinion leaders in the community.

A second exception is the study by Celentano et al. (2000), also from Thailand, which tested the diffusion model in a different way. The researchers designed a field experiment among Royal Thai Army conscripts, including an intervention group, a "diffusion group" (men housed in barracks at the same base but who did not receive the intervention) and controls at a distant base. The intervention promoted condom use, reduced alcohol consumption and brothel patronage, and improved sexual negotiation and condom skills. Whereas the intervention reduced sexually transmitted diseases among the intervention group, it did not produce results in the diffusion group.

Celentano and colleagues are currently involved in a five-country randomized trial of DOI through popular opinion leaders in China, India, Peru, Russia, and Zimbabwe (Celentano, personal communication). However, the research is ongoing, and the results are not yet available.

Given the relevance of numerous elements (e.g., homophily, channels of communication, attributes of the program, information-decision process) and mention of DOI as a key theory for HIV/AIDS prevention in several review articles, why is DOI not more prominent in the literature on HIV/AIDS in developing countries?

Several explanations seem plausible. First, DOI is largely a sociological theory that uses social roles, norms, and networks to explain behavior. It does not provide an answer to the key question "what triggers a given individual to action?" Rather, those designing programs have tended to look to the psychosocial theories for guidance on changing deeply rooted sexual mores and behaviors (e.g., the Health Belief Model, Theory of Reasoned Action, Social Learning [modeling] theory, and Prochaska's stages of change theory, to name a few).

Second, the DOI model implies a certain rationality of purpose and sequencing of behavior (i.e., awareness, knowledge, persuasion, adoption, and implementation). Adoption of safer sex diffused effectively through the highly educated, cohesive community of gay men in San Francisco. However, critics of Western-based models are quick to point out that sexual behavior is often irrational (Airhihenbuwa & Obregon, 2000; UNAIDS, 1999). Emotions and sexual arousal may overtake the best of intentions (Perloff, 1995), especially where alcohol, drugs, or fear of violence are also involved. Given that adolescents represent a major target audience for prevention programs in developing countries worldwide, this criticism is particularly relevant.

Third, structural and environmental factors strongly influence sexual behavior (Sweat & Denison, 1995). Migrant workers and truck drivers by definition live apart from their families for significant portions of time, increasing their likelihood of seeking out other partners. Poverty causes the families of young girls to sell them into prostitution, and it prompts mothers to accept transactional sex to provide the bare essentials for their children. School girls whose parents can't afford school fees are more vulnerable to the advances of "sugar daddies." As Perloff (1995) stated, "individuals simply may not be in a position to undo the circumstances that led them to the activity in the first place."

Fourth, cultural norms also dictate sexual behavior. As Singhal & Rogers (2003) explained, culture can be a barrier or a facilitator in controlling the epidemic. One aspect of culture—the role of women in a given society—is recognized as central to HIV/AIDS prevention. In many societies the inferior status of women makes them particularly vulnerable to HIV/AIDS. A faithful wife who suspects her husband of having multiple partners cannot refuse to have sexual relations with him or negotiate condom use. Young women are often the victims of forced sexual relations, including by members of their own family. Indeed, there is a growing literature on sexual violence related to women's efforts to protect themselves from HIV/AIDS.

Fifth, leaders in a position to be highly influential at the local or national level may not model appropriate behavior. Such individuals lose their credibility by preaching one behavior but practicing another (e.g., the school teacher who teaches about responsible sexual behavior but then seduces his students after class). A similar problem arises when a prominent national figure engages in high-risk behavior (e.g., the King of Swaziland, who takes on a new adolescent wife every year, implicitly legitimizing the practice of multiple sexual partners).

Sixth, the innovation-decision process may derail in the face of new situations. For example, the introduction of antiretroviral drugs has caused many young gay men to let down their guard vis-a-vis preventive behaviors. They may be highly knowledgeable about the HIV risk, but the introduction of drugs has caused them to minimize this risk. Some gay men may perceive certain benefits of being HIV positive, such as a strong sense of community with others living with HIV/AIDS and special medical treatment for those participating in clinical trials.

In sum, the preventive interventions for HIV/AIDS increasingly address the context in which behavior change must take place. This approach is highly consistent with Roger's basic definition of the elements of DOI: an innovation, communicated via certain channels, over a period of time, to members of a social system (Rogers, 1995). Certain concepts from DOI have been central to prevention initiatives in countries worldwide (e.g., homophily, communication channels,

opinion leadership). One possible reason that DOI has not been more prominent in the literature on HIV/AIDS prevention in developing countries is that it recognizes context as an important factor but does not provide explicit guidance on addressing the social, cultural, and economic obstacles related to context. Another reason is the seeming preference for cognitive or psychosocial models that directly address the question: "What triggers behavior?" As the field of prevention gradually shifts from a predominant focus on individual behavior to recognition of the importance of social norms in defining sexual behavior, DOI may reemerge as a useful theory in the fight against HIV/AIDS.

REFERENCES

Airhihenbuwa, C. O., & Obregon, R. (2000). A critical assessment of theories/models in health communication for HIV/AIDS. *Journal of Health Communication, 5,* 5–15. Celentano, D. (2003, personal communication).

Celentano, D., Bond, K. C., Lyles, C. M., Eiumtrakul, S., Go, V., Beyrer, C., Chiangmai, C., Nelson, K., Kahamboonruang, C., & Vaddhanaphuti, C. (2000). Preventive intervention to reduce sexually transmitted infections. A field trial in the Royal Thai Army. *Archives of Internal Medicine, 160,* 535–540.

Elford, J., Sherr, L., Bolding, G., Serle, F., & Maguire, M. (2002). Peer-led HIV prevention among gay men in London: Process evaluation. *AIDS CARE, 14*(3), 351–360.

Hogue, Jan (ed). (2002). Project lessons learned case study: What happened in Uganda? In *Declining HIV prevalence, behavior change, and the national response.* Washington, DC: The Synergy Project. pp. 1–13.

Kelly, J. A., St. Lawrence, J. S., Diaz, Y. E., Stevenson, L. Y., Hauth, A. C., Brasfield, T. L., Kalichman, S. C., Smith, J. C., & Andrew, M. E. (1991). HIV risk behavior reduction following intervention with key opinion leaders of population: an experimental analysis. *American Journal of Public Health, 81,* 168–171.

Kelly, J. A., St. Lawrence, J. S., Stevenson, L. Y., Hauth, A. C., Kalichman, S. C., Diaz, Y. C., Brasfield, T. L., Koob, J. J., & Morgan, M. G. (1992). Community AIDS/HIV risk reduction: The effects of endorsements by popular people in three cities. *American Journal of Public Health, 82,* 1483–1489.

Kelly, J. A., Winett, R. A., Roffman, R. A., Solomon, L. J., Sikkema, K. J., Kalichman, S. C., Stevenson, L. Y., Koob, J. J., Desiderato, L. J., Perry, M. J., Norman, A. D., Lemke, A. L., Hauth, A. C., Flynn, B. S., Yaffe, D. M., Steinder, S., & Morgan, M. G. (1993). Social diffusion models can produce population-level HIV risk behavior reduction: Field trial results and mechanisms underlying change. Paper presented at 9th International Conference on AIDS, Berlin, June.

King, R. 1999. Sexual behavior change for HIV: Where have theories taken us? Geneva: UNAIDS.

Lamptey, P., Wigley, M., Carr, D., & Collymore, Y. (2002). Facing the AIDS pandemic. *Population Bulletin, 57*(3), 3–38.

McKee, N., Bertrand, J. T., & Benton-Becker, A. (forthcoming 2004). *Strategic communication in the HIV/AIDS epidemic.* New Delhi: Sage Publications.

Miller, R. L., Klotz, D., & Eckholdt, H. M. (1998). HIV prevention with male prostitutes and patrons of hustler bars: Replication of an HIV preventive intervention. *American Journal of Community Psychology, 26*(1), 97–131.

Perloff, R. M. (2001). *Persuading people to have safer sex. Applications of social science to the AIDS crisis.* Mahwah, NJ: Lawrence Erlbaum Associates.

Rao, N., & Svenkerud, P. J. (1998). Effective HIV/AIDS prevention communication strategies to reach culturally unique populations: Lessons learned in San Francisco, U.S.A. and Bangkok, Thailand. *International Journal of Intercultural Relations, 22*(1), 85–105.

Rogers, E. M. (1995). *Diffusion of innovations* (4th ed.). New York: Free Press.

Rogers, E. M. (2003). *Diffusion of innovations* (5th ed.). New York: Free Press.

Singhal, A., & Rogers, E. (2003). *Combating AIDS: Communication strategies in action.* New Delhi: Sage Publications.

Steinfatt, T. M. (2002). *Working at the bar: Sex work and health communication in Thailand.* Westport, CT: Ablex.

Svenkerud, P. J., & Singhal, A. (1998). Enhancing the effectiveness of HIV/AIDS prevention programs targeted to unique population groups in Thailand: Lessons learned from applying concepts of diffusion of innovations and social marketing. *Journal of Health Communication, 3,* 193–216.

Sweat, M., & Dennison, J. (1995). Reducing HIV incidence in developing countries with structural and environmental interventions. AIDS 9,(suppl A), S251–S257.

UNAIDS (2002). Report on the Global HIV/AIDS epidemic. Geneva: Joint United Nations Programme on HIV/AIDS.

Wohlfeiler, D. (1998). Community organizing and community building among gay and bisexual men: The STOP AIDS Project. In M. Minkler (ed.), *Community organizing and community building for health* (pp. 230–243).

Article Source: Bertrand, J. (2004). Diffusion of Innovation and HIV/AIDS. *Journal of Health Communication, 9,* 113–121. Reprinted with permission.

QUESTIONS

1. What were the relative advantages of the innovation identified in the article?
2. Which advantages were in the article that you didn't think of?
3. What were the compatibility issues you identified? How did these compare with the ones identified in the article?
4. How complex did you perceive this innovation to be? How and why was your assessment the same or different from what was proposed in the article?
5. To what extent did you determine trialability to be an issue in the adoption of this innovation? How did your assessment compare with the assessment presented in the article?
6. To what extent did you determine that this innovation is observable? How does your assessment of this match with the one presented in the article?
7. Compare your assessment of the likelihood of adoption of this innovation with that presented in the article. Is there a difference of opinion, and if so, why?

CHAPTER REFERENCES

Barker, K. (2004). Diffusion of Innovations: A world tour. *Journal of Health Communication, 9,* 131–137.

Backer, T.E., & Rogers, E.M. (1998). Diffusion of innovation theory and work-site AIDS programs. *Journal of Health Communication, 3,* 17–28.

Burke, J. (2004). Infant HIV infection: Acceptability of preventive strategies on Tanzania. *AIDS Education and Prevention, 16*(5), 415–425.

Centers for Disease Control and Prevention. (2007). Cover your cough. Retrieved March 17, 2007, from http://cdc.gov/flu/protect/covercough.htm.

Dukes, R.L., Stein, J.A., & Ullman, J.B. (1997). Long-term impact of Drug Abuse Resistance Education (D.A.R.E.). *Evaluation Review, 21,* 483–500.

Dukes, R.L., Ullman, J.B., & Stein, J.A. (1996). A three-year follow-up of Drug Abuse Resistance Education (D.A.R.E.). *Evaluation Review, 20,* 49–66.

Eshkevari, L., & Heath, J. (2005). Use of acupuncture for chronic pain. *Holistic Nursing Practice, 19*(5), 217–221.

Food and Drug Administration. (2004). Lasik eye surgery. Retrieved December 5, 2004, from http://www.fda.gov/cdrh/LASIK/default.htm.

Haider, M., & Kreps, G. (2004). Forty years of Diffusion of Innovations: Utility and value in public health. *Journal of Health Communication, 9,* 3–11.

Hollander, D. (2004). Long-term use of female condom may hinge partly on depth of instruction. *International Family Planning Perspectives, 30*(1). Retrieved December 8, 2004, from http://www.agi-usa.org/pubs/journals/3004904b.html.

Israel-Ballard, K., Chantry, C., Dewey, K., Lonnerdal, B., Sheppard, H., Donovan, R., Carlson, J., Sage, A., & Abrams, B. (2005). Viral, nutritional, and bacterial safety of flash-heated and pretoria-pasteurized breast milk to prevent mother-to-child transmission of HIV in resource-poor countries: A pilot study. *Journal of Acquired Immune Deficiency Syndromes, 40*(2), 175–181.

Janssen, P.A., Holt, V.L., & Sugg, N.K. (2002). Introducing domestic violence assessment in a postpartum clinical setting. *Maternal and Child Health Journal, 6*(3), 195–203.

Kane, M., & Mittman, R. (2002). *Diffusion of Innovation in Health Care.* Oakland, CA: California HealthCare Foundation. Retrieved October 30, 2004, from http://www.chcf.org/documents/ihealth/DiffusionofInnovation.pdf.

Lounsbury, B. (2006). Why don't we do it in our sleeves? Retrieved March 17, 2007, from http://www.coughsafe.com/index.html.

Lynam, D.R., Milich, R., Zimmerman, R., Novak, S.P., Logan, T.K., Martin, C., Leukefeld, C., & Clayton, R. (1999). Project DARE: No effects at ten year follow-up. *Journal of Consulting and Clinical Psychology, 67*(4), 590–593.

McCarthy, K.A., & Milus, T. (2000). Patient education viewed through the lens of Diffusion of Innovations research. *Topics in Clinical Chiropractic, 7*(4), 15–24.

National Cancer Institute. (2003). *Theory at a Glance: A Guide for Health Promotion Practice.* Washington, DC: U.S. Department of Health and Human Services.

Nguygen, H.Q., Carrieri-Kohlman, V., Rankin, S.H., Slaughter, R., & Stubarg, M.S. (2004). Supporting cardiac recovery through health technology. *Journal of Cardiac Nursing, 19*, 200–208.

O'Malley, K. (2006, June 13). Merck & Co: The marketing machine behind Gardasil. *Pharmaceutical Business Review.* Retrieved May 25, 2007, from http://www.pharmaceutical-business-review.com/article_feature .asp?guid=463AB18E-B911-4CC6-BD44-FB9CC69C6561.

Piot, P. (1998). *The Female Condom and AIDS: UNAIDS Point of View.* Geneva: UNAIDS. Retrieved October 30, 2004, from ftp://lists.inet.co.th/ pub/sea-aids/gend/gend129.txt.

Rogers, E.M. (2003). *Diffusion of Innovation.* New York: Free Press.

Rogers, E.M. (2004). A prospective and retrospective look at the diffusion model. *Journal of Health Communication, 9*, 13–19.

Rogers, E.M., & Scott, K.L. (1997). The Diffusion of Innovations model and outreach from the National Network of Libraries of Medicine to Native American communities. Retrieved October 30, 2004, from http://nnlm. gov/pnr/eval/rogers.html.

Ryan, B., & Gross, N. (1943). The diffusion of hybrid seed corn in two Iowa communities. *Rural Sociology, 8*, 15–24.

Yee, D. (2007). Hand sanitizers becoming popular. Retrieved March 17, 2007, from http://www.abqtrib.com/news/2007/jan/05/hand-sanitizer-becoming-popular.

CHAPTER 9

Emerging Theories

Theory Essence Sentences

Ecological models: Factors at many levels influence health behavior.

Social Capital Theory: Behavior is influenced by who we know and how we know them.

STUDENT LEARNING OUTCOMES

After reading this chapter the student will be able to:

1. Explain how ecological models differ from other theories and models.

2. Discuss the different levels of factors used in ecological models.

3. Give an example of factors at each level in ecological models.

4. Use an ecological approach to explain one of their health behaviors.

5. Discuss the ideas that form the basis of Social Capital Theory.

6. Differentiate among the three types of relationships in Social Capital Theory.

7. Use Social Capital Theory to explain one of their health behaviors.

ECOLOGICAL MODELS

In the preceding chapters, we have seen the many ways in which health behavior can be explained. The explanations are based on many factors, categorized as being either internal, such as beliefs, attitudes, skills, perceptions, and expectations, or external in the social environment, such as social supports, significant others, models, and rewards or consequences. Similar to the other theories and models, ecological models also explain behavior using these same factors. The difference is that ecological models use both internal and external factors, rather than one or the other. In addition, ecological models view the external environment as being composed of not only the social but also the physical environment (Sallis & Owen, 1997), focusing on environmental causes of behavior. Therefore, when ecological models are used in health promotion, the intent is to change the environment (social or physical), since changes in the environment change individual behavior (McLeroy et al., 1988).

Because ecological models are a point of view or perspective, they do not have constructs per se, unlike the other theories and models (Sallis & Owen, 2002). The internal and external factors that underpin behavior are presented as levels (McLeroy et al., 1988). Perceptually, these levels are like concentric circles (Figure 9.1), with the smallest at the center representing the internal or intrapersonal level; moving to the external levels, which include the interpersonal level; and widening to the community, institutional, and finally the societal level. The basis of ecological models is the recognition that the dynamic interplay among the various factors at dif-

FIGURE 9.1 An ecological model.

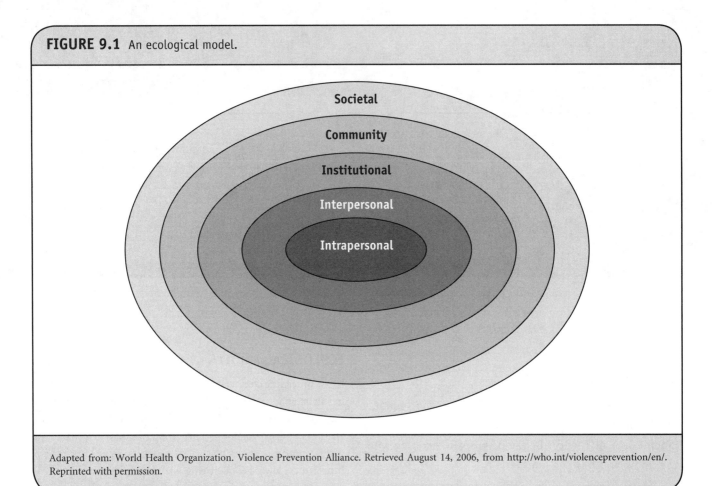

Adapted from: World Health Organization. Violence Prevention Alliance. Retrieved August 14, 2006, from http://who.int/violenceprevention/en/. Reprinted with permission.

ferent levels affects behavior (Stokols, 1992). Because of this interplay between and among the many levels of influence, changing one can have an impact on them all (Spence & Lee, 2003). This concept is similar to reciprocal determinism in the Social Cognitive Theory.

Although this multilevel perspective is consistent in all ecological models, the specific terms used to describe the levels or factors may differ slightly. The level designations presented here are those commonly used in health education and health promotion.

Intrapersonal Level

All ecological models recognize the contribution intrapersonal-level factors make to health behavior. The impact of intrapersonal-level factors cannot be understated. In fact, historically, they have been the foundation for explaining health behavior and the basis for health promotion interven-

tions (Novilla et al., 2006). Intrapersonal-level factors include knowledge, attitudes, beliefs, personality traits (McLeroy et al., 1988), skills, perceptions (Novilla et al., 2006), personal history (World Health Organization [WHO], 2006), self-efficacy, and perceptions (Sallis & Owen, 1999), to name but a few of the more common ones.

An example of how individual factors, or those at the intrapersonal level, affect health is seen in violent behavior. The intrapersonal factors in this case may include the personality trait of impulsivity, a personal history of being a victim of child abuse, or alcohol or drug abuse (WHO, 2006). Another example of an intrapersonal factor affecting health behavior is the impact of gender on physical exercise. When girls reach puberty, there is a 50% reduction in their physical activity levels. The reason for this may be physiological, in that a simultaneous reduction in energy expenditure occurs at this time (Goran et al., 1998).

Interpersonal Level

The next set of factors in ecological models is at the interpersonal or relationship level. These are external factors included in the relationships we have with our relatives, friends, and peers. These people provide our social identity, make up our support systems, and define our role within the social structure (McLeroy et al., 1988; WHO, 2006).

Our relationships with others at this level influence our health behavior. For example, in the case of smoking, the strongest predictor of this behavior is having parents, siblings, or peers who smoke. Thus, if your friends and parents smoke, it is more likely that you will too (von Bothmer, Mattsson, & Fridlund, 2002). The same is true of drug-taking behavior. The peer group and family have a major influence on whether or not someone will engage in this behavior (Eddy et al., 2002).

Institutional Level

In some ecological models, there are factors at the institutional level that constrain or promote certain behaviors. These are the rules, regulations, and policies of informal structures (McLeroy, et al., 1988; Eddy, 2002) that are often associated with the workplace environment. Examples of institutional-level factors include policies providing flex time to enable employees to attend health programs, healthy food selections in the cafeteria (Eddy et al., 2002), corporate sponsorship of health initiatives, incentives for participation in health activities, and use of worksite communication networks (Watt et al., 2001).

Community Level

The community-level factors include the social networks, norms, or standards of behavior that exist formally or informally among individuals, groups, or organizations (Eddy et al., 2002; McLeroy et al., 1988; WHO, 2006). The norms of the community are associated with specific behaviors. For instance, they might include involvement in health initiatives such as the Great American Smokeout or the Five a Day campaign (Watt et al., 2001), participation in organized sports, volunteering on the local fire department, driving children to school rather than allowing them to walk, forbidding the use of alcohol, or not cutting your lawn on Sunday morning.

Looking at violent behavior again, associated factors at this level include high population density, people frequently moving in and out, and great diversity relative to age and income. These factors result in a community with little social glue holding it together. Violence is more likely to occur in a community with these characteristics. It is also more likely in communities where there is drug trafficking, a high level of unemployment, and where people do not know their neighbors and are not involved in local community activities (WHO, 2006).

Societal Level

At the societal level we find broader factors that encourage or discourage specific behaviors. These include economics, social policies, social or cultural norms of behavior, and attitudes. Going back to the violence example, factors at the societal level would be the cultural acceptability of resolving conflicts through violent means, parental rights overriding child welfare, and male dominance over women and children (WHO, 2006).

If we look at smoking behavior from the societal level, laws are now in effect in many states banning indoor smoking in public places and making the sale of cigarettes to minors illegal. These laws affect behavior and ultimately health. Another example of factors at the policy or societal level that change behavior at the individual level are the May 2006 federal guidelines aimed at addressing childhood obesity. The guidelines restrict the types of beverages that can be sold in schools to water, certain juices with no added sweeteners, and fat-free or low-fat regular and flavored milks (American Heart Association, 2006).

In summary, ecological models explain behavior as the result of an interplay between internal and external factors.

Internal and external factors affect behavior.

Application of the Social Ecological Model in Folic Acid Public Health Initiatives

LISA A. QUINN, SHARON J. THOMPSON, AND M. KATHERINE OTT

Lisa A. Quinn, MSN, CRNP, is an assistant professor in the Villa Maria School of Nursing, Gannon University, Erie, Pennsylvania.

Sharon J. Thompson, PhD, RN, MPH, is an assistant professor in the Villa Maria School of Nursing, Gannon University, Erie, Pennsylvania.

M. Katherine Ott, MS, CHES, is a teaching fellow at Kent State University, Kent, Ohio.

ABSTRACT

All women of childbearing age who are capable of becoming pregnant should consume 0.4 mg/400 μcg of folic acid daily. Folic acid decreases the incidence of neural tube defects in newborns. Despite continued public health initiatives, many women still do not consume the recommended daily requirement. This article analyzes the use of the social ecological model in folic acid public health initiatives and emphasizes assessing the outcomes of such initiatives. *JOGNN, 34,* 672–681; 2005. DOI: 10.1177/0884217505281877

Each year, 4,000 pregnancies in the United States are complicated by neural tube defects. The most common preventable neural tube defects are spina bifida, which occurs in 1 in 2,000 births, and anencephaly, which occurs in 1 in 8,000 births. Neural tube defects result in varying degrees of physical disability, ranging from a mild curvature of the spine to incompatibility with life. Neural tube defects account for 14% of infant deaths in the United States each year (Merseraeu, 2000).

Folic acid, or folate, was first discovered to have a connection with neural tube defects in the early 1960s (Centers for Disease Control and Prevention [CDC], 2001; Kadir & Economides, 2002; Rose & Mennutie, 1994). Folate plays a significant role in cell division and cell growth, which links folate deficiency to the incidence of neural tube defects (Perlow, 1999). Folic acid, a component of the vitamin B complex, is the synthesized compound used in dietary supplements and fortified foods. Folate occurs naturally in some foods, such as oranges, dark green leafy vegetables, and liver (Oakley, 1997).

Descriptive epidemiologic studies provided evidence that the occurrence of neural tube defects is linked to inadequate intake of folic acid, both preconceptionally and prenatally (Lewis & Nash, 1997; March of Dimes, 2001; Oakley, 1997; Platzman, 1998). A nonrandomized intervention study conducted in the late 1970s and early 1980s reported a sevenfold reduction in the incidence of neural tube defects among babies born to women who took daily multivitamin supplements containing folic acid (Smithells, Seller, & Harris, 1986). Additional study confirmed these findings, and researchers reported that if women of childbearing age had an adequate intake of folic acid, 50% to 75% of neural tube defects could be prevented (Czeizel & Dudas, 1992; Reifsnider & Gill, 2000; Schartz & Johnson, 1996).

Folic acid decreases the incidence of neural tube defects in newborns, but despite continued public health initiatives, many women still do not consume the recommended daily requirement. This article analyzes the use of the social ecological model in folic acid public health initiatives and emphasizes assessing the outcomes of such initiatives.

RECOMMENDATIONS FOR FOLIC ACID SUPPLEMENTATION

In 1992, with support from the National Institute of Medicine, the U.S. Public Health Service recommended that "all women of childbearing age who are capable of becoming pregnant should consume 0.4 mg, 400 μcg, of folic acid daily" (CDC, 1992; Schartz & Johnson, 1996). In March 1996, after extensive review and debate, the U.S. Food and Drug Administration issued a regulation requiring that, by January 1, 1998, all enriched cereal grain products must contain a minimum 140 µcg of folic acid for every 100 g of grain.

These two measures serve as population-based health promotion strategies that can be examined with the social ecological model (Green, Richard, & Potvin, 1996). The first is an "active" measure, as women of childbearing age must actively make the decision to ensure adequate daily folic acid intake—either through dietary intake or a multivitamin. The second is a "passive" measure, as women of childbearing age are provided folic acid every time they consume enriched cereal grain products, regardless of whether or not they make the decision to ensure adequate daily folic acid intake.

Healthy People 2010 Objectives Specific to Folic Acid Supplementation

Healthy People 2010 (U.S. Department of Health and Human Services, 2000) includes objectives specific to folic acid supplementation. Overall, the aim is to "reduce neural tube defects by 50%," "increase the number of women who consume 400 µcg of folic acid from 21% in the early 1990s to 80% by 2010 among nonpregnant women," and "increase the proportion of pregnancies begun with an optimum folic acid level" (p. 42). Healthy People 2010 objectives build on initiatives from the past two decades. Current objectives challenge individuals, communities, and health care professionals to take specific steps to ensure that good health and a long life are enjoyed by all (Hobbins, 2003).

Healthy People 2010 objectives related to folic acid serve as indicators of population-based health standards to be met. To assist in meeting identified health standards, objectives provide direction for the development of health promotion initiatives, including specific health promotion strategies. Application of the social ecological model to folic acid health promotion initiatives based on Healthy People 2010 objectives can best be accomplished at the organizational, community, and public policy levels.

THE SOCIAL ECOLOGICAL MODEL

The social ecological model provides a set of conceptual and methodological principles, drawn largely from systems theory, for organizing comprehensive, community-based, health promotion initiatives (Glanz, Lewis, & Rimer, 1997). Ecological models specific to health promotion are multifaceted—targeting environmental, behavioral, and social policy changes that help individuals adopt healthy behaviors. Ecological models are unique in that they take into account the physical environment and its relationship to people at intrapersonal, interpersonal, organizational, community, and public policy levels. This perspective is based on the major philosophical

construct of the model: Behavior does not occur in a vacuum (Glanz et al., 1997).

The intrapersonal level of the social ecological model takes into account an individual's knowledge, attitudes, values, skills, behavior, self-concept, and self-esteem. Strategies to intervene include mass media campaigns, social marketing, and skills development (Health, 1992; McLeroy, Bibeau, Steckler, & Glanz, 1988). The interpersonal level includes an individual's social networks, social supports, families, work groups, peers, and neighbors. Intervention strategies include enhancement of social supports and social networks, changing group norms, and increasing access. The organizational level includes norms, incentives, organizational culture, management styles, organizational structure, and communication networks. Strategies to intervene include incentive programs, process consultation, coalition development, and agency linkage. The community level includes community resources, neighborhood organizations, social and health services, organizational relationships, folk practices, governmental structures, and informal and formal leadership practices. Intervention strategies include community development, community coalitions, empowerment, conflict resolution, and mass media campaigns. Finally, the public policy level includes legislation, policies, taxes, and regulatory agencies. Strategies to intervene include mass media campaigns, policy analysis, political change, and lobbying (Health, 1992; McLeroy et al., 1988).

Social ecology initiatives do not target individuals who are making specific health-significant decisions. Instead, to promote healthful choices, social ecology engages the social processes and agencies that have a major influence on the health-significant decisions made by individuals. The goal is to establish a health-promoting environment within the social space in which individuals make health-significant decisions (Stokols, 1992; Stokols, Allen, & Bellingham, 1996; Wasserman, Shaw, Selvin, Gould, & Syne, 1998).

Ecological models address multiple layers of influences on behavior. This provides a comprehensive approach to health promotion initiatives. Many of the predominant theories and models of behavior focus on one dimension of health promotion, such as knowledge, attitudes, or skills. Health promotion strategies based on ecological models target individual behaviors and environmental influences to behavior (Green et al., 1996). Ecological models have been used with success in work-site health promotion initiatives, food-labeling requirements, roadway improvement campaigns, and smoking and alcohol prevention strategies (Green et al., 1996). These systems models have been advanced by the CDC and the American Cancer Association (2002) as an appropriate public health approach to advance the health of communities.

THE SIGNIFICANCE OF THE SOCIAL ECOLOGICAL MODEL TO FOLIC ACID PUBLIC HEALTH INITIATIVES

Many birth defects have only recently been linked to individual behaviors and environmental influences. For example, contact with the rubella virus by a rubella-negative pregnant woman during early pregnancy can lead to congenital rubella syndrome (Hasenau & Covington, 2002). Maternal consumption of alcohol during pregnancy can lead to fetal alcohol syndrome. Maternal folic acid deficiency, preconceptionally and during pregnancy, can lead to neural tube defects. The incidence of each of these birth defects can be significantly reduced, even prevented, if women of childbearing age change their health-significant decisions (Hasenau & Covington, 2002).

Application of the principles of social ecology to folic acid public health initiatives is an appropriate use of this health promotion model. An ongoing health promotion initiative specific to folic acid and the prevention of neural tube birth defects links individual behaviors to environmental influences. This linkage is key to applying principles of social ecology to establish a health-promoting environment to ensure that women of childbearing age make healthful choices specific to folic acid consumption (Oakley, 1997). In fact, a social ecological approach is necessary as health promotion programs that are narrow in scope and rely solely on interventions aimed at individuals and small groups are not likely to effect change (Stokols et al., 1996). An example of a social ecological approach—from the intrapersonal to the public policy levels—specific to a folic acid health promotion initiative is presented in Table 1.

FOLIC ACID PUBLIC HEALTH INITIATIVES USING A SOCIAL ECOLOGICAL APPROACH

This review included statewide programs specific to folic acid education. A search of several databases, including MEDLINE, PsychINFO, and CINAHL, was conducted for articles containing the search term *folic acid education*, published in English, between 1990 and 2003. The search yielded 56 articles. The articles were screened, and any article that did not identify an ecological approach in meeting educational needs specific to folic acid was rejected. After this process, 10 articles were included in this review. These articles identify folic acid public health initiatives from 1999 through 2003. An overview of these statewide folic acid health promotion initiatives is presented in Table 2.

The initial CDC recommendation specific to folic acid supplementation was made in 1992. Unfortunately, the rec-ommendation largely went unheeded by the public, by health care providers, and by public health officials. A 1995 survey conducted by the March of Dimes indicated that 52% of women reported awareness of folic acid, but only 32% were taking some sort of folic acid supplementation (Howse, 1999). This finding prompted the CDC, the March of Dimes, and the National Council on Folic Acid to collaborate on the National Folic Acid Campaign, a public health initiative that was launched in 1999. The collaborative members of the initiative designed and developed media campaigns, public and professional educational materials, and community programs to promote neural tube defect prevention in the United States (CDC, 1999b).

The goal of the National Folic Acid Campaign was to educate all women who could possibly become pregnant to consume 400 μcg of synthetic folic acid daily from vitamin supplements, fortified foods, or both in addition to eating foods high in folate in a healthful diet (CDC, 1999b). The campaign targeted all women of reproductive age, health care professionals, and community advocacy groups. Among women of reproductive age, research identified two primary target groups for the initial thrust of the campaign: (a) women who were planning a pregnancy (contemplators) and (b) women who were not planning a pregnancy (noncontemplators) (CDC, n.d.).

Campaign strategies were developed with input from women, community partners, agencies, and advocacy groups supporting the health promotion initiative. The CDC developed specific campaign messages based on this input and on information gathered from an extensive review of research specific to health communication. These messages were incorporated into all campaign materials provided to agency partners within the community (CDC, n.d.).

A new era in public health initiatives came about in 1984 with the inception of the Ottawa Charter for Health Promotion, which went well beyond the physical and environmental health risks that exist within communities to emphasize the social causes of illness (Ottawa Charter Committee, 1986). The Ottawa charter presented an ecological approach to disease prevention. This approach includes advocacy, collaboration, and multisector processes—all of which require public policy initiatives specific to health and wellness, a supportive environment, community action in the development of personal skills, and a reorientation of health services.

According to the Ottawa charter (Ottawa Charter Committee, 1986), health is created and lived by people within the settings of their everyday life: where they learn, work, play, and live. Health is created by caring for oneself and others, by being able to make decisions and have control over one's life

TABLE 1 A Social Ecological Approach to a Folic Acid Health Promotion Initiative

Ecological Level	Strategy	Description	Example
Intrapersonal	Program→client	Strategies aimed at building clients' competencies, knowledge, beliefs, attitudes, or values	A folic acid campaign aimed at increasing knowledge among women of childbearing age of the need to take folic acid before becoming pregnant
	Program→ [client—client]	Establishment of relationships between clients to have them share ways to restore or promote their own health	A focus group session to have women share folic acid information
Interpersonal	Program→ [groups]→client	Strategies aimed at modifying the clients' interpersonal environment (other individuals and small groups of individuals who regularly interact with the client)	Folic acid education sessions offered to women with the objective of changing their family's intake of daily multivitamins in addition to eating a healthy diet
	Program→ [groups—groups]→client	Establishment of relationships between members of the clients' interpersonal environment to have them share ways to restore or promote clients' health	Self-help groups of women gathering to prevent neural tube defects
Organizational	Program→ organization→ client	Organizational change programs aiming to modify health-compromising aspects of an organization	Provision of foods rich in folic acid at the cafeteria and "take your daily multivitamin" campaigns in the workplace
		Training programs whose objectives are to increase health promotion–relevant competencies of important actors in organizations	A training program aimed at improving health care providers' folic acid promotion skills
		Creation of a new organization	The creation of a national organization for the prevention of neural tube defects
	Program→ [organization—organization]→ client	Establishment of relationships between organizations devoted to—or interested in—a specific health issue	A community coalition between a women's organization and the March of Dimes
Community	Program—community—client	Training programs whose objectives are to increase health promotion–relevant competencies of a community's representatives	Training community health department personnel to be effective in providing health information specific to folic acid use to all women of childbearing age
	Program→ [community—community]→ client	Establishment of relationships between communities to promote health	Developing a coalition between cities and counties to share resources to promote folic acid use
Public policy	Program→political system→client	Programs aimed at influencing political representatives to have them legislating on a health-related issue	A program aimed at convincing health care professionals to lobby elected officials specific to increasing folic acid knowledge and use
	Program→[political system—political system]→client	Establishment of relationships between political representatives with the objective of improving health of a given targeted population	Lobbying for availability of folic acid–rich foods in programs serving the poor; lobbying for affordable multivitamins

TABLE 2　Examples of Statewide Folic Acid Health Promotion Initiatives

Initiative (Reference Source)	Target Population	Intervention	Ecological Level	Evaluation
Southwestern Virginia: the Folic Acid Campaign and Evaluation: 1977–1999 (Centers for Disease Control and Prevention, 199a)	All women capable of becoming pregnant	Year-long community intervention campaign in a four-county area: TV and radio public service announcements, news conference, newspaper ads, billboard ads, printed materials, focus group helped to develop food labeling, information cards, grocery stores involved and promoted folic acid foods, green ribbons to signify folic acid, folic acid education for grades 5–12 and at the college level	Intrapersonal, interpersonal, organizational, community	Evaluation using precampaign and postcampaign random sample telephone survey Survey assessed folic acid knowledge and awareness pre- and postcampaign Findings: Knowledge increased up from 77% in 1998 to 81% in 1999 Awareness increased up from 54% in 1998 to 75% in 1999
Alaska Folic Acid Coalition (Alaska Folic Acid Coalition, 2001)	Women of reproductive age	Broad-based community education	Intrapersonal, organizational community	No evaluation plan identified
Ohio Chapter of the March of Dimes Folic Acid Education Campaign (March of Dimes of Ohio, Miami Valley Division, 2001)	Women of childbearing age Physicians Health care providers	Television, public service announcements Stork Nest Program Legislation; Healthy Baby Bill	Intrapersonal, interpersonal, organizational community public policy	No evaluation plan identified As a chapter of the March of Dimes, a National Gallup Survey will evaluate the campaign
Middle Tennessee Folic Acid Council (Tennessee Department of Health, 2001)	General public Health care professionals Women of childbearing age	Displays Health fairs Statewide toll-free folic acid information line Multivitamin distribution to women who could not afford them	Intrapersonal, interpersonal, organizational, community	No evaluation plan identified
Wisconsin Health Care Education and Training (Health Care Education & Training, Inc., 2002)	Family planning clinic staff	Development of folic acid educational materials TV broadcast: folic acid presentation statewide	Intrapersonal, interpersonal, organizational, community	No evaluation plan identified
North Carolina: "Educating Providers" (Association of State and Territorial Health Officials, 2003)	Health care providers	Folic acid curriculum: "Reconsidering Multi-vitamin Supplementation: mailed to 7,500 health care providers, spring 2002	Intrapersonal, interpersonal, organizational community	No evaluation plan identified

(continued)

TABLE 2 (Continued)

Initiative (Reference Source)	Target Population	Intervention	Ecological Level	Evaluation
		Display boards placed at professional conferences and at health care settings to attract providers Health department personnel made visits to offices of local providers, serving as folic acid ambassadors Mass mailings to members of North Carolina Perinatal Association Presentations at Women's Wellness Centers		
Montana Folic Acid Campaign (Association of State and Territorial Health Officials, 2003) Collaboration/coalition of state health departments, hospitals, March of Dimes, advocacy groups, 350 national and regional chain stores in more than 100 communities, 34 family-planning clinics, WIC clinics	Women of childbearing age	Health Families campaign: distributed information, folic acid guidelines "September is Folic Acid Month" campaign to increase the number of people buying/taking multivitamins Media: TV, radio, newspapers Retail/grocery stores: highlighted foods with folic acid, distributed March of Dimes folic acid fact sheets Governor made public service announcements	Intrapersonal, interpersonal, organizational, community, public policy	Indicated: informal evaluation showed an increase in the sale of multivitamins since the campaign began Formal evaluation in progress and is expected to provide an accurate assessment of the campaign's impact on Montana's rate of birth defects Results are to be available in 2005
Puerto Rico: Starting Early (Association of State and Territorial Health Officials, 2003)	All women between the ages of 10 and 50 years who are capable of becoming pregnant *Rate of neural tube defects is higher in Puerto Rico than in most areas of the United States	Three strategies: folic acid message in school health curricula in elementary, intermediate, and high school; school nutritionists increased high-folate foods in school lunches; training of adolescent peer leaders	Intrapersonal, interpersonal, organizational, community	There was a significant increase in the percentage of women who knew about implications of folic folic acid consumption 1 year after campaign began: up from 49% in 1996 to 62% in 1997
South Carolina: Reducing Disparities (Association of State and Territorial Health Officials, 2003)	African American women South Carolina Department of Health partnered with state agencies and programs aimed at improving birth out-	Public awareness efforts: education campaigns, community initiatives Local health departments distributed folic acid information to health	Intrapersonal, interpersonal, organizational, community	Not evaluated yet Indicated: evaluation plan is in place

TABLE 2 (Continued)

Initiative (Reference Source)	Target Population	Intervention	Ecological Level	Evaluation
The South Carolina folic acid campaign is integral to the state's infant mortality reduction initiative Major goal: to stress what communities can do to improve birth outcomes	comes among African American women	care providers Involvement of community-based organizations, churches Media campaign Print materials: brochures, flyers		
Delaware Folic Acid Coalition (Christian Care Health System, 2003)	Women of childbearing age	Multivitamin distribution to women Vitamins donated by Happy Harry's, regional pharmacy chain, to women who could not afford them	Interpersonal, organizational	No evaluation plan identified
California Preconception Care Initiative: Every Woman, Every Time (Cullum, 2003)	Health care providers	Education packet distributed at conferences Presentations Targeted mailings Newsletters Advertisements in newspapers and professional journals Online information Computer network sharing among providers	Intrapersonal, interpersonal, organizational, community, public policy	Responses from 187 providers: 75% indicated the material in the packet would change how they provided information in their practice; 62% found information useful; 80% would distribute handouts; 75% would provide billing codes; 77% found presentation useful
Georgia Folic Acid Initiative (March of Dimes of Georgia, 2003)	Women of childbearing age Women who have had an infant with spina bifida, anencephaly Health care professionals Health care policy makers	Media/community health education outreach campaign Media campaigns Community education programs Special education campaigns for at-risk women Outreach education for health care providers	Intrapersonal, interpersonal, organizational, community, public policy At the public policy level: Department of Community Health General Budget, 2003: allocation of 2.1 million dollars for comprehensive folic acid campaign	Not evaluated yet Indicated: evaluation plan to identify the effectiveness of initiative is in place As a chapter of the March of Dimes, a National Gallup Survey will evaluate campaign
Washington State Folic Acid Council (Washington State Folic Acid Council, 2003)	General public Health care providers State policy makers	Education Resource referral Advocacy regarding the impact of folic acid	Intrapersonal, interpersonal, organizational, community, public policy	Not evaluated yet Indicated: will evaluate effectiveness of folic acid projects and programs and share the lessons learned

circumstances, and by ensuring that the society one lives in creates conditions that allow the attainment of health by all its members. Societies are complex and interrelated. Health cannot be separated from other societal concerns. The inextricable link between people and their environment constitutes the basis for a social ecological approach to health. Within an ecological approach to disease prevention, society must go beyond individual behaviors to inclusion of multiple facets of the environment (Green et al., 1996).

As a comprehensive community-based health promotion program, the National Folic Acid Campaign supports a social ecological approach to health promotion. Strategies in the campaign specific to an ecological approach are evident in (a) coalition development and approaches to community involvement; (b) educational approaches used, including social marketing techniques and mass media campaigns; and (c) policy development regarding folic acid.

Most statewide folic acid campaigns do not incorporate all levels of the social ecological model into the design of their health promotion programs. However, most include interventions in at least two levels. An overview of several state-sponsored folic acid health promotion initiatives is presented in tabular format, including information specific to (a) the title of the initiative, (b) the target population, (c) intervention strategies, (d) social ecological levels used, and (d) evaluation of the initiative (see Table 2).

In addition to statewide folic acid health promotion initiatives, there are many programs and campaigns initiated at the local level. An example is the Salud Campaign in Hartford, Connecticut. This program targets Latino children and their caregivers, promoting increased consumption of fresh fruits and vegetables for better health, including the prevention of neural tube defects. Intervention strategies, based on principles of social ecology, ranged from the intrapersonal through the community level of intervention and included public service announcements in the media—television, radio, newspapers, local magazines—and on mass transit—advertisement boards within buses and taxicabs as well as on bus and taxicab exteriors. Evaluation indicated that the program was effective in increasing public awareness of neural tube defects and sources of folate (Perez-Escamilla et al., 2000). However, the authors did not include any evaluation specific to the model used to develop intervention strategies, nor did they include specific evaluation data that led to the determination that the program was effective.

The programs reviewed in this article, and those summarized in Table 2, have used in varying degree principles of the social ecological model. Regardless of how many levels of

the model were incorporated, each of the initiatives has gone beyond the individual level and has moved toward a population-based approach to health promotion. Although still aiming to change the health-significant behavior of individuals, social ecology focuses on the environmental influences on health decisions.

CONTINUED EFFORTS NEEDED SPECIFIC TO FOLIC ACID PUBLIC HEALTH INITIATIVES

In a 2003 Gallup Poll sponsored by the March of Dimes, a nationwide sample of 2,006 women between the ages of 18 and 45 years were surveyed. Findings indicated that 33% of the women who had seen folic acid public service announcements on television believed the information was (a) intended for women who were trying to get pregnant or (b) intended for women in a different age group—the information was not intended for them.

It is estimated that only 32% of women in the United States who are between the ages of 18 and 45 years take a multivitamin containing 400 μcg of folic acid on a daily basis (March of Dimes, 2003). These findings should lead planners of folic acid public health initiatives, whether they are revising current programs or developing new ones, to direct their efforts in developing strategies that will more effectively reach the target population: all women of childbearing age. A social ecological approach is recommended. If women want health information from their health care providers, strategies can be initiated at the interpersonal level, at the point of service for health and wellness care. Increasing access to folic acid information from sources women view as having the requisite knowledge to guide them in making healthful choices can increase the number of women of childbearing age who take a daily multivitamin containing 400 μcg of folic acid.

The National Council on Folic Acid (n.d.), in its Strategic Plan 2002–2005, included education strategies specific to all levels of the social ecological model. Although this is a positive step, continued effort is required. Further research should be conducted using the social ecological model as a theoretical framework. In addition, further study is required of the model itself. Evaluating the relationship between the various constructs of the model and public health initiative outcomes is required. Doing so can serve as effective mechanisms for promoting use of the social ecological model in organizing comprehensive, community-based, health promotion initiatives including future initiatives specific to folic acid requirements for all women of childbearing age.

SUMMARY

All programs and health initiatives using an ecological framework identify health promotion strategies that target individual behaviors and environmental influences on behavior. The campaigns and initiatives identified throughout this article used an ecological approach to improving folic acid intake among women of childbearing age.

Evaluation of the effectiveness of campaigns and health initiatives aimed at improving folic acid consumption among women of childbearing age have focused on identifying the behavior itself, rather than on which campaign strategies were effective in changing the behavior. For example, state and national campaigns have evaluated program effectiveness by identifying an increase in folic acid knowledge or folic acid intake among women of childbearing age, without identifying which campaign strategies effected any identified increases to folic acid knowledge or folic acid intake.

All programs require rigorous evaluation. Programs using a social ecological approach are challenging to evaluate because this approach simultaneously addresses multiple layers of influences on behavior. Although addressing multiple layers of influences on behavior may be key to the success of programs aimed at improving public health, it may also make isolation and evaluation of specific components of the program extremely difficult. However, this evaluation is necessary. Investigating ways to isolate components that offer the most effective approaches to helping individuals make healthy lifestyle choices in their daily lives is a challenge that must be addressed.

REFERENCES

Alaska Folic Acid Coalition. (2001). *Folic acid campaign.* Retrieved September 18, 2003, from http://www.epi.hss.state.ak.us/mchepi/abar/preved/afac/default.stm

Association of State and Territorial Health Officials. (2003). State efforts to increase folic acid consumption and reduce neural tube defects. Retrieved September 18, 2003, from http://www. dphhs.state.mt.us/news/press_releases/march/ folic_acid_best_practices.pdf

Centers for Disease Control and Prevention. (1992). Recommendations for use of folic acid to reduce the number of cases of spina bifida and other neural tube defects. *Morbidity and Mortality Weekly Report, 48,* RR-14.

Centers for Disease Control and Prevention. (1999a). Folic acid campaign and evaluation: Southwestern Virginia, 1997–1999. *Morbidity and Mortality Weekly Report, 48,* 914–917.

Centers for Disease Control and Prevention. (1999b). *Preventing neural tube birth defects: A prevention model and resource guide.* Atlanta, GA: Author.

Centers for Disease Control and Prevention. (2001). Knowledge and use of folic acid among women of reproductive age: Michigan, 1998. *Morbidity and Mortality Weekly Report, 50,* 185–189.

Centers for Disease Control and Prevention. (n.d.). *Folic acid now.* Retrieved September 5, 2003, from http://www. cdc.gov/ncbddd/folicacid/folcamp.html

Centers for Disease Control and Prevention and the American Cancer Society. (2002). Harnessing public health knowledge: Beyond comparisons and control groups [Video recording]. Atlanta, GA: Author.

Christian Care Health System. (2003). *Community-based women's and children's health services.* Retrieved September 18, 2003, from http://www.christiancare.org/health_guide/ health_guide_pmri_material.cfm

Cullum, A. (2003). Ongoing provider practices to enhance preconception wellness. *Journal of Obstetric, Gynecologic, and Neonatal Nursing, 32,* 543–549.

Czeizel, A. E., & Dudas, J. (1992). Prevention of the first occurrence of neural tube defects by periconceptual vitamin supplementation. *New England Journal of Medicine, 327,* 32–35.

Glanz, K., Lewis, M. L., & Rimer, B. K. (1997). *Health behavior and health education* (2nd ed.). San Francisco: Jossey-Bass.

Green, L., Richard, L., & Potvin, L. (1996). Ecological foundations of health promotion. *American Journal of Health Promotion, 10,* 270–281.

Hasenau, S. M., & Covington, C. (2002). Neural tube defects prevention and folic acid. *Maternal Child Nursing, 27,* 87–92.

Health. (1992). Health and education research: Theory and practice—Future directions. *Health Education Research: Theory and Practice, 7*(1), 1–6.

Health Care Education & Training, Inc. (2002). Folic acid: Getting the word out. Retrieved September 2, 2003, from http://www.hcet.org/resource/postconf/folicapst.html

Hobbins, D. (2003). Full circle: The evolution of preconception health promotion in America. *Journal of Obstetric, Gynecologic, and Neonatal Nursing, 32,* 516–522.

Howse, J. L. (1999). Stopping neural tube defects: Nurses and folic acid partner for awareness. *AWHONN Lifelines, 3*(3), 10.

Kadir, R., & Economides, D. (2002). Neural tube defects and periconceptual folic acid. *Canadian Medical Association Journal, 167,* 255–257.

Lewis, C., & Nash, A. (1997). The factors associated with effective folic acid prophylaxis in the periconceptual period in women attending an antenatal clinic. *Journal of Obstetric, Gynecologic, and Neonatal Nursing, 17,* 248–253.

March of Dimes. (2001). *Folic acid and the prevention of birth defects: A national survey of pre-pregnancy awareness and behavior among women of childbearing age, 1995–2001.* White Plains, NY: Author.

March of Dimes. (2003). *Why don't women take folic acid? Forgetfulness and denial: The latest survey finds.* Retrieved September 24, 2003, from http://www.marchofdimes.com

March of Dimes of Georgia. (2003). *The Georgia folic acid initiative.* Retrieved September 18, 2003, from http//www.marchofdimesga.com/affairs/folic.html

March of Dimes of Ohio, Miami Valley Division. (2001). *2001 annual report.* Retrieved September 18, 2003, from http://www.mvmod.org/2001annualreport

McLeroy, K. R., Bibeau, D., Steckler, A., & Glanz, K. (1988). An ecological perspective on health promotion. *Health Education Quarterly, 15,* 351–377.

Mersereau, P. (2000). Preventing neural tube defects: A national campaign. *Small Talk, 12,* 1–2, 4–5.

National Council on Folic Acid. (n.d.). *Strategic plan 2002–2005.* Retrieved September 18, 2003, from http://www.folicacidinfo.org/finalstrategies

Oakley, G. P. (1997). Doubling the number of women consuming vitamin supplement pills containing folic acid: An urgently needed birth defect prevention complement to the folic acid fortification of cereal grains. *Reproductive Toxicology, 11,* 579–581.

Ottawa Charter Committee. (1986). *Health Promotion I: iii–iv.* Ottawa, Canada: Author.

Perez-Escamilla, R., Himmelgreen, D., Bonello, H., Peng, Y., Mengual, G., Gonzalez, A., et al. (2000). Marketing nutrition among urban Latinos:

The Salud campaign. *Journal of the American Dietetic Association, 100,* 698–701.

Perlow, J. (1999). Education about folic acid: The OB/GYN's role in preventing neural tube defects. *Contemporary Obstretrics and Gynecology, 44,* 39–53.

Platzman, A. (1998). Folic acid: Once overlooked, now a nutrient on the brink of stardom. *Environmental Nutrition, 21*(1), 1–2.

Reifsnider, E., & Gill, S. (2000). Nutrition for the childbearing years. *Journal of Obstretric, Gynecologic, and Neonatal Nursing, 29,* 43–55.

Rose, N. C., & Mennutie, M. T. (1994). Periconceptual folate supplementation and neural tube defects. *Clinical Obstetrics and Gynecology, 37,* 605–620.

Schartz, R. H., & Johnson, R. B. (1996). Folic acid supplementation: When and how? *Obstetrics and Gynecology, 88,* 886–887.

Smithells, R. W., Seller, M. J., & Harris, R. (1986). Further experience of vitamin supplementation for prevention of neural tube defect recurrences. *Lancet, 1,* 648–669.

Stokols, D. (1992). Establishing and maintaining healthy environments. *American Psychologist, 47,* 6–22.

Stokols, D., Allen, J., & Bellingham, R. L. (1996). The social ecology of health promotion: Implications for research and practice. *American Journal of Health Promotion, 10,* 247–251.

Tennessee Department of Health. (2001). *Folic acid: A vitamin that could change a life forever.* Retrieved September 18, 2003, from http://www2 .state.th.us/health/mch/folic acid/lessonplan.htm

U.S. Department of Health and Human Services. (2000). *Healthy people 2010* (Conference edition in two volumes). Washington, DC: Author.

U.S. Food and Drug Administration. (1996). Food standards: Amendment of standard of identity for enriched grain products to require addition of folic acid. *Federal Register, 61,* 8761–8797.

Washington State Folic Acid Council. (2003). *About the folic acid council.* Retrieved September 18, 2003, from http://www.folic acid council.org/ about/index.htm

Wasserman, C., Shaw, G., Selvin, S., Gould, J., & Syme, L. (1998). Socioeconomic status, neighborhood social conditions, and neural tube defects. *American Journal of Public Health, 88,* 1674–1680.

Article Source: Quinn, L.A., Thompson, S.J., & Ott, M.K. (2005). Application of the social ecological model in folic acid public health initiatives. *Journal of Obstetric, Gynecologic and Neonatal Nursing, 34*(6), 672–681. Copyright 2005, Association of Women's Health, Obstetric and Neonatal Nurses. Reprinted with permission.

QUESTIONS

1. Why was it determined that a social ecological approach was appropriate for a folic acid intervention?

2. What strategies in the National Folic Acid Campaign are evidence of an ecological approach?

3. What ecological levels and specific interventions were used in the Southwestern Virginia Folic Acid Campaign? How effective were they?

4. What ecological levels and specific interventions were used in the Starting Early program in Puerto Rico? How effective were they?

5. What are the similarities and differences between the Virginia and Puerto Rico programs and the results of your brainstorming session?

SOCIAL CAPITAL THEORY

The notion of social capital is relatively new, with its relationship to and impact on health being the focus of research only since the mid-1990s (Wakefield & Poland, 2005). From a community perspective, *social capital* refers to the networks, norms, and trust people need to cooperate with each other, in a reciprocal fashion, for the benefit of all (Putnam, 2000; Putnam, Leonardi, & Nanetti, 1993). Social capital includes the resources we have available to us by virtue of our relationships or connections with others in these networks. The extent (or amount, if you will) of our social capital, then, depends on the "richness" of the people in our network, their connections, and their resources (money, education, clout, etc.) (Carpiano, 2006). However, before the network resources (i.e., the social capital) can be used or accessed, trusting, reciprocal relationships must exist between the members of the social network (Carpiano, 2006).

Trust and reciprocity are at the very core of Social Capital Theory. They lead to the expectations and obligations that come with being part of a particular network (Hawe & Shiell, 2000). Without trust and reciprocity, there is no social capital. Perhaps it is in this way that social capital influences health behavior.

The networks of social capital are diverse: they are what make up our social environment. They may be whole societies, communities, neighborhoods, civic associations, organizations, schools, religious affiliations, or families, to name but a few. Think of all the groups to which you belong and the resources (connections, clout, money, jobs) available to you as a result of your relationships with the people in these networks.

Social capital can also include one's social skills or ability to negotiate and work with others to find solutions to common problems (Szreter & Woolcock, 2004). It may refer to styles and forms of leadership, structure of service delivery, and social unity among communities (Szreter & Woolcock, 2004).

As you can see, social capital can be many things. Consequently, it is often used as an umbrella term that takes into account social cohesion (which includes trust and reciprocity), support, and integration or participation (Almedon, 2005) in social networks. It is the connectedness that people have to the people around them (Carpiano, 2006). When people feel connected to each other, they develop behaviors and attitudes that benefit themselves and their society as a whole (Putnam, 2000).

Because social capital includes caring relationships and the extent of their impact on health (Szreter & Woolcock,

FIGURE 9.2 Neighbors watching out for each other.

2004; Wakefield & Poland, 2005), a community in which people are more connected to each other is better able to support positive health behaviors and dissuade negative ones (Berkman & Kawachi, 2000). As a case in point, in a neighborhood where everyone knows everyone else and each person watches out for the other, there may be lower tolerance for illegal behavior, drug use, or crime (Figure 9.2) (Berkman & Kawachi, 2000; Ross & Jang, 2000).

Greater social capital in communities has been linked to improved child development and adolescent well-being; better mental health; lower crime rates; less youth delinquency; overall reduced mortality; lower susceptibility to binge drinking, depression, and loneliness; and higher perceptions of well-being and health. In communities where social capital is low, we find higher rates of stress and isolation and lower rates of child well-being, ability to respond to environmental health hazards, and receipt of effective health interventions (Szreter & Woolcock, 2004). A neighborhood or community with greater social capital is better able to organize itself and is better positioned to fight with one voice in one direction (Veenstra et al., 2005).

The more people you know, the more connected you are to a variety of others in a number of ways and the more resources you have at your disposal. This is akin to the old saying, "It's not what you know but who you know that counts." There are three different types of social capital depending on the strength of the relationships between the people who make up the social network: bonding, bridging, and linking.

Bonding Social Capital

Bonding social capital refers to those relationships between people who see themselves as being similar in terms of their shared social identity (Szreter, 2002; Szreter & Woolcock, 2004; Woolcock, 2001), origin, or status or position in society (Szreter, 2002). An example of this is the network of ties that holds families and groups together (Wakefield & Poland, 2005). Think about the behaviors, attitudes, expectations, and obligations that come with being part of your family. How do these things impact your health behavior?

Social networks, in general, facilitate and support bonding between people. This support may directly or indirectly, positively or negatively affect health. This occurs directly by their impact on stress levels, self-esteem, exercise, sexual activity, or the utilization of health services. Bonding relationships also influence health more indirectly through their effects on the larger social, economic, political, and environmental determinants of health (Berkman et al., 2000). They may affect the types of jobs and housing available in a neighborhood, as well as neighborhood wealth (Veenstra et al., 2005).

Being connected to others and needing to conform to the group norm is not always possible or always a good thing (Crow, 2002). When people don't or can't conform to the group norms, they are excluded and barred from accessing the social capital of the network (Wakefield & Poland, 2005). Think of the social network of a particular religious affiliation. When some people in a community are not part of the network, they are not able to access the social capital of that church, mosque, temple, or synagogue.

Exclusion from a social network and not having access to its social capital are important in terms of understanding health behaviors. Unless people can be "named, blamed and shamed" (Rose, 2000, p. 1407) for unacceptable behavior (health or otherwise), there is little incentive to conform or behave in acceptable ways (Wakefield & Poland, 2005). People with higher levels of social capital tend to be healthier than those with lower levels of social capital (Bolin, Lindgren, Lindstrom, & Nystedt, 2003) because greater social capital is linked to lower rates of overall mortality. It is specifically linked to reduced mortality from cardiovascular disease and cancers (Kawachi et al., 1997).

Needing to conform to the group norms, and in so doing remaining part of the network, does not always result in positive health outcomes. In fact, conformity with the group norms may support unhealthy or inappropriate behaviors. Take the case of a woman enduring sexual harassment in the workplace. She may be reluctant to report it for fear of losing her job, being blacklisted within the network, and consequently becoming unemployable (Wakefield & Poland, 2005). Similarly, in cultures where spousal abuse is considered the norm, women tolerate repeated beatings because it is the norm of the group not to complain about such treatment. Complaining may result in a divorce. Although bringing relief from the beatings, a divorce may also mean losing her children to her ex-husband and his family and being an outcast in her society.

Bridging Social Capital

Bridging social capital refers to networks of people who come together as acquaintances. They are from different social groups and differ in some sociodemographic sense, be it age, ethnicity, education, or self-esteem (Wakefield & Poland, 2005). People become part of these networks to engage in an activity with mutually beneficial outcomes that were not possible within their bonded relationships. Examples of this type of relationship are those among sports team members, a choir, people working on a group project, students in a class, and tenants in an apartment building (Szreter, 2002). These relationships may affect health behavior by virtue of a desire to do what the group does, or to be a "team player," in order to have access to the resources of the group.

Linking Social Capital

The weakest social capital relationships are *linking* relationships. In these, we have norms of respect and networks of trusting relationships, but they are between people who interact across power or authority gradients representing formal institutions. These are the relationships seen between teacher and student, physician and patient, and police officer and crime victim (Szreter & Woolcock, 2004). Although there is a relationship, the extent of social capital is limited by the power gradient.

In summary, according to Social Capital Theory, trust impacts norms, expectations, and relationships and, therefore, affects behavior (Figure 9.3).

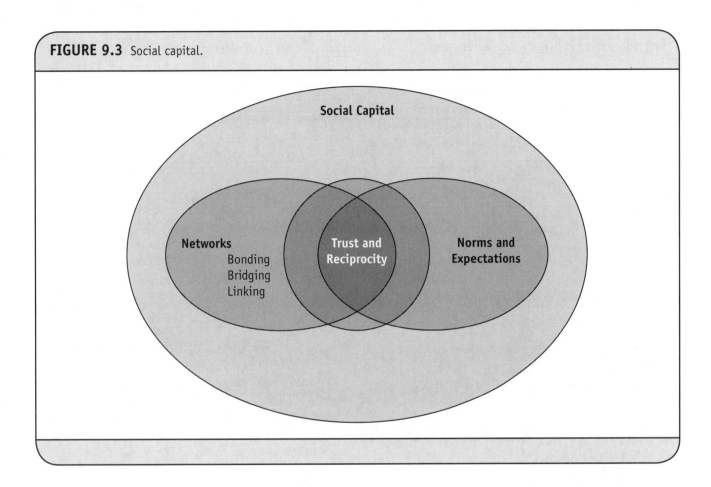

FIGURE 9.3 Social capital.

THEORY IN ACTION: CLASS ACTIVITY

Make a list of all the networks or groups to which you belong. For example, you may be part of a family, religious group, a campus community, fraternity or sorority, and so forth. For each of these, identify the type of relationship— that is, bonding, bridging, or linking. Next, make a list of the resources (social capital) that come with each of these relationships. The resources are whatever you deem to be valuable, whether it be money, job opportunities, travel opportunities, housing, internship sites, references, or so on. When you have finished, read the following article and answer the questions at the end.

Social Capital and Substance Use Among Swedish Adolescents—An Explorative Study

PETTER LUNDBORG

Lund University Centre for Health Economics (LUCHE)

ABSTRACT

Cross-sectional survey data on Swedish adolescents aged 12–18 was used to estimate the link between individual social capital and smoking, illicit drug use and binge drinking. Major conclusions drawn were (1) that social capital, indicated by measures of social participation and trust, was negatively correlated with the probability of smoking and illicit drug use, but (2) that social capital showed no statistically significant correlation with the probability of binge drinking.

INTRODUCTION

Social capital has been recognised as an important determinant of health. It has been found, for instance, that US states with low levels of aggregate social capital have higher rates of mortality than states with higher levels of social capital (Kawachi, Kennedy, Lochner, & Prothow-Stith, 1997; Subramanian, Kawachi, & Kennedy, 2001). At the individual level, it has been found that higher levels of social capital are positively correlated with self-assessed health (Bolin, Lindgren, Lindström, & Nystedt, 2003).

Social capital has been defined as the set of rules, norms, obligations, reciprocity, and trust embedded in social relations, social structures, and society's institutional arrangements which enable members to achieve their individual and community objectives (Coleman, 1990). In the words of Putnam (1995), social capital represents "features of social life—networks, norms, and trust—that enable participants to act together more effectively to pursue shared objectives." As indicators of social capital, researchers have often used individuals' participation in social organisations and levels of interpersonal trust. Social participation is usually regarded as most central to the concept of social capital, whereas trust is viewed as a consequence of social capital (Putnam, 2001; Woolcock, 2001).

Social capital has been conceptualised as a property of individuals, small groups, communities, or even larger entities. In Macinko and Starfield (2001) four different levels for the analysis of social capital were defined, ranging from the macro-level to the micro-level. The choice of level for the analysis has varied according to academic subject and author (Lindström, 2004a). At the individual level, social capital has been conceptualised as access to and membership in social networks and/or trust. These different conceptualisations of social capital need not be mutually exclusive and social capital may be properties of both the individual and the larger community (Pevalin & Rose, 2003).

An individual-oriented approach may be appropriate for a number of reasons. As pointed out by Glaeser (2001), the decision to invest in social capital is made by individuals, not communities. Individuals invest in social capital by spending time and energy interacting and forming links with other people (Glaeser, Laibson, & Sacerdote, 2002). The return of the investments is both the direct utility from socialising and the indirect utility that comes from the extended resources that increased social capital generates (Bolin et al., 2003). Furthermore, there exists substantial heterogeneity in social capital, as measured by social participation and trust, across individuals. Glaeser et al. (2002) showed that only a few percent of observed individual level heterogeneity in social capital— both when measured as trust and social participation—was explained by group-level variables.

The mechanism behind the relationship between social capital and health is less well understood. One explanation that has been offered is that social capital reduces unhealthy habits like smoking and excessive alcohol consumption, or other deviant health behaviours. Thus, risky health behaviours may mediate the relationship between social capital and health. Individuals with high levels of personal social capital may be more able to receive social support when facing difficulties and/or stressful events in life compared to individuals with low levels of social capital (Cohen & Wills, 1985; Tsutsumi, Tsutsumi, Kayaba, & Igaraschi, 1998). The support may be of both practical and emotional character. However, if social capital is a scarce resource, substance use may function as an alternative coping behaviour in the presence of stress, since it produces relaxation (Lindström, 2000, p. 25). Consequently, individuals with low levels of social capital may be less able to handle stress by receiving support and may be more inclined to resort to substance use as a coping behaviour.

At the individual level people are thus able to gain access to extended resources through their access/membership in social networks (Portes, 1998; Locher et al., 2005). Portes (1998), for instance, notes that 'the consensus is growing in the [sociological] literature that social capital stands for the ability of actors to secure benefits by virtue of membership in social networks or other social structures' and that the 'greatest theoretical promise of social capital lies at the individual level.' The access to social networks, and thus social capital, may however vary systematically between individuals, as revealed in Glaeser et al. (2002).

Furthermore, an individual with a large social network, being an indicator of social capital, may be more monitored and controlled compared to an individual with no or small social network. The network may thus regulate and exert social control over deviant health-related behaviour, such as smoking and drinking (Bolin et al., 2003). The social network may facilitate diffusion of health-related information and adopt norms regarding health-related behaviour, which may be costly for the members of the network to deviate from. Healthy norms tend to be reinforced in social networks; individuals who are socially isolated are more likely to smoke, drink, overeat, and engage in various health-damaging behaviours (Putnam, 2000, p. 327). Consequently, higher social capital may increase the cost of substance use (or increase the cost of whatever purpose substance use fulfils). It should also be noted that in a community context with declining smoking prevalence, smoking may also become more and more of a social stigma, thus increasing the cost of smoking for the individual (Lindström, 2003).

Finally, trust in other people has been found to be related to institutional trust (Lindström, 2003). Individuals with low levels of trust in public institutions may thus be more reluctant to take advice, such as health-related advice, from friends, physicians, and public institutions.

A number of empirical studies have analysed social capital at the individual level and its relationship with health and health-related behaviours. In Pevalin and Rose (2003), most individual-level measures of social capital were associated with a significant reduction in the likelihood of common mental illnesses and poor self-reported health. Also conceptualising social capital at the individual level, Locher et al. (2005) found that low levels of social capital were associated with nutritional risk among black men. Positive correlations between individual-level social capital and self-reported health were reported in Rose (2000), Bolin et al. (2003), and Lindström (2004a). Similar findings were reported by Veenstra (2000) for elderly people. Regarding health-related behaviours, Lindström (2003) found that social participation and trust were negatively related to daily smoking, and Lindström, Hansson, Ostergren, and Berglund (2000) found that high levels of individual-level social capital were a significant predictor of maintenance of smoking cessation. In Lindström (2004b) low levels of individual-level social capital, measured as low levels of trust, and the combination of low trust and high social participation, were associated with cannabis smoking among young adults.

Conceptualising social capital at an aggregate level, Weitzman and Kawachi (2000) found that social capital was negatively correlated with the probability of binge drinking at college campuses in the U.S. Social capital was measured as average daily time volunteering in different activities and the individual responses were then aggregated. The outcome measure, binge drinking, however, was on the individual level. Not explicitly focusing on social capital, Carlsson and Vågerö (1998) found a positive correlation between low levels of family social capital and heavy drinking among Russian males. It should be noted that different kinds of social capital, obviously, may be more or less beneficial. Focusing on negative aspects of social capital, Lowell (2002) examined injection patterns among drug users and found that drug users that belonged to networks of drug users were more likely to engage in risky injection patterns.

In this paper, we examine the relationship between social capital and smoking, binge drinking, and illicit drug use among Swedish adolescents, using an individual-level approach. An explorative empirical approach is adopted and the aim is not to build a formal economic model of individual health-related behaviour and social capital. Using a cross-sectional data set, we test the hypothesis that social capital, here measured as social participation and trust, reduces adolescent substance use.

The data used is presented in the next section, while the following section describes the empirical model. The penultimate section reports on the results, and the paper ends with a discussion in the final section.

DATA

Cross-sectional data was collected from a survey conducted in 2001 in Trelleborg, a medium-sized town on the south coast of Sweden. All pupils in grades 6, 8 and 9 at the compulsory schools and grades 1 and 2 at the upper secondary schools participated in the survey, which was filled in by the pupils anonymously in a classroom setting. Respondents were 12–18 years old at the time of the survey.[1] A total of 1719 questionnaires were collected.[2] Due to incomplete survey responses, the number of observations used for the analyses was 1346 for binge drinking, 1330 for smoking, and 1443 for illicit drug use. The reason for the different sample sizes was that different variables were used for the regressions on binge drinking, smoking, and illicit drug use, and individuals with missing values for any of the variables included in the particular regression were omitted from the analyses. Consequently, between 77 percent and 84 percent of the sample could be used for the analyses. Two variables accounted for 359 of the missing observations. These were income and smoking risk perceptions. An analysis of missing responses showed that individuals with both parents born outside Sweden and individuals aged 12–15 were significantly more likely to have missing responses. For a detailed account of the survey and for a translation into English of the questionnaire, see Lundborg (2003).

Social Capital

Social participation and trust were used as indicators of social capital. Both indicators were measured at the individual level. Trust was measured by asking the respondent to state his/her attitude towards the following statement: "Most people can be trusted." The respondent was asked to state whether he/she totally disagreed, disagreed, agreed, or totally agreed to the statement. A dichotomous variable was created, taking the value 1 if the respondents agreed or totally agreed, and 0 otherwise.

Social participation refers to what extent the individual takes part in formal and/or informal activities and/or organisations in society. The respondent was asked whether he or she during the previous year participated in a political meeting (party meeting or demonstration), participated in a meeting of an association (athletic club, scouts, etc.), attended a theatrical show or a movie, attended an art exhibition, attended a religious activity, attended a sporting event (for instance a match or competition), wrote a letter to the press, visited a restaurant or disco, attended a larger family gathering (larger = more than 10 persons), attended a party at someone else's place, or none of the above. The variety of categories included aimed at capturing a broad range of different activities and associations that were relevant to adolescents. A variable was created, ranging from 0 to 10, indicating the number of activities in which the respondent participated.

Dependent Variables

Dependent variables were binge drinking, smoking, and illicit drug use. All three were dichotomous variables taking the value 1 if the individual participated in the activity of interest and 0 otherwise.

The smoking question was stated as: "Do you smoke?". The alternatives were: "(1) Yes, every day, (2) Yes, almost every day, (3) Yes, but only at parties, (4) Yes, but very rarely, (5) Did smoke but have quit, (6) Have only tested, (7) Have never smoked." When studying the smoking decision we defined a smoker as an individual who reported smoking every or almost every day. Thus, a dummy variable was created, assigning the value one to individuals reporting smoking every or almost every day and zero otherwise.

A binge drinker was defined as an individual who during the past month, on one or several occasions, consumed something of the following: six cans of low alcohol content beer or more, four cans of beer or more, one bottle of wine or more, half a bottle of spirits or more.[3] A user of illicit drugs was defined as an individual who reported that he/she had used illicit drugs during the past six months.

The fraction of smokers, binge drinkers, and illicit drug users in the sample were 0.16, 0.38, and 0.05, respectively.

---

[1] The 6th, 8th and 9th grade students in elementary school were aged 12–13, 14–15, and 15–16, respectively, at the time of the survey. Grade 1 and grade 2 students in upper secondary school were 16–17 and 17–18 years old, respectively.

[2] The response rate was 91.6 percent. Non-responders constituted mainly those who were absent the day in which the survey was conducted. Reasons included being sick, truancy, and on job-training.

---

[3] Low alcoholic content beer is defined as beer with an alcohol content exceeding 2.8 but not 3.5 percent by volume, while beer consists of beer with an alcohol content exceeding 3.5 percent. A can consists of 50 centilitres beer. A bottle of wine consists of 75 centilitres, while a half bottle of spirits consists of 35 centilitres.

Explanatory Variables

As additional explanatory variables besides social capital, personal characteristics such as age, gender, and whether born in Sweden were included. Age was coded as 6 different dummy variables with the omitted category reference group being the oldest age group (ages 17–18). Other explanatory variables included were variables indicating whether the individual lived in a single-parent household, personal income,[4] and a number of dummy variables indicating the respondents housing situation. The variables were selected since they have been found to affect substance use in previous studies (Norton, Lindrooth, & Ennet, 1998; DeCicca, Kenkel, & Mathios, 2000; Lundborg, 2002; Lundborg & Lindgren, 2002).

In the case of binge drinking and smoking, the perceived risks of alcoholism and lung cancer, respectively, were included as additional explanatory variables. For illicit drug use, variables that indicated the perceived risk were, unfortunately, lacking from the data set. Descriptive statistics are shown in Table 1.

EMPIRICAL MODEL

For person i, the substance-use decision can be written as

$$Substance_i^* = \beta_0 + \beta_1 Y_{1i} + \beta_2 S_i + \varepsilon_i. \tag{1}$$

The latent variable $SUBSTANCE_i^*$ is not observable in practice, and, instead, we define a dummy variable, $SUBSTANCE_i$, taking the value 1 if $SUBSTANCE_i^* > 0$ and zero otherwise. Further, Y_{1i} represents a vector of explanatory variables, S_i represents the social capital variables, β_j is the associated vector of coefficients, and ε_i is a random term. Included in Y_{1i} were the other explanatory variables besides social capital, as described in the data section. Eq. (1) was estimated using a *probit-model*.[5] In order to facilitate interpretation of the results, marginal effects were calculated and reported.

RESULTS

Smoking

In the first column of Table 2, the results from the smoking equation are reported. Clearly both trust and social participation showed significant negative correlations with the prob-

[4] Personal income was assessed by asking the following question: "How much money are you able to spend each month (monthly pocket money + other income)."

[5] A logit model was also tested, but the results were similar.

TABLE 1 Descriptive statistics

Variable	Mean (sd.) Smoking	Illicit drug use	Binge drinking
Substances	0.161 (0.368)	0.055 (0.229)	0.383 (0.486)
Female	0.492 (0.500)	0.489 (0.500)	0.495 (0.500)
Born outside Sweden	0.088 (0.283)	0.087 (0.282)	0.087 (0.282)
One parent born outside Sweden	0.089 (0.286)	0.089 (0.284)	0.088 (0.284)
Two parents born outside Sweden	0.102 (0.303)	0.104 (0.305)	0.101 (0.301)
Age group 17–18	0.194 (0.396)	0.189 (0.392)	0.192 (0.394)
Age group 16–17	0.197 (0.398)	0.196 (0.397)	0.199 (0.399)
Age group 15–16	0.207 (0.405)	0.208 (0.406)	0.208 (0.406)
Age group 14–15	0.211 (0.408)	0.207 (0.405)	0.209 (0.407)
Age group 12–13	0.192 (0.394)	0.200 (0.400)	0.192 (0.394)
Co-operative flat	0.067 (0.250)	0.070 (0.255)	0.070 (0.255)
Terrace-house	0.120 (0.325)	0.121 (0.326)	0.120 (0.325)
House/farm	0.614 (0.487)	0.613 (0.487)	0.612 (0.487)
Rented room/ student's lodging	0.006 (0.077)	0 —	0.006 (0.077)
Live with mother only	0.172 (0.378)	0.171 (0.377)	0.174 (0.379)
Live with father only	0.035 (0.185)	0.035 (0.185)	0.035 (0.184)
Social participation	4.59 (1.96)	4.556 (1.983)	4.575 (1.959)
Trust	0.492 (0.500)	0.486 (0.500)	0.493 (0.500)
Income	8.294 (7.190)	8.317 (7.487)	8.342 (7.372)
Lung cancer risk perception	0.449 (0.291)	—	—
Alcoholism risk perception	—	—	24.950 (21.474)
Number of observations	1330	1443	1346

ability of smoking. High level of trust was correlated with a 0.06 decrease in the probability of smoking.

Being female was correlated with an increase in the probability of smoking with 0.04. The variable indicating being born outside Sweden, and the two variables indicating having one or two parents being born outside Sweden, showed no correlation with the probability of smoking. Furthermore, the three youngest age groups, i.e. ages 15–16, 14–15, and 12–13, were significantly less likely to be smokers.

Living in a terrace-house or a house/farm were correlated with a lower probability of smoking compared to the omitted reference category, living in a rented flat. Respondents living with only their father showed an increased risk of smoking, while living only with a mother showed no correlation with the probability of smoking. Higher income was associated with a significantly higher probability of smoking. Finally, perceived lung-cancer risks showed a significant negative correlation with the smoking probability.

Illicit Drugs

The second column of Table 2 presents the results from the estimation of the illicit drugs equation. High level of trust was associated with a decrease in the probability of having used illicit drugs with 0.029. Social participation however was only significant at the 10 percent level, although the sign was as expected.

Females were significantly less likely to have used illicit drugs. The probability decreased by 0.019. Being born outside Sweden, or having parents born outside Sweden, showed no statistically significant correlation with the probability of having used illicit drugs. However, belonging to the two youngest age groups, 14–15, and 12–13, was correlated with a lower probability.

Regarding living conditions, living in a house or farm was significantly correlated with a lower probability of illicit drug use. Furthermore, living with only a mother or father showed no statistically significant effect on the probability of illicit drug use. Finally, income showed a significant and positive correlation with the probability of having used illicit drugs.

Binge Drinking

In the third column of Table 2, the results from the binge drinking equation are shown. Trust did not show any statistically significant correlation with the probability of binge drinking. This is also true for the variable measuring social participation.

Being female was associated with a 0.07 lower probability of participating in binge drinking. Being born outside Sweden showed a negative correlation with the probability of binge drinking, although only significant at the 10 percent

TABLE 2 Probit model for smoking, illicit drug use, and binge drinking

Variable	Marginal effect (std. error)		
	Smoking[a]	Illicit drug use[a]	Binge drinking[a]
Female	0.044 (0.023)*	−0.019 (0.007)*	−0.071 (0.031)*
One parent born outside Sweden	0.047 (0.036)	0.005 (0.014)	0.110 (0.053)*
Both parents born outside Sweden	0.028 (0.059)	0.012 (0.018)	−0.105 (0.066)
Born outside Sweden	−0.030 (0.040)	−0.007 (0.015)	−0.129 (0.067)
Age group 16–17	−0.057 (0.027)	−0.012 (0.010)	−0.110 (0.048)*
Age group 15–16	−0.065 (0.020)**	−0.006 (0.011)	−0.180 (0.046)**
Age group 14–15	−0.090 (0.023)**	−0.034 (0.009)**	−0.293 (0.041)**
Age group 12–13	−0.167 (0.018)**	−0.047 (0.009)**	−0.455 (0.028)**
Co-operative flat	−0.043 (0.030)	−0.015 (0.010)	−0.077 (0.066)
Terrace-house	−0.066 (0.022)*	−0.016 (0.008)	−0.047 (0.048)
House/farm	−0.050 (0.025)*	−0.024 (0.013)*	−0.109 (0.042)*
Rented room/ student's lodging	−0.052 (0.057)	— —	0.098 (0.193)
Live with mother	0.022 (0.026)	0.011 (0.010)	0.023 (0.040)
Live with father	0.121 (0.066)*	−0.010 (0.016)	0.057 (0.088)
Social participation	−0.014 (0.004)**	−0.003 (0.002)	0.005 (0.008)
Trust	−0.061 (0.017)**	0.029 (0.010)**	−0.018 (0.031)
Income	0.005 (0.001)**	0.001 (0.000)**	0.004 (0.003)
Lung cancer risk perception	−0.074 (0.034)*	— —	— —
Alcoholism risk perception	— —	— —	−0.002 (0.001)*
Observations	1330	1443	1346

*Significant at 5% level; **significant at 1% level.
[a]Robust standard errors in parentheses.

level. However, having one parent being born outside Sweden was correlated with a higher probability of binge drinking. All the age variables were statistically significant and negative with the magnitude of the marginal effect increasing with younger age.

Respondents living in a house or farm had a significantly lower probability of participating in binge drinking. Living only with a father or a mother showed no correlation with the probability of binge drinking. Furthermore, income was not statistically significant. Finally, perceived risks of alcoholism showed a significant and negative correlation with the probability of binge drinking.

DISCUSSION AND CONCLUSIONS

According to the results from this study, social capital was negatively correlated with the probability of adolescent smoking and illicit drug use, but no statistically significant correlation with the probability of binge drinking was observed. Similar results in the case of smoking have been found in prior studies on an adult population (Lindström, 2003). The results for illicit drug use, however, have, to the knowledge of the author, not been obtained elsewhere. The finding that social capital showed no statistically significant correlation with binge drinking was in contrast to the finding of Weitzman and Kawachi (2000). However, both the measurement and the level of aggregation of social capital were different in their study. Also, their study was conducted in the United States and on an older age group (18–24) than in this study.

One explanation for the negative correlation found between social capital and substance use in the case of smoking and illicit drug use may be that individuals with high levels of social capital could more easily receive practical or emotional support in times when life is tough and/or stressful. Individuals facing a scarcity of social capital, however, could be more prone to utilise alternative stress-reducing factors, such as substance use, when facing stress. An additional explanation may be that individuals with large social networks, being an indicator of social capital, would be more monitored and controlled compared to an individual with no or small social network. Higher social capital would then increase the full cost of substance use.

It should be noted that the effects of social capital on adolescent substance use may be less clear-cut that suggested above. A large network may also increase the availability of substances for adolescents. For instance, adolescents with a larger social network may be more able to get hold of alcohol compared to adolescents with smaller social networks. Consequently, the latter effect may equal out the potential negative effect of social capital on binge drinking. This may explain why social capital showed no statistically significant effect on binge drinking in this paper. It remains to be settled, however, why this explanation should apply to binge drinking, but not to smoking or illicit drug use. One possibility is that even though a large social network may increase the availability of these substances as well, there may be strong countervailing effects of social capital on the consumption. As discussed above, adolescents with a large social network may be more monitored and controlled compared to adolescents with a small social network, and this effect of social capital may be stronger in the case of consumption of illicit drugs and smoking. This would, for instance, occur if these behaviours were less accepted by persons in the adolescent's social network than binge drinking. Since smoking and illicit drug use is much less common than binge drinking, this could indicate less acceptance and, thus, stronger regulating and monitoring effects of social capital than in the case of binge drinking.

Furthermore, substance use may affect social capital. In order to gain access to certain networks, the adolescent may have to behave in accordance with the members of the network in order to gain acceptance. This may include conforming to certain behaviours, which may include substance use. Peer effects in substance use has been documented in a number of studies (Bauman & Ennet, 1996; Norton et al., 1998; Gaviria & Raphael, 2001). Thus, further studies should investigate the potential for reverse causality in the relationship between social capital and substance use.

In accordance with a number of prior studies, individual levels of trust and social participation were used as indicators of social capital (Veenstra, 2000; Lindström, 2003; Locher et al., 2005). The use of trust as an indicator has been challenged, however. It has been found in a simple experimental trust game that the answers to trust questions do not predict trusting behaviour (Glaeser et al., 2002). It should also be acknowledged that other proxies for social capital, such as social support, have been used. In this study, however, the most commonly used indicators in the literature, social participation and trust, were used.

Living only with a father was positively correlated with smoking. As suggested by Coleman (1990), living in a single-parent family may indicate lower within-family social capital. If this is the case, the correlation between living in a single-parent family and substance is expected. However, living in a single-parent household may also act as a proxy for having divorced parents. Events such as divorces may be related to increased stress and, thus, to increased risk of the adolescent resorting to substance use in order to produce stress-relief.

Social capital may also be reflected in the variables measuring the housing situation of the respondent. The results showed that living in a house or farm was associated with a lower probability of participating in smoking, illicit drug use, and binge drinking. Prior studies have found that house-owners have higher levels of social capital (Glaeser et al., 2002). This has been explained by the reduced mobility following from owning a house and the increased social capital following from low mobility. Obviously, the higher social capital of house-owners may spill over to their children.

Among other variables, it was found that income was positively and significantly correlated with the probability of smoking and illicit drug use, but not to the probability of binge drinking. Furthermore, the perceived risks of lung-cancer and alcoholism were associated with a lower probability of smoking and binge drinking, respectively. This was expected since a significant portion of the "full price" of substance use is the risk of facing future health hazards. Such effects were also found in Lundborg and Lindgren (2004) and Viscusi (1990, 1991) for the case of smoking, and in Lundborg and Lindgren (2002) for the case of alcohol consumption.

Further studies should examine whether there are differential effects on substance use from formal and informal social participation. For instance, both participation in political meetings and visiting parties were included in the questions on social capital. It is certainly possible that the effect of these two activities on substance use differs.

The results from this study should be viewed as explorative, rather than saying something about the causality involved. Consequently, one should be careful in drawing policy conclusions based on the results. In order to say something about the causality between social capital and substance use, a theoretical framework is needed. Such a theory should describe how decisions about substance use and investments in social capital and health are made simultaneously and in a dynamic perspective. Future economic research in the area should be devoted to development of theory and testing, using longitudinal data.

ACKNOWLEDGMENTS

The author would like to thank Kristian Bolin, Sören Höjgård, Björn Lindgren, Katarina Steen-Karlsson, and two anonymous referees for helpful comments. The financial support from the Swedish Social Research Council and Handelsbankens forskningsstiftelser is gratefully acknowledged.

REFERENCES

Bauman, K. E., & Ennet, S. T. (1996). On the importance of peer influence for adolescent drug use: Commonly neglected considerations. *Addiction*, *91*, 85–198.

Bolin, K., Lindgren, B., Lindström, M., & Nystedt, P. (2003). Investments in social capital—implications of social interactions for the production of health. *Social Science & Medicine*, *56*, 2379–2390.

Carlsson, P., & Vågerö, D. (1998). The social pattern of heavy drinking in Russia during transition. Evidence from Taganrog. *European Journal of Public Health*, *8*, 280–285.

Cohen, S., & Wills, T. A. (1985). Stress, social support, and the buffering hypothesis. *Psychological Bulletin*, *98*, 310–357.

Coleman, J. S. (1990). *Foundations of social theory*. Cambridge, MA: Harvard University Press.

DeCicca, P., Kenkel, D. S., & Mathios, A. (2000). Racial difference in the determinants of smoking onset. *Journal of Risk and Uncertainty*, *21*, 311–340.

Gaviria, A., & Raphael, S. (2001). School-based peer effects and juvenile behaviour. *Review of Economics and Statistics*, *83*, 257–268.

Glaeser, E. L. (2001). The formation of social capital. In ch. 16 in *The Contribution of Human and Social Capital to Sustained Economic Growth and Well-Being*, International Symposium Report, Human Resources Development Canada (HRDC) and Organisation for Economic Co-operation and Development (OECD).

Glaeser, E. L., Laibson, D., & Sacerdote, B. (2002). The economic approach to social capital. *Economic Journal*, *112*, 811–846.

Kawachi, I., Kennedy, B. P., Lochner, K., & Prothow-Stith, D. (1997). Social capital, income inequality and mortality. *American Journal of Public Health*, *87*, 1491–1498.

Lindström, M. (2000). *Social participation, social capital, and socioeconomic differences in health-related behaviours. An epidemiological study*. Doctoral dissertation, Department of Community Medicine, Lund University.

Lindström, M. (2003). Social capital and the miniaturization of community among daily and intermittent smokers: A population-based study. *Preventive Medicine*, *36*, 177–184.

Lindström, M. (2004a). Social capital, the miniaturisation of community and self-reported global and psychological health. *Social Science & Medicine*, *59*, 595–607.

Lindström, M. (2004b). Social capital, the miniaturization of community and cannabis smoking among young adults. *European Journal of Public Health*, *14*, 204–208.

Lindström, M., Hansson, B. S., Östergren, P., & Berglund, G. (2000). Socioeconomic differences in smoking cessation: The role of social participation. *Scandinavian Journal of Public Health*, *28*, 200–208.

Locher, J., Ritchie, C. S., Roth, L. D. L., Baker, P. S., Bodner, E. V., & Allman, R. M. (2005). Social isolation, support, and capital and nutritional risk in an older sample: Ethnic and gender differences. *Social Science & Medicine*, *60*, 747–761.

Lowell, A. M. (2002). Risking risk: The influence of types of capital and social networks on the injection practices and social capital. *Social Science & Medicine*, *55*, 803–821.

Lundborg, P. (2002). Young people and alcohol: An econometric analysis. *Addiction*, *97*, 1573–1582.

Lundborg, P. (2003). *Risky health behaviours among adolescents*. Doctoral dissertation, Department of Economics, Lund University.

Lundborg, P., & Lindgren, B. (2002). Risk perceptions and alcohol consumption among young people. *Journal of Risk and Uncertainty*, *25*, 165–183.

Lundborg, P., & Lindgren, B. (2004). Do they know what they are doing? Risk perceptions and smoking behaviour among teenagers. *Journal of Risk and Uncertainty*, *28*, 261–286.

Macinko, J., & Starfield, B. (2001). The utility of social capital in research on health determinants. *The Milbank Quarterly*, *79*, 387–427.

Norton, E. C., Lindrooth, R. C., & Ennet, S. T. (1998). Controlling for the endogeneity of peer substance use on adolescent alcohol and tobacco use. *Health Economics*, *7*, 439–453.

Pevalin, D. J., & Rose, D. (2003). *Social capital for health. Investigating the links between social capital and health using the British Household Panel Survey.* Research report, Health Development Agency.

Portes, A. (1998). Social capital: Its origins and applications in modern sociology. *Annual Review of Sociology, 24,* 1–24.

Putnam, R. (1995). Bowling alone: America's declining social capital. *Journal of Democracy, 6,* 65–78.

Putnam, R. (2000). *Bowling alone: The collapse and revival of American community.* New York: Simon and Schuster.

Putnam, R. (2001). Social capital: Measurement and consequences. *Canadian Journal of Policy Research, 2,* 41–51.

Rose, R. (2000). How much does social capital add to individual health? A survey study of Russians. *Social Science & Medicine, 51,* 1421–1435.

Subramanian, S. V., Kawachi, I., & Kennedy, B. P. (2001). Does the state you live in make a difference? Multilevel analysis of self-rated health in the US. *Social Science & Medicine, 53,* 9–19.

Tsutsumi, A., Tsutsumi, K., Kayaba, K., & Igaraschi, M. (1998). Health-related behaviours, social support and community morale. *International Journal of Behavioural Medicine, 5,* 166–182.

Veenstra, G. (2000). Social capital, SES and health: An individual-level analysis. *Social Science & Medicine, 50,* 619–629.

Viscusi, W. K. (1990). Do smokers underestimate risks? *Journal of Political Economy, 98,* 1253–1268.

Viscusi, W. K. (1991). Age variations in risk perceptions and smoking decisions. *The Review of Economics and Statistics, 73,* 577–588.

Weitzman, E. R., & Kawachi, I. (2000). Giving means receiving: The protective effect of social capital on binge drinking on college campuses. *American Journal of Public Health, 90,* 1936–1939.

Woolcock, M. (2001). The place of social capital in understanding social and economic outcomes. *Canadian Journal of Policy Research, 2,* 11–17.

Article Source: Lundborg, P. (2005). Social capital and substance use among Swedish adolescents—an exploratory study. *Social Science & Medicine, 61*(12), 1151–1158.

QUESTIONS

1. What were the indicators of social capital used in this article?
2. What did the author find the relationship to be between social capital and drinking, smoking, and drug use?
3. Explain how your social capital affects your own alcohol, smoking, and drug use.
4. What were the explanations offered for these outcomes in the article?
5. How are these explanations similar or different from the ones you proposed to explain the relationship between your own social capital and your drinking, smoking, and drug use behavior?

CHAPTER REFERENCES

Almedon, A. (2005). Social capital and mental health: An interdisciplinary review of primary evidence. *Social Science & Medicine, 61*(5), 943–964.

American Heart Association. (2006). Alliance for a Healthier Generation and industry leaders set healthy school beverage guidelines for U.S. schools. Retrieved May 8, 2006, from http://www.americanheart.org/presenter.jhtml?identifier=3039339.

Berkman, L., Glass, T., Brissette, I., & Seeman, T. (2000). From social integration to health: Durkheim in the new millennium. *Social Science & Medicine, 51,* 843–857.

Berkman, L., & Kawachi, I. (2000). *Social Epidemiology.* New York: Oxford University Press.

Bolin, K., Lindgren, B., Lindstrom, M., & Nystedt, P. (2003). Investments in social capital—implications of social interactions for the production of health. *Social Science & Medicine, 56*(12), 2379–2390.

Carpiano, R.M. (2006). Toward a neighborhood resource-based theory of social capital for health: Can Bourdieu and sociology help? *Social Science and Medicine, 62,* 165–175.

Crow, G. (2002). The relationship between trust, social capital and organizational success. *Nursing Administration Quarterly, 26*(3), 1–11.

Eddy, J.M., Donahue, R.E., Webster, R.D., & Bjornstad, E. (2002). Application of an ecological perspective in worksite health promotion: A review. *American Journal of Health Studies, 17*(4), 197–202.

Goran, M.I., Gower, B.A., Nagy, T.R., & Johnson, R.K. (1998). Developmental changes in energy expenditure and physical activity in children: Evidence for a decline in physical activity in girls before puberty. *Pediatrics, 101*(5), 887–891.

Hawe, P., & Shiell, A. (2000). Social capital and health promotion. A review. *Social Science & Medicine, 51,* 871–885.

Kawachi, I., Kennedy, B.P., Lochner, K., & Prothrow-Stith, D. (1997). Social capital, income inequality and mortality. *American Journal of Public Health, 87,* 1491–1498.

McLeroy, K.R., Bibeau, D., Steckler, A., & Glanz, K. (1988). An ecological perspective on health promotion programs. *Health Education Quarterly, 15,* 351–377.

Novilla, M.L.B., Barnes, M.D., DeLaCruz, N.G., Williams, P.N., & Rogers, J. (2006). Public health perspectives on the family: An ecological approach to promoting health in the family and community. *Family and Community Health, 29*(1), 28–42.

Putnam, R.D. (2000). *Bowling Alone: The Collapse and Revival of American Community.* New York: Simon and Schuster.

Putnam, R.D., Leonardi, R., & Nanetti, R.Y. (1993). *Making Democracy Work: Civic Traditions in Modern Italy.* Princeton, NJ: Princeton University Press.

Rose, N. (2000). Citizenship and the third way. *American Behavioral Scientist, 43,* 1395–1411.

Ross, C.E., & Jang, S.J. (2000). Neighborhood disorder, fear, and mistrust: The buffering role of social ties with neighbors. *American Journal of Community Psychology, 28*(4), 401–420.

Sallis, J.F., & Owen, N. (1997). Ecological models of health behavior. In K. Glanz, B.K. Rimer, & F.M. Lewis (Eds.), *Health Behavior and Health Education* (2nd ed., pp. 403–424). San Francisco: Jossey-Bass.

Sallis, J.F., & Owen, N. (1999). *Physical Activity and Behavioral Medicine.* Thousand Oaks, CA: Sage Publications.

Sallis, J.F., & Owen, N. (2002). Ecological models of health behavior. In K. Glanz, B.K. Rimer, & F.M. Lewis (Eds.), *Health Behavior and Health Education* (3rd ed, pp. 462–484). San Francisco: Jossey-Bass.

Spence, J.C., & Lee, R.E. (2002). Toward a comprehensive model of physical activity. *Psychology of Sport and Exercise, 4,* 7–24.

Stokols, D. (1992). Establishing and maintaining healthy environments: Toward a social ecology of health promotion. *American Psychologist, 47*(1), 6–22.

Szreter, S. (2002). The state of social capital: Bringing back in power, politics, and history. *Theory and Society, 31*(2), 573–621.

Szreter, S., & Woolcock, M. (2004). Health by association? Social capital, social theory and the political economy of public health. *International Journal of Epidemiology, 33*(4), 650–667.

Veenstra, G., Luginaah, L., Wakefield, S., Birch, S., Eyles, J., & Elliott, S. (2005). Who you know, where you live: Social capital, neighborhood and health. *Social Science & Medicine, 60,* 2799–2818.

von Bothmer, M.I.K., Mattsson, B., & Fridlund, B. (2002). Influences on adolescent smoking behaviour: Siblings' smoking and norms in the social environment do matter. *Health and Social Care in the Community, 10*(4), 213–220

Wakefield, S.E.L., & Poland, B. (2005). Family, friend or foe? Critical reflections on the relevance and role of social capital in health promotion and community development. *Social Science & Medicine, 60,* 2819–2832.

Watt, G.F., Donahue, R.E., Eddy, J.M., & Wallace, E.V. (2001). Use of an ecological approach to worksite health promotion. *American Journal of Health Studies, 17*(3), 144–147.

Woolcock, M. (2001). The place of social capital in understanding social and economic outcomes. *Canadian Journal of Policy Research, 2*(1), 1–17.

World Health Organization. (2006). Ecological framework. Retrieved May 6, 2006, from http://www.who.int/violenceprevention/approach/ecology/en.

Choosing a Theory

After reading this chapter the student will be able to:

1. Explain how theory is applied in practice.

2. Use a set of guidelines to choose a theory.

3. Determine whether a chosen theory is appropriate for the given situation.

GUIDELINES FOR CHOOSING A THEORY

Knowing some of the many different theories and models that can be used to explain health behavior is one thing—knowing which theory to use when is another. Unfortunately, there is no magic formula or chart to tell you which of the theories is just right for a given situation, because there are no right or wrong theories. Some may work better than others in a particular situation, with a certain population, to address a specific health problem, or to produce a desired result.

With this said, the following guidelines may help you narrow down the choices:

1. Identify the health issue or problem and the population affected.
2. Gather information about the issue or population or both.
3. Identify possible reasons or causes for the problem.
4. Identify the level of interaction (intrapersonal, interpersonal, or community) under which the reasons or causes most logically fit.

5. Identify the theory or theories that best match the level and the reasons or causes.

Identify the Health Issue and the Population Affected

The first and most logical step in identifying a theory is to identify the health issues you are trying to address and the population affected. Is the issue alcohol use at the high school, a head lice outbreak at the local day care center, or falls among the elderly? Each problem and population may require a different theory. The same problem in different populations may also require different theories.

Gather Information

Next, do a literature search to learn what others have found and done about the issue. A literature search is not limited to a search of the Internet (Figure 10.1). You need to search the professional literature using an appropriate database. Ones commonly used for health education and health promotion include the following:

- CINAHL (Cumulative Index to Nursing and Allied Health Literature): Available through a university or college library or a public library
- Academic Premier Search: Accessed through a university or college library
- PubMed: Maintained by the National Library of Medicine and National Institutes of Health; accessed directly at http://www.pubmed.gov

FIGURE 10.1 Conduct a literature search.

- ERIC (Education Resource Information Center): The database for school health information; accessed directly at http://www.eric.ed.gov

Identify Possible Reasons or Causes for the Problem

Third, take the information you found in the literature and combine it with the information you have from your community. This will enable you to identify possible causes for the problem, that is, to answer the question "Why does this problem exist?" Remember, theories help explain the *why* of health behavior, that is, why people do what they do. Why is it that some people fall, use alcohol, get head lice, go for mammograms, or do self testicular exams, and others do not?

Identify the Level of Interaction

Once you have determined possible causes or reasons why the health issue exists, it is time to determine under which level of interaction these reasons fall—intrapersonal, interpersonal, community, or all three. Identifying the level helps you determine which theories would most likely explain the behavior and therefore would best serve as the basis for change.

Identify the Theory or Theories That Match Best

Use the Theory Chart that accompanies this chapter to help you identify which theories would most likely explain the

behavior and enable you to plan an intervention to change the behaviors you have identified. Remember, for a theory to be most effective, all of it should be used (Hochbaum, Sorenson, & Lorig, 1992), although sometimes health educators do mix and match aspects from the different theories.

Let's say that the health issue is a high rate of influenza among the elderly in your community. After assessing the situation, you find that the reasons for this are poor compliance with influenza vaccination, lack of transportation to the health department, and inadequate parking facilities. An ecological approach would be appropriate in this situation to explain the poor compliance behavior, but it might also be explained by the perceived barriers construct of the Health Belief Model.

When you think you have determined which theory would fit best, see how it answers the following questions (National Cancer Institute [NCI], 2003):

- Is it logical given the situation you are trying to address?
- Is it similar to the theories others have used successfully in similar situations, as you found in the literature?
- Is it supported by research?

Choosing a theory is a lot like choosing your clothes. All of your clothes do the same thing—they cover your body—but they do so in different ways. You choose which clothes to wear depending on a host of factors, such as time of day, climate, occasion, and what your friends are wearing (if you're female, it may depend on whether you have the right shoes to wear). For example, you wouldn't wear a bathing suit to shovel snow. Once you have decided on which clothes to wear, you need to try them on to see whether they fit.

Theories, just like clothes, all do the same thing. They all help explain why people do what they do, but they do it in different ways. You choose a theory depending on a host of factors such as behavioral causes of the health issue or problem, the level of interaction (intrapersonal, interpersonal, or community), the target population, and the desired outcomes or change. Once you decide on which theory to use, you need to apply it to see whether it fits.

Theory Chart

Level	Theory	Constructs
Intrapersonal	*Self-Efficacy Theory:* People will only try to do what they think they can do, and people won't try what they think they can't do.	Mastery experience Vicarious experience Verbal persuasion Emotional state
	Theory of Reasoned Action and Theory of Planned Behavior: Health behavior results from intention influenced by attitude, norms, and control.	Attitudes Subjective norms Behavioral control Volitional control
	Health Belief Model: Personal beliefs influence health behavior.	Perceived seriousness Perceived susceptibility Perceived benefits Perceived barriers Cues to action Modifying variables Self-efficacy
	Attribution Theory: There is a cause or explanation for things that happen.	Locus of control Stability Controllability
	Transtheoretical Model or Stages of Change: Behavior change is a process that occurs in stages.	Stages of change Processes of change Self-efficacy
Interpersonal	*Social Cognitive Theory:* Behavior, personal factors, and environmental factors interact with each other, and changing one changes them all.	Self-efficacy Observational learning Expectations Expectancies Emotional arousal Behavioral capability Reinforcement Locus of control
Community	*Diffusion of Innovation:* Behavior changes as innovations are adopted.	Innovation Communication channels Time Social system
	Ecological Models: Factors at many levels influence health behavior.	Intrapersonal level Interpersonal level Community level Institution level Societal level
	Social Capital Theory: Behavior is influenced by who we know and how we know them.	Bonding relationships Bridging relationships Linking relationships

THEORY IN ACTION: CLASS ACTIVITY

In small groups, brainstorm possible causes for the low level of physical activity among female students on your campus. In your discussion, take into account the ethnic diversity of your small group, as well as that of the student population on your campus in general. List the possible causes or reasons for the lack of physical activity. Based on this (limited) information, use the theory chart in this chapter to identify a theory or theories that may be appropriate to explain the behavior and which can then be used as the basis for an intervention to increase their physical activity level. Provide a rationale for why you made this choice.

Now read the following article and answer the questions at the end.

Camine con Nosotros: Connecting Theory and Practice for Promoting Physical Activity Among Hispanic Women

FRANCISCO G. SOTO MAS, MD, MPH

WILLIAM M. KANE, PhD

SCOTT GOING, PhD

EARL S. FORD, MD, PhD

JAMES R. MARSHALL, PhD

LISA K. STATEN, PhD

JOAN E. SMITH, BSN, MBA

Francisco G. Soto Mas, MD, MPH, is at the University of New Mexico College of Education, Albuquerque, NM.

William M. Kane, PhD, is an associate professor in the health education program at the University of New Mexico College of Education, Albuquerque, NM.

Scott Going, PhD, is an associate research scientist in the Department of Nutritional Sciences, at the University of Arizona, Tucson, AZ.

Earl S. Ford, MD, PhD, is in the Division of Nutrition and Physical Activity at the Centers for Disease Control and Prevention.

James R. Marshall, PhD, is a professor of public health at the Arizona Cancer Center, Tucson, AZ.

Lisa K. Staten, PhD, is a research assistant professor of public health at the Arizona Cancer Center, Tucson, AZ.

Joan E. Smith, BSN, MBA, is an adult program operations administrator in the Office of Chronic Disease Prevention, Bureau of Prevention and Health Promotion, Arizona Department of Health Services, Phoenix, AZ.

ABSTRACT

Despite the popularity and widespread use of theory in health education, practitioners still find it difficult to design and implement theory-based interventions. This is especially true when working with ethnic/racial minority groups, including Hispanic groups. Practitioners working with Hispanic communities face additional barriers that may often discourage them from using theories when planning interventions. These barriers include the diversity that exists within the Hispanic population, lack of reliable data, and issues related to cross-cultural applicability of current behavior theories. However, the use of theory constitutes a valuable tool for developing more effective programs, and theorist researchers should be more sensitive to practitioners' needs. By explaining the processes for selecting and applying theory in the same detail as outcome results, researchers will contribute to increasing practitioners' interest in theory. This article describes *Camine con Nosotros*, a theory-based physical activity program for Hispanic women, and explains the process of selecting the theoretical framework of the program and connecting theory and practice.

Over the past 30 years, the fields of health education and health promotion have shown significant development, particularly in program planning and evaluation. A considerable contributing factor has been the application of behavioral and social science theory, which facilitates the planning and evaluation of programs. However, practical explanation of the processes by which theories are selected and applied is lacking in the literature. As a consequence, practitioners find it difficult to connect theory and practice and to design and implement theory-based programs. The recognition of the difficulties faced in applying theory in everyday practice is not new: In the 1980s and early 1990s, theorist researchers made some effort to address the issue (D'Onofrio, 1992; Turner, 1987; van Ryn & Heaney, 1992). Nevertheless, there is still a recognized need for bridging the gap between theory and practice (Bartholomew, Parcel, & Kok, 1998; Glanz, Lewis, & Rimer, 1997), and innovative models to facilitate the process of selecting and applying theories are being proposed (Bartholomew et al., 1998).

Despite efforts to overcome utilization barriers, connecting theory and practice is, in many cases, a challenge for health educators, especially for those working with Hispanic populations. Lack of familiarity with cultural and psychosocial issues can lead practitioners to choose theories that are inconsistent with the particular characteristics of the participant population or to inappropriately predict the relationship between their key variables. It is the responsibility of the program planner to understand the cultural and psychological contexts of the population subject to intervention, and to select theories that properly address the factors related to the behavior to be studied. From this perspective, it has been suggested that researchers who belong to the same ethnic group being studied are better able to understand and analyze the cultural and psychosocial realities of that group (Marín & VanOss, 1991; Rogler, Malgady, & Rodríguez, 1989). Other researchers argue that some of the differences between Hispanics and non-Hispanics in epidemiological studies can, in part, be explained by the misinterpretation of data by professionals who are not familiar with Hispanic cultural issues (Good & Good, 1986). The recognized lack of Hispanic public health professionals, including researchers (Cantor, Bergeisen, & Baker, 1998; Palepu et al., 1998; Soto Mas & Papenfuss, 1997), may constitute a considerable barrier to the use of theory with Hispanic communities.

Practitioners working with Hispanics face additional barriers that may discourage them from considering the use of theory. First, the Hispanic population is composed of a variety of groups, with different national origins, acculturation levels, language skills, races, and life experiences. Second, the health status of Hispanics is still imprecisely known and insufficiently analyzed; contradictions exist not only in reported mortality and morbidity but also in risk factors and behavior data (Soto Mas, Papenfuss, & Guerrero, 1997). This makes it more difficult for practitioners to find the resources for developing a sound theoretical framework for a particu-

lar Hispanic group and to understand the circumstances that influence the health behaviors of the participant population. It may also be the reason why some authors point out that, in planning and delivering health education and promotion programs, practitioners usually depend on models that have not been developed to meet the needs of Hispanic communities (National Coalition of Hispanic Health and Human Services Organizations [COSSMHO], 1995).

Practitioners working with Hispanics may have other reasons to be confused about the appropriateness of using theory. Generalization across populations is considered by some authors to be a characteristic of formal theory (Green, 1991; van Ryn & Heaney, 1992), and studies have found that the combination of elements from different models has broad applicability across ethnic groups (Pasick, 1997). On the other hand, the lack of cultural sensitivity has been cited as a main weakness of current health behavior theories (Pasick, 1997; Pasick, D'Onofrio, & Otero-Sabogal, 1996). The literature also alerts researchers to the danger of assuming universality of theoretical concepts or constructs, and recommends the distention between what is ethnic or universal and what is emic or group specific (Marín & VanOss, 1991). Although teasing apart these conflicting views and agreeing on the cross-cultural applicability of theory are essential to research in social and behavioral sciences and health education, the discourse confuses practitioners and discourages them from using theory.

Nevertheless, we should insist on the benefits of developing theory-based interventions for Hispanic populations. Although using theories and models cannot guarantee the success of a program, they provide a framework in which programmers can better plan, implement, and evaluate an intervention. They also contribute to the understanding of conditions affecting specific behaviors and help us identify factors and circumstances that are most likely to produce particular results (D'Onofrio, 1992). Therefore, we should commit to building practitioners' confidence in theory and to providing them with the resources to select and apply theory in a rational way. *Camine con Nosotros* (Come Walk with Us), the program described here, is an example of a theory-based intervention that was developed following a rational process that facilitates the selection and practical application of a theoretical framework.

CAMINE CON NOSOTROS

Background

The first surgeon general's report on physical activity and health (U.S. Department of Health and Human Services,

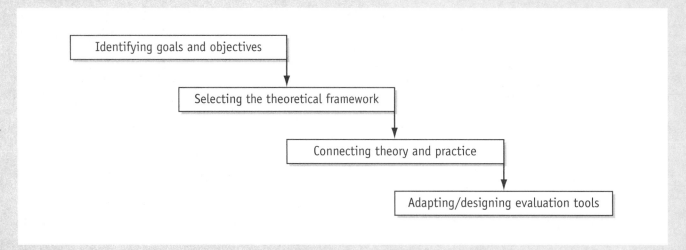

FIGURE 1 From Theory to Practice

1996) declares the need for promoting physical activity among minority populations and developing theory-based strategies that facilitate the planning, implementation, and evaluation of physical activity interventions. One group in need of effective programs promoting regular physical activity is the Hispanic adult population. Regional and national data demonstrate that Hispanic adults have lower levels of physical activity than Whites (Burchfield et al., 1990; Centers for Disease Control and Prevention [CDC], 1992, 1994; Crespo, Keteyian, Heath, & Sempos, 1996; Hovell et al., 1991; Perez-Stable, Marín, & Marín, 1994). In addition, the *Healthy People 2000 Review, 1997* (National Center for Health Statistics [NCHS], 1997) shows that Hispanics are far from reaching the year 2000 physical activity objectives: 34% of Hispanics age 18 years and older are sedentary (year 2000 target = 25%), and only 13.6% engage in vigorous physical activity and 20% in moderate physical activity (year 2000 target = 17% and 25%, respectively). Within the Hispanic population, adult women merit particular attention. The prevalence of physical inactivity is higher among Hispanic women than among Hispanic men. In comparison with White women, Hispanic women have been shown to have lower levels of leisure-time physical activity and lower levels of light to moderate and vigorous physical activity (CDC, 1991a, 1991b). Sixty-one percent of Hispanic women report a sedentary lifestyle (defined as less than 3 sessions of leisure-time physical activity a week), compared with 56.4% of White women ("Prevalence of Selected Risk Factors," 1994).

Given the demonstrated relationship between physical activity and health, the promotion of physical activity among Hispanic women should become a public health priority. Although health promotion programs aimed at His-

panic women have traditionally focused on maternal health (CDC, 1994), the prevalence of chronic diseases among this group calls for a different approach. Coronary heart disease, stroke, breast and colorectal cancer, diabetes, and hypertension are the leading causes of morbidity and mortality among Hispanic women (CDC, 1994), all of which point to physical activity as a particularly effective prevention strategy. In addition, the impact of chronic conditions on this group is expected to increase during the next two decades. As more Hispanics move into an older age group, more women will be living with chronic disease and disability for longer periods of time (Soto Mas, 1999).

Camine con Nosotros is a theory-based physical activity program for Hispanic women age 50 years and older in Maricopa County, Arizona. The program selected a theoretical framework through a step-by-step process that began with the identification of the goals and objectives of the intervention (see Figure 1).

Identifying Goals and Objectives

The goal of *Camine con Nosotros* was to decrease risk factors for cardiovascular disease by increasing participants' daily physical activity level. Because the qualifying requirements for participation included not having medical insurance or not qualifying for state medical assistance, it was expected that the participating population would include mainly low-income women from underserved communities. Because of the region's proximity to the border, a high percentage of Mexican-descendent participants were expected.

Focus groups and a review of the literature assisted in the identification of the measurable objectives of the program. Several studies have demonstrated that the level of intensity

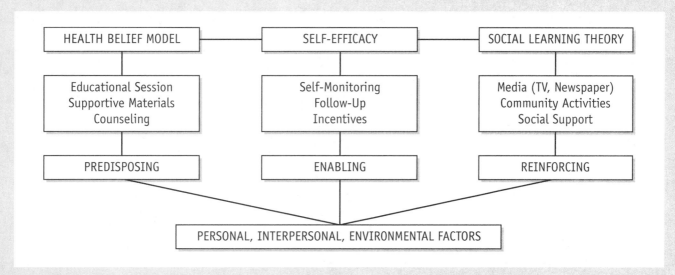

FIGURE 2 *Camine con Nosotros* Theoretical Design

is related to participation in physical activities. Low to moderate intensity, home-based activities are more likely to be adopted (King, Haskell, Young, Oka, & Stefanick, 1995; Pollock, 1998), especially if cognitive-behavioral strategies and regular follow-up support are included (e.g., self-monitoring, personal contact, and feedback) (King et al., 1997). In addition, walking is one of the preferred types of leisure-time physical activity of U.S. adults, including Mexican Americans (Crespo et al., 1996), and it is well suited to the population in this study, which faces limited availability of and access to exercise facilities. Therefore, a home-based program was identified as the most feasible approach for this group. To be consistent with current recommendations for physical activity in healthy adults, the objective of the program was established as engaging participants in 30 minutes of walking, 5 days a week, during the period of the intervention (1 year). A moderate intensity level was adopted (between 50% and 70% of the age-predicted maximum heart rate, defined as 220 minus age).

Selecting the Theoretical Framework

Through focus groups made up of community lay health advisers (*promotoras*), prospective participants, and health education specialists, key issues related to physical activity in the population studied by *Camine con Nosotros* were identified. Although the idea of exercising appealed to focus group participants, program planners found three main issues of concern: (a) lack of knowledge of the relationship between moderate physical activity and health, (b) perceived lack of personal resources for engaging in regular physical activity,

and (c) lack of environmental support (family, friends, and community) for performing the intended behavior. Three theoretical frameworks were selected to address these factors: the Health Belief Model (HBM), self-efficacy (SE), and the Social Learning Theory (SLT) (see Figure 2).

HBM. According to the HBM, a person's health-related behavior depends on his or her perception of (a) the severity of the problem or illness, (b) his or her vulnerability to that problem, and (c) the benefits and barriers to taking preventive action (Houchbaum, 1958). Although the model focuses on cognitive-perceptive variables, which have been questioned as predictors of physical activity behaviors (Dishman & Sallis, 1994; Mirotznik, Feldman, & Stein, 1995; Oldridge & Streiner, 1990), researchers recommended the use of the HBM for a number of reasons. It is known that knowledge and information vary across populations (Finnegan, Viswanath, Kahn, & Hannan, 1993; Tichenor, Donohue, & Olien, 1970), and due to language and cultural barriers, Hispanics may have less access than other groups to quality health information (Jacobson, 1999). This may influence their health-related knowledge, perceptions, attitudes, and behaviors. The San Antonio Heart Study found that Mexicans were significantly less informed than non-Hispanic Whites on how to prevent heart attacks and on the benefits of regular exercise (Hazuda, Stern, Gaskill, Haffner, & Gardner, 1983). Other studies have found that Hispanics have more misconceptions about the health consequences of certain risk behaviors than Anglos (Ford & Jones, 1991; Perez-Stable, Sabogal, Otero-Sabogal, Hiatt, & McPhee, 1992). Therefore, a theoretical model such as the HBM, which emphasizes knowledge and perception, seemed appropriate for a population to which the health outcome of a preventive behavior (e.g., physical activity) may never have been properly presented. Other studies have shown an association between the knowledge of and belief in the health benefits of physical activity and the adoption and maintenance of an exercise program in men and women (Dishman & Gettman, 1980; Dishman & Steinhardt, 1990; Sallis et al., 1986). In addition, positive (benefits) and negative (barriers) behavioral outcome expectations, both principal constructs of the HBM, have been associated with physical activity among adults (Ali & Twibell, 1995; Neuberger, Kasal, Smith, Hassanein, & DeViney, 1994). It has been proposed that decreasing the perceived barriers to exercise may facilitate walking among healthy middle-class Hispanic adults (Hovell et al., 1991). All of these issues can be addressed through an educational component based on the HBM.

SE. SE is the confidence that people have in performing a behavior in a specific situation (Bandura, 1977). SE has been found to be significantly associated with the adoption and maintenance of an exercise program (Caspersen, Christenson, & Pollard, 1986; Sallis, Hovell, & Hofstetter, 1992; Sallis et al., 1989). It has also been positively correlated with physical activity among older adults, women (Sallis et al., 1989), and Hispanics (Hovell et al., 1991). SE is a major construct in SLT, and Bandura (1986) considers SE to be the most important prerequisite for behavioral change. Performance accomplishments, vicarious experiences, verbal persuasion, and physiological feedback are factors influencing SE (Bandura, 1977). It has been suggested that feelings of low SE may be more common among racial/ethnic minority groups, including Hispanics. Some authors relate this lower SE among Hispanics to misconceptions about the relationship between certain risk behaviors and disease, given that misconceptions can give a false perception of the need for change (Jackson, Proulx, & Pelican, 1991).

SLT. Finally, Bandura's (1986) SLT depicts human behavior as an interactive model between environmental, personal, and behavioral factors. Reinforcement, observational learning, self-control, expectations, behavioral capability, and emotional coping responses, together with SE, are principal constructs in SLT (Bandura, 1977). Another construct is the environment, or the external factors that affect behavior. These factors can be particularly important for promoting physical activity among Hispanic women for several reasons. First, the term *environment* includes the social environment, such as family members, friends, and peers, who are part of the cultural legacy of Hispanics. In Hispanic culture, the family constitutes an emotional support system that includes both immediate and extended members. This broad conception includes the community, which generally serves as a support network (COSSMHO, 1995). Second, environment also refers to factors such as place, time, or facilities, which are also crucial in health promotion programs for underserved Hispanic communities. More than 26% of Hispanic families live in poverty (U.S. Bureau of the Census, 1993) and in neighborhoods that are likely to be lacking in available spaces for exercise and recreational activities. They may also live in areas with critical social problems and safety concerns. All of these factors influence the adoption and maintenance of a physical activity program.

The three theories discussed above were deemed appropriate for this program, given the particular characteristics of the problem to be addressed, the population, and the identified socioeconomic and environmental factors.

Connecting Theory and Practice

The next question that a program planner confronts after deciding on a theoretical framework is how to connect theory and practice, that is, how to develop an intervention that is consistent with the concepts and variables of the selected theory or theories. *Camine con Nosotros* took a comprehensive approach to addressing the modifiable determinants of physical activity. The intervention considered individual, interpersonal, and environmental approaches.

To be consistent with the HBM, an educational session based on the three key variables of the model was developed. This included a lesson plan with goals and measurable learning objectives. The leading causes of mortality and morbidity within the Hispanic female adult population and their relation to physical inactivity served as a basis for addressing perceived susceptibility. Perceived severity was addressed by presenting the most common illnesses among this population for which a sedentary lifestyle constitutes a risk factor. Preventive action to be taken (increasing daily physical activity through walking) and specific instructions on how, where, and when were included for developing a positive effect on expectations (perceived benefits). Perceived barriers, such as the identification of an appropriate location, safety issues, and walking equipment, were also addressed. Activities for SE, such as assessing the heart rate while walking, preventing injury, and self-monitoring, were included as part of the educational component. In addition to the educational session, a bilingual booklet containing information learned during the session was developed and distributed to participants.

Other intervention components included a mail-delivered packet that was sent to participants monthly during the yearlong intervention (see Table 1). The packet included three items.

The first item was a self-monitoring daily activity log that participants were instructed to fill out and return by mail at the end of each month. The number of minutes walked and whether the target heart rate was reached were the two main sections that participants were asked to complete. Self-monitoring is considered an effective behavioral management technique for starting a physical activity program (Weber & Wertheim, 1989), and it provides internal reinforcement. A space for comments was provided on this form, which allowed participants to provide feedback on the program.

The second item was a component to provide incentive for participation and maintenance, and it consisted of a contest in which participants responded to monthly questions related to well-known Hispanic people and cultural and historical events. Incentives have been identified as a way of reducing perceived barriers and motivating people to act (Bandura, 1986). In addition, the questions allowed family members and friends to be involved, promoting a positive social environment.

The third item was a newsletter to provide information about the program and to help participants maintain motivation and a positive attitude toward behavior, both of which have been positively correlated with physical activity (Dishman & Steinhardt, 1990; Kimiecik, 1992). Other topics that were expected to appeal to family members and friends (e.g., child development) were included to contribute to a positive social environment.

These components of the intervention focused on perception and SE, the core constructs within the theoretical framework chosen by *Camine con Nosotros*. Knowledge, attitudes, and skills, which are also predisposing and enabling factors that facilitate the initiation and adoption of health behaviors, were crucial factors addressed in these activities and materials.

An additional environmental component was developed to create positive social support related to community, family, friends, and peers. Social support is a core component of SLT and an important reinforcing factor that has been positively related to adult physical activity (Felton & Parson, 1994; Minor & Brown, 1993). Instrumental in this effort was the involvement of *promotoras de salud* or lay health advisers. The use of lay workers has gained recognition as a valuable health promotion strategy (Eng, 1993; Eng & Young, 1992; Israel, 1985; Meister, Warrick, Zapién, & Wood, 1992). This approach has been proposed as a way of overcoming cultural and linguistic barriers between health providers and community groups (Baker et al., 1997). As active community members, *promotoras* were involved in television and radio promotional activities, community health fairs, school and church meetings, and clinical activities that were organized for recruitment, promotion, and retention purposes. They assisted participants in filling out recruitment forms and evaluation questionnaires, and they served as facilitators for the educational session and follow-up activities, which included regular phone contacts and personal one-to-one interaction. As peers, many *promotoras* participated in the walking program and provided vicarious support and modeling for participants. The *promotora* activities and the family involvement pursued through the contest and newsletter were directed toward creating a positive neighborhood and family climate for the promotion of physical activity.

Finally, a main concern of program planners should always be the cultural and linguistic competence of the intervention. Focus groups and *promotoras* provided continuous feedback during the assessment and preparation stages of the program, and a Hispanic health promotion specialist was involved in the planning stage and contributed to the development of the intervention and evaluation protocols. Materials were initially developed in Spanish by a Hispanic health education specialist and translated into English by a professional translator. The final version was then revised by a bilingual staff (*promotoras* and health professionals) to ensure appropriate language level and health information accuracy. All written materials were bilingual, and the educational session was offered in both Spanish and English.

Evaluation

The overall project included three levels of evaluation: process, impact, and outcome. The study involved a control group that received standard provider interaction with no specific walking message. However, given that the purpose of this article is to describe and justify the theoretical design of the intervention, only process and impact evaluation protocols will be described here. Outcome protocols and results will be subsequently reported.

TABLE 1 Program Components

Educational session

Booklet

Mail-delivered monthly packet

Daily activity log

Contest

Newsletter

Staff telephone calls

As previously discussed, the heterogeneous characteristics of Hispanic populations and the lack of agreement as to the cross-cultural sensitivity of health behavior theories represent special concerns for practitioners when considering the use of theory. An additional barrier is the lack of available evaluation tools (Green, 1991), including social behavior instruments. Evaluation tools are particularly problematic when dealing with Hispanic groups because existing instruments must often be culturally and/or linguistically adapted, which changes their internal structure and compromises their validity and reliability (VanOss & Marín, 1991). In many cases, researchers working with minority groups have to choose an instrument, adapt it, and use it, because validating an instrument requires additional time and resources that are often unavailable.

For *Camine con Nosotros*, we developed an evaluation protocol that included the implementation of existing instruments, the adaptation of existing instruments, and the development of new instruments by the investigators. The Arizona Activity Frequency Questionnaire was used for assessing physical activity levels (related to the goal and general objectives of the program). This questionnaire is a bilingual instrument developed by the University of Arizona, and it is in the process of being validated. The instrument measures the total daily energy expenditure, amount of time spent on various activities, and metabolic-equivalent threshold (MET) levels. The instrument was not modified in this project. SE and attitudes-perceptions questionnaires were used to assess the overall impact of the intervention. The SE questionnaire was adapted from the Exercise Efficacy Instrument developed by Sallis, Pinski, Grossman, Patterson, and Nader (1988), and it consisted of a bilingual, seven-item protocol (e.g., "How confident are you that you could increase your physical activity without it interfering with things you like to do?"), using a 5-point Likert-type scale ranging from *I am sure I could* to *I can't*. The attitudes-perceptions questionnaire was developed by the investigators, and it is composed of a bilingual, five-item protocol (e.g., "I believe that simply walking can provide me with health benefits"), using a 5-point Likert-type scale ranging from *strongly agree* to *strongly disagree*. These three assessments were used in a pretest-posttest protocol over a 1-year period.

The impact of the educational session on knowledge and skills was also assessed using a pretest-posttest design. Two different questionnaires were developed by the investigators. These questionnaires were also bilingual, and the contents were based on the lesson plan and consistent with the learning objectives established for the educational session. Knowledge was assessed using a 10-item protocol (e.g., "Daily walking can prevent diabetes") and a true-false scale. Skills were assessed using a five-item protocol (e.g., "One thing I can do to stick to this program is") and a multiple five-choice scale.

The process evaluation focused not only on assessing participation but also on receiving feedback from participants and *promotoras* regarding the feasibility of the program, quality of materials and information, and their personal evaluation of the program. Three bilingual questionnaires were developed by the investigators, two for collecting participants' feedback and one for collecting *promotoras'* feedback. Five process evaluation activities were scheduled over the 12-month intervention period.

CONCLUSIONS

Although, traditionally, the Hispanic population has been concentrated in certain areas of the United States, the growth of this group is projected to increase in every region throughout the country. It has been estimated that, by the year 2020, persons of Hispanic origin will comprise 29% of the population in the west, 14% in the south, 12% in the northeast, and 6% in the Midwest (Campbell, 1994). This demographic change is already having a great impact at the community level. Latino students make up more than 13% of the public school population, although they sit in about half of the desks in many urban schools (Soto Mas, 1999). In terms of labor force participation, the number of Hispanic workers will increase to more than 16 million by the year 2005, up from 10 million in 1992 (Soto Mas et al., 1997).

It is essential that health promotion programs be sensitive to these facts and develop programs that meet the needs of this growing population. Health behavior theories are a recommended resource for practitioners working with Hispanic communities, although it is the responsibility of researchers to provide constructs and evaluation tools that are consistent with the social, cultural, and linguistic characteristics of different Hispanic groups. In the meantime, existing theories constitute a valuable tool for practitioners who understand how to justify the selection of a theory and properly connect theory and practice.

Health behavior researchers can make a significant contribution toward this effort by focusing more on the process. Describing the rationale for program design, defining intervention components in detail, and providing accurate information on process and impact evaluation protocols are as important as the outcome and should be given equal importance in reporting. This is particularly critical for studies involving Hispanics and other ethnic/racial minority groups, because it will facilitate the use of theory and the design of more effective programs.

REFERENCES

Ali, N. S., & Twibell, R. K. (1995). Health promotion and osteoporosis prevention among postmenopausal women. *Preventive Medicine, 24,* 528–534.

Baker, E. A., Boulding, N., Durham, M., Escobar Lowell, M., González, M., Jodaitis, N., Negrón Cruz, L., Torres, I., Torres, M., & Trillio Adams, S. (1997). The Latino health advocacy program: A collaborative lay health advisor approach. *Health Education and Behavior, 24,* 495–509.

Bandura, A. (1977). *Social Learning Theory.* Englewood Cliffs, NJ: Prentice Hall.

Bandura, A. (1986). *Social foundations of thought and action: A social-cognitive theory.* Englewood Cliffs, NJ: Prentice Hall.

Bartholomew, L. K., Parcel, G. S., & Kok, G. (1998). Intervention mapping: A process for developing theory-and evidence-based health education programs. *Health Education and Behavior, 25,* 545–563.

Burchfield, C. M., Hamman, R. F., Marshall, J. A., Baxter, J., Kahn, L. B., & Amirani, J. J. (1990). Cardiovascular risk factors and impaired glucose tolerance: The San Luis Valley Diabetes Study. *American Journal of Epidemiology, 131,* 57–70.

Campbell, P. (1994). *Population projections of the United States, by age, race, and sex: 1993 to 2020* (Current Population Reports Series P25-1111). Washington, DC: Bureau of the Census.

Cantor, J. C., Bergeisen, L., & Baker, L. C. (1998). Effect of an intensive educational program for minority college students and recent graduates on the probability of acceptance to medical school. *Journal of the American Medical Association, 280,* 772–776.

Caspersen, C. J., Christenson, G. M., & Pollard, R. A. (1986). Status of the 1990 physical fitness and exercise objectives—evidence from NHIS 1985. *Public Health Reports, 101,* 587–592.

Centers for Disease Control and Prevention. (1991a). *National Health Interview Survey, 1991* [Public use data tapes]. Atlanta, GA: National Center for Health Statistics, Centers for Disease Control and Prevention.

Centers for Disease Control and Prevention. (1991b). *National Health and Nutrition Examination Survey (NHNES III) (1988–1991)* [Public use data tapes]. Atlanta, GA: National Center for Health Statistics, Centers for Disease Control and Prevention.

Centers for Disease Control and Prevention. (1992). *1992 BRFSS summary prevalence report.* Atlanta, GA: Department of Health and Human Services, Public Health Service, National Center for Chronic Disease Prevention and Health Promotion, Centers for Disease Control and Prevention.

Centers for Disease Control and Prevention. (1994). *Chronic disease in minority populations.* Atlanta, GA: Author.

Crespo, C. J., Keteyian, S. J., Heath, G. W., & Sempos, C. T. (1996). Leisure-time physical activity among U.S. adults: Results from the Third National Health and Nutrition Examination Survey. *Archives of Internal Medicine, 156,* 93–98.

Dishman, R. K., & Gettman, L. R. (1980). Psychobiologic influences on exercise adherence. *Journal of Sport and Exercise Psychology, 2,* 295–310.

Dishman, R. K., & Sallis, J. F. (1994). Determinants for physical activity and exercise. In C. Bouchard, R. J. Shephard, & T. Stephens (Eds.), *Physical activity, fitness, and health: International proceeding and consensus statement.* Champaign, IL: Human Kinetics.

Dishman, R. K., & Steinhardt, M. (1990). Health locus of control predicts free-living, but not supervised, physical activity: A test of exercise-specific control and outcome-expectancy hypotheses. *Research Quarterly for Exercise and Sport, 61,* 383–394.

D'Onofrio, C. N. (1992). Theory and the empowerment of health education practitioners. *Health Education Quarterly, 19,* 385–403.

Eng, E. (1993). The Save our Sisters Project: A social network strategy for reaching rural Black women. *Cancer, 72,* 1071–1077.

Eng, E., & Young, R. (1992). Lay health advisors and community change agents. *Family and Community Health, 15,* 24–40.

Felton, G. M., & Parson, M. A. (1994). Factors influencing physical activity in average-weight and overweight young women. *Journal of Community Health Nursing, 11,* 109–119.

Finnegan, J. R., Viswanath, K., Kahn, E., & Hannan, P. (1993). Exposure to sources of heart disease prevention information: Community type and social group differences. *Journalism Quarterly, 70,* 569–584.

Ford, E. S., & Jones, D. H. (1991). Cardiovascular health knowledge in the United States: Findings from the National Health Interview Survey, 1985. *Preventive Medicine, 20,* 725–736.

Glanz, K., Lewis, F. M., & Rimer, B. (Eds.). (1997). *Health behavior and health education: Theory, research, and practice.* San Francisco, CA: Jossey-Bass.

Good, B. J., & Good, M. J. (1986). The cultural context of diagnosis and therapy: A view from medical anthropology. In M. R. Miranda & H. Kitano (Eds.), *Mental health research and practice in minority communities: Development of culturally sensitive training programs* (pp. 1–27). Washington, DC: National Institute of Mental Health.

Green, L. W. (1991). Everyone has a theory, few have measurement. *Health Education Research, 6,* 249–250.

Hazuda, J. P., Stern, M. P., Gaskill, S. P., Haffner, S. M., & Gardner, L. I. (1983). Ethnic differences in health knowledge and behaviors related to the prevention and treatment of coronary heart disease: The San Antonio Heart Study. *American Journal of Epidemiology, 117,* 717–728.

Houchbaum, G. M. (1958). *Public participation in medical screening programs: A sociopsychological study* (USPHS Publication No. 572). Washington, DC: Public Health Service.

Hovell, M., Sallis, J., Hofstetter, R., Barrington, E., Hackley, M., Elder, J., Castro, F., & Kilbourne, K. (1991). Identification of correlates of physical activity among Latino adults. *Journal of Community Health, 16,* 23–36.

Israel, B. (1985). Social network and social support: Implications for natural helper and community level interventions. *Health Education Quarterly, 12,* 65–80.

Jackson, M. Y., Proulx, J. M., & Pelican, S. (1991). Obesity prevention. *American Journal of Clinical Nutrition, 53,* 1625S–1630S.

Jacobson, H. (1999). La comunicación con pacientes hispanohablantes [Communicating with Spanish-speaking patients]. *Médico Interamericano, 18,* 12–16. Available: http://www.users.interport.net/~icps/medico/medico99/january/

Kimiecik, J. (1992). Predicting vigorous physical activity of corporate employees: Comparing the theories of reasoned action and planned behavior. *Journal of Sport and Exercise Psychology, 14,* 192–206.

King, A. C., Blair, S. N., Bild, D. E., Dishman, R. K., Dubbert, P. M., Marcus, B. H., Oldridge, N. B., Paffenbarger, R. S., Powell, K. E., & Yeager, K. K. (1997). Determinants of physical activity and interventions in adults. *Medicine and Science in Sports and Exercise, 24,* S221–S236.

King, A. C., Haskell, W. L., Young, D. R., Oka, R. K., & Stefanick, M. L. (1995). Long-term effects of varying intensities and formats of physical activity on participation rates, fitness, and lipoproteins in men and women aged 50 to 65 years. *Circulation, 91,* 2596–2604.

Marín, G., & VanOss Marín, B. (1991). *Research with Hispanic populations.* Newbury Park, CA: Sage.

Meister, J., Warrick, L. L., Zapién, J., & Wood, A. (1992). Using lay health workers: Case study of a community-based prenatal intervention. *Journal of Community Health, 17,* 37–51.

Minor, M. A., & Brown, J. D. (1993). Exercise maintenance of persons with arthritis after participation in a class experience. *Health Education Quarterly, 20,* 83–95.

Mirotznik, J., Feldman, L., & Stein, R. (1995). The Health Belief Model and adherence with a community center-based, supervised coronary heart disease exercise program. *Journal of Community Health, 20,* 233–247.

National Center for Health Statistics. (1997). *Healthy people 2000 review, 1997* (DHHS Publication No. PHS 98-1256). Hyattsville, MD: Department of Health and Human Services.

National Coalition of Hispanic Health and Human Services Organizations (COSSMHO). (1995). Meeting the health promotion needs of Hispanic communities. *American Journal of Health Promotion, 9*, 300–311.

Neuberger, G. B., Kasal, S., Smith, K. V., Hassanein, R., & DeViney, S. (1994). Determinants of exercise and aerobic fitness in outpatients with arthritis. *Nursing Research, 43*, 11–17.

Oldridge, N. B., & Streiner, D. L. (1990). The Health Belief Model: Predicting compliance and dropout in cardiac rehabilitation. *Medicine and Science in Sports and Exercise, 22*, 678–683.

Palepu, A., Carr, P. L., Friedman, R. H., Amos, H., Ash, A. S., & Moskowitz, M. A. (1998). Minority faculty and academic rank in medicine. *Journal of the American Medical Association, 280*, 767–771.

Pasick, R. J. (1997). Socioeconomic and cultural factors in the development and use of theory. In K. Glanz, F. M. Lewis, & B. K. Rimer (Eds.), *Health behavior and health education: Theory, research, and practice* (pp. 425–440). San Francisco, CA: Jossey-Bass.

Pasick, R. J., D'Onofrio, C. N., & Otero-Sabogal, R. (1996). Similarities and differences across cultures: Questions to inform a third generation for health promotion research. *Health Education Quarterly, 23*, S142–S161.

Perez-Stable, E. J., Marín, G., & Marín, B. V. (1994). Behavioral risk factors: A comparison of Latinos and non-Latino whites in San Francisco. *American Journal of Public Health, 84*, 971–976.

Perez-Stable, E. J., Sabogal, F., Otero-Sabogal, R., Hiatt, R. A., & McPhee, S. J. (1992). Misconceptions about cancer among Latinos and Anglos. *Journal of the American Medical Association, 268*, 3219–3223.

Pollock, M. L. (1998). Prescribing exercise for fitness and adherence. In R. K. Dishman (Ed.), *Exercise adherence* (pp. 259–277). Champaign, IL: Human Kinetics.

Prevalence of selected risk factors for chronic disease by education level in racial/ethnic populations—United States, 1991–1992. (1994). *Morbidity and Mortality Weekly Report, 43*, 894–899.

Rogler, L. H., Malgady, R. G., & Rodríguez, O. (1989). *Hispanics and mental health: A framework for research.* Malabar, IL: Robert E. Krieger.

Sallis, J. F., Haskell, W. L., Fortmann, S. P., Vranizan, K. M., Taylor, C. B., & Solomon, D. S. (1986). Predictors of adoption and maintenance of physical activity in a community sample. *Preventive Medicine, 15*, 331–341.

Sallis, J. F., Hovell, M. F., & Hofstetter, C. R. (1992). Explanation of vigorous activity during two years using social learning variables. *Social Science and Medicine, 34*, 25–32.

Sallis, J. F., Hovell, M. F., Hofstetter, C. R., Faucher, P., Elder, J. P., Blanchard, J., Carpensen, C. J., Powell, K. E., & Christenson, G. M. (1989). A multivariate study of determinants of vigorous exercise in a community sample. *Preventive Medicine, 18*, 20–34.

Sallis, J. F., Pinski, R. B., Grossman, R. M., Patterson, T. L., & Nader, P. R. (1988). The development of self-efficacy scales for health-related diet and exercise behaviors. *Health Education Research, 3*, 283–292.

Soto Mas, F. (1999). Salud para todos en el año 2000: Una agenda de salud pœblica hispana para el siglo XXI [Health for all by the year 2000: A Hispanic public health agenda for the 21st century]. *Médico Interamericano, 18*, 6–10. Available: http://www.users.interport.net/~icps/ medico/medico99/january/

Soto Mas, F., & Papenfuss, R. (1997). El médico hispano y la promoción de la salud [The role of the Hispanic physician in health promotion]. *Médico Interamericano, 16*, 206–209.

Soto Mas, F., Papenfuss, R. L., & Guerrero, J. J. (1997). Hispanics and worksite health promotion: Review of the past, demands for the future. *Journal of Community Health, 22*, 361–371.

Tichenor, P. J., Donohue, G. A., & Olien, C. N. (1970). Mass media flow and differential growth in knowledge. *Public Opinion Quarterly, 34*, 159–170.

Turner, B. S. (1987). *Medical power and social knowledge.* Newbury Park, CA: Sage.

U.S. Bureau of the Census. (1993). *Income, poverty and health insurance, 1992.* Washington, DC: Author.

U.S. Department of Health and Human Services. (1996). *Physical activity and health: A report of the surgeon general.* Atlanta, GA: Department of Health and Human Services, Centers for Disease Control and Prevention, National Center for Chronic Disease Prevention and Health Promotion.

van Ryn, M., & Heaney, C. A. (1992). What's the use of theory? *Health Education Quarterly, 19*, 315–330.

Weber, J., & Wertheim, E. H. (1989). Relationships of self-monitoring, special attention, body fat percent, and self-motivation to attendance at a community gymnasium. *Journal of Sport and Exercise Psychology, 11*, 105–114.

Article Source: Soto Mas, F.G., Kane, W.M, Going, S., Ford, E.S., Marshall, J.R., Staten, L.K., & Smith, J.E. (2000). *Camine con Nosotros*: Connecting theory and practice for promoting physical activity among Hispanic women. *Health Promotion Practice, 1*(2), 178–187. Reprinted with permission.

QUESTIONS

1. What were the three main causes or reasons for low physical activity identified by the authors?

2. How were these similar or different from what your group identified?

3. What theories were chosen as the basis for the program, and what was the rationale the authors gave for choosing these theories?

4. How similar or different were these from yours?

5. How did the authors use the constructs of the theories in practice?

REFERENCES

Hochbaum, G.M., Sorenson, J.R., & Lorig, K. (1992). Theory in health education. *Health Education Quarterly, 19*(3), 295–313.

National Cancer Institute. (2003). *Theory at a Glance: A Guide for Health Promotion Practice.* Washington, DC: U.S. Department of Health and Human Services.

Index